How to Be a More Creative Executive

How to Be a More Creative Executive

JOSEPH G. MASON

New York   Toronto   London   1960
McGRAW-HILL BOOK COMPANY, INC.

HOW TO BE A MORE CREATIVE EXECUTIVE

To my wife, Ann
whose cheerful acceptance
of "typewriter widowhood"
made this book possible

Preface

This will not be the easiest book you have ever read. It is not about an easy subject.

Nowhere in the book will you find any statement to the effect that creative thinking—the active use of imagination—is an easy task.

Nor will you find any secret formulas or magic phrases that can produce million-dollar ideas for you. In fact, if the writer occasionally makes a categorical statement that appears to be *the* answer, it was not intended that way. By its nature, creativity is infinite—there is always a better way and always a worse way. Therefore, there are no real *answers*. There are preferred ways, and apparently better ways. But not answers.

The book was planned to do several things:

To help you develop an increased sensitivity to problems, needs, and opportunities in business

To build your knowledge of problem-solving procedures, and the aids to thinking more creatively

By removing some of the "mystery" that has always clouded the subject of creativity, to help you to gain self-confidence in applying principles and using techniques that have helped others

To explain some of the background that is necessary to create the kind of "climate" that will encourage more creative kinds of thinking on the part of associates and subordinates.

You will find some basic theories and psychological principles —enough, it is hoped, to help you achieve understanding of the "whys" behind certain recommendations. At the same time, however, this is primarily a "technician's" book, rather than a "scientist's"—the emphasis is on how to do it. If, upon completion of this book, you wish to delve more deeply into the subject, the Appendix contains the Bibliography compiled by Dr. Sidney J. Parnes and his staff at the University of Buffalo—certainly one of the most comprehensive listings of material relevant to creativity so far developed.

The Appendix also contains a chapter-by-chapter compilation of review questions which you may use to check or increase your understanding of the text. They were purposely put into a separate appendix, rather than spread throughout the book, however, so that you may, if you wish, just "read" the book. In other words, you may make as much of this book as you like—or as little. In that respect, the book is a great deal like your own imagination:

What you get out of it will depend upon what you put into using it.

Acknowledgments

To attempt to acknowledge individually all the persons who have in some way contributed to this book would involve a listing verging on the edge of infinity.

It would, of necessity, have to include all members of the University of Buffalo's annual Creative Problem Solving Institutes. It would include, very particularly, the students in creative problem-solving courses, conferences, and workshops conducted by the author. Even members of luncheon and dinner audiences who have been subjected to experiments in dynamic techniques and presentation methods would have to be singled out for their contributions in spontaneous evaluation and criticism. And so, certainly, would dozens of talented and creative business associates over the last fourteen years. To all these, a general, but nevertheless sincere, acknowledgment is made.

Certain individuals, however, must be mentioned for specific contributions:

Paul Russell and Phil Kobbe, responsible for first encouraging me into a serious study of this fascinating subject of creativity.

Alex Osborn and Bobb Chaney for their continuing support and encouragement.

Don Mitchell, Herb True, and John Arnold—creative teachers whose philosophies and methods undoubtedly find some reflection in these pages.

Editors Paul McCrea, of *Nation's Business*, and Raymond Fremed, of *Chemical Engineering*, who have not only published this writer's articles in the past, but have also generously given permission to adapt much material from those articles to this book.

Finally, my wife, Ann, for her contributions as a research assistant.

To all of these, my special thanks.

Joseph G. Mason

Contents

Preface　　　　　　　　　　　　　　　　　　　　　　　　　　　vii

1. Why Be Creative?　　　　　　　　　　　　　　　　　　　1

Life in a changing world · Old problems needing new solutions
· The need for leadership

2. What Is Creative?　　　　　　　　　　　　　　　　　　15

Creativeness, talent, aptitudes, originality · Novelty, Discovery,
Chance · The arts, science, business · The dual nature of creativity

3. Characteristics of Creative People　　　　　　　　　31

Problem sensitivity · Idea fluency · Originality · Flexibility ·
Drive · Other characteristics

4. Blocks to Creativeness　　　　　　　　　　　　　　　47

Perceptual · Cultural · Emotional · Habits—ways to overcome
them

5. The Nature of Creative Thought　　　　　　　　　　68

Creative minds in action · Steps in the creative thinking process

6. The Nature of Problems　　　　　　　　　　　　　　84

Commonness of problems · Where problems come from · How
to measure them · How to think about them

xi

1

Why Be Creative?

Late in 1957, a group of twenty-four working scientists were asked to predict what they thought our world would be like in twenty years. The scientists represented different industries and came from different parts of the country. They were, for all practical purposes, men who are actually shaping the "world of tomorrow" for us. Here are some of the predictions they agreed upon for the year 1977:

Any new house built will have an all-metal framing with a plastic exterior. Interior lighting in houses will be full-wall or full-ceiling. An interior color scheme will be changed by turning a dial. The house will require practically no upkeep, because it will be built and furnished with nearly indestructible materials. And it will be heated by an atomic-reactor furnace.

People in 1977 will be wearing clothes much different from what we are used to today. They will be either one-trip disposable garments or, for a permanent wardrobe, temperature-controlled year-round garments that can warm or cool the wearer as desired. And these permanent garments will be soilproofed.

Automobiles, said the scientists, will be crashproof, automatic-control models, powered by either wireless electricity or an exotic fuel—a tankful of which will last all year. Roads will be snow-proofed for year-round safer driving. Almost every family will have a second car that converts to either an airplane or a helicopter. However, if a person is really in a hurry to get somewhere, the prediction was that he will be able to take an atomic-reactor airliner which will get him there at 2,500 miles an hour.

They predicted that by 1977 everyone will be making telephone calls over private-line TV sets, and that the family TV will have a screen covering one whole wall of the room and be in both color and 3D.

On the questions of diet and health, these predictions were made: individual diets will include fresh meat and vegetables which will be stored in cupboards—no refrigerators or freezers will be needed. A large portion of every person's diet will be made up of synthetic foods, grown in the mass-production version of test tubes. Every infant born will be vaccinated against the common cold. However, they also pointed out, there is a good possibility that the atmosphere, at least in our cities, will be virus-free in the first place, so a person's chances of catching a cold will be greatly reduced. If anything goes wrong with an individual's heart, kidneys, or other vital organ, the organ can be replaced. Both heart disease and cancer will be eliminated as killers.

A few other predictions: a lawn will stay green even through the driest part of the summer. Grass will grow to a height of about 1½ inches and will never need mowing. The droughts in some areas will no longer be problems, because we will be making fresh water out of the ocean. The newest military weapon in 1977, they predicted, will be a superray or disintegrating gun, and everyone will have more time to worry about the Russians using it first, because the thirty-hour work week will be universal.

It is important to remember that the men making these predictions were not science-fiction writers, nor were they the publicity men of giant corporations. They had all spent years acquiring knowledge and experience in research and product development and were actively engaged in those pursuits at that time. This, of course, made their predictions quite interesting. In retrospect, however, those scientific guesses become even more interesting. The predictions were all based on a future twenty years away. But less than fifteen *months* later, the following things had happened:

A national magazine reported that four manufacturers were in production with "electroluminescent" lamps—metal panels that gave off light and could be made to glow "in any color of the rainbow." One company, Sylvania, was reported to have produced over 300,000 of these panels for radio and telephone dials, bedside clocks, house numbers, thermometers, light switches, and airplane seat-belt signs.

Minnesota Mining and Manufacturing Company received national publicity for their development of a 5-pound atomic reactor that could produce electricity directly from atomic energy, with a companion "heat pump" that operated from the electrical power so produced. The company admitted that they were probably ten years away from having a "commercially usable" product, but they had "high hopes" for their new development.

It was reported that a major airline had begun to treat all the uniforms worn by their stewardesses with a new chemical stain repellent and that, as a result, their monthly dry-cleaning bills were running only a sixth of what they had been previously.

General Motors introduced their new experimental car, "Firebird III," across the country, and made a great point of showing the equipment that would permit the car to be guided automatically on an "electronic highway" which was then being tested.

A large chemical-products company had a display board in their research center with packages of meat and vegetables that had been there for six months at room temperature without visible deterioration, because they had been irradiated with the gamma rays produced by spent nuclear materials.

And another chemical producer devoted a full summer to field-testing a chemical grass inhibitor on one of our large Eastern turnpikes.

One thing none of those twenty-four scientists predicted, probably because they felt it would be too fantastic, was the repeal of the law of gravity. But in that same fifteen-month period, it was announced that new advances in the development of a unified field theory of physics now have scientists suspecting that the earth's gravity is an electromagnetic force. If this proves to be so, then the force can be shielded, neutralized, or utilized to produce a counterforce. In other words, gravity could well be "on the way out"—and in less than twenty years.

Where these educated and experienced technical specialists had been led astray in their predictions was in underestimating one of the most dynamic and powerful forces at work in the world today: the speeding up of our "rate of change." Today, we are acquiring new knowledge and technological skills at such a rapidly increasing rate that developments and discoveries which used to take twenty years can now be accomplished in ten; events which formerly took ten years to bring about now become realities in two or three years. At the time those twenty-four scientists made their predictions, the fastest man-made machine was an airplane which traveled at about 750 miles an hour. Within two months, man-made satellites were in orbit at 18,000 mph, and within the fifteen-month period, a Russian rocket had escaped the earth's gravitational field at 25,000 mph!

It has been estimated that we are currently advancing our technological knowledge at a rate of 22 per cent a year. This means that we more than double our knowledge every four years. Whether this estimate is accurate or not, it is safe to say that never before in history has man's knowledge of his nature and environment increased so fast or in so many different directions. In fact, so rapidly are we moving today that even man's oldest and most useful invention, the wheel, can't keep up any more. The wheel isn't going to disappear completely overnight, of course, and possibly not even in our lifetime. But it is significant that there are now at least two models of wheelless automobiles, both of which depend on jets of air to propel them along *above* the road. And in new electronic computers, the old wheel number counters are being replaced by electronic switches and tubes which are faster and more dependable.

So what does this mean to you as a business executive? Aren't these all signs of progress? And isn't progress inevitable?

These are all signs of progress, of course. They are also signs of *change* and changes to come. But all changes are not progressive. And progress isn't inevitable—only change is inevitable. We just hope that, through the resourcefulness and decency of man, the changes will also be progressive. Today, in the midst of our looking into and anticipating the future, we can, simply by looking at the "old" problems we have never adequately solved, see definite proof that change doesn't have to be for the good. In fact, many of these "old" problems are, if anything, going from bad to so much worse that they could, in time, destroy our nation.

For example: By 1970, according to Dr. Arthur R. Upgren, Director of the Bureau of Economic Studies, Macalester College, our gross national product in the United States will be at the phenomenally high figure of $700-billion a year. However, Dr. Upgren reports the liquidity of our banks—the sum of cash and reserves and United States government securities as a proportion of percentage of deposits—has been declining since 1945 from a high of 83 per cent. Says Dr. Upgren, "If we now make loans in the next ten years to expand deposits by the growth we need, I estimate that the liquidity ratio will be down to the danger point again of 23 per cent . . . where we were in 1929." And, he points out, "If this problem isn't solved, we will have a money shortage too severe for our economy to withstand in 1970."

Our natural resources—metals, chemicals, fuels—are being exhausted at fantastic rates to support the growth of our expanding economy and standard of living. We are, in many fields, already turning to substitute and synthetic materials to supply our basic needs. But the big danger is that our children's children will have to get along without even these if we continue to consume and waste them at the present rate. Much of this exhaustion of resources is preventable, that we do know. As an example, consider the wasteful use of coal—for years one of our basic natural resources. If we could solve the problems of efficient conversion of coal into energy, just one kilogram—about two pounds—of coal could yield us 25-billion kilowatt hours of electricity—as much as all the power plants in the United States in 1958 could generate by running steadily for two months!

Our growing labor force is caught in a squeeze between its increase in size and the decrease in need. Industrial productivity is such today that fewer workers are needed, and fewer still will be needed in the future, to maintain our manufacturing output. In view of this situation, one economist reported that unemployment may easily become our greatest national problem in future years. As examples, he reported that between April and October of 1958, our production went up 10 per cent, but production-worker payrolls increased only 5 per cent. When General Motors went into full production on their 1959 lines, their production increase was 25 per cent. But they hired only 5 per cent more workers.

On an international scale, broad-thinking authorities are pointing out signs in our relationship to Soviet Russia that could, if they prove out, ultimately end in our defeat by Russia in world economic battles. They are greatly concerned that we, in America, have adopted the attitude that the dangers do not exist: we prefer to praise our country's power and look hopefully to its glorious future. Yet the fact remains that in every corner of the globe the United States is being outmaneuvered by Russia, both economically and sociologically. And the story of history is a repetitive story of the rise and fall of great nations. If America is to survive, we have to face up to the fact that somehow we must convince Americans in general of the necessity of paying the price of survival. That price will include change of attitudes, removal of old prejudices and misconceptions, and certainly the sacrifice of some of our much-guarded self-interests.

At lesser than national and international levels, we have dozens of problems in every field of living that require new and different solutions, and require those solutions soon, before they also assume the proportions of national crisis. Most of these are old problems that we have, for expediency or for the sake of personal or political self-interests, let degenerate to the point where they are now major problems. And by virtue of their severity, they have assumed the aspect of new problems requiring new solutions. As examples:

Every eight seconds a new American baby is born. Every morning we have 7,000 more American mouths to feed. Every year we add the equivalent of a new state of Maryland to our population. These new people are all hungry—they've all got to be fed. Problem: where is the food coming from?

By 1970, we will need more new college plants in this country than we have built in the 300 years since the founding of Harvard. In our elementary and secondary schools we are at least 75,000 classrooms short of our minimum needs today. By 1970, another big jump in our school-age population will catch up with us. Problem: How do we get out from under, let alone get ahead?

Our major cities are having problems that were never even dreamed of by their founding fathers: they are riddled by slums, strangled by traffic, and, in common with their parent states, starved for income. And yet our growing population puts ever-growing demands for more services, supplies, protection, and health needs upon these cities. Problem: Unless something is done to reverse the trend, we face the complete deterioration of our cities as centers of culture, commerce, and living over the next ten to twenty years.

And what about our people? America's greatest resource has always been the ingenuity and resourcefulness of its people. Won't these come through in our times of trouble to help us out of our difficulties? At present, there seems little indication of it. In May, 1958, Charles H. Brower, President of Batten, Barton, Durstine & Osborn, Inc., the national advertising agency, gave a talk before the National Sales Executives Convention in Washington, D.C. Included in his talk was this statement:

> This, in America, is the high tide of mediocrity, the great era of the goof-off, the age of the half-done job. The land from coast-to-coast has been enjoying a stampede away from responsibility. It is populated with laundrymen who won't iron shirts, with waiters who won't serve, with carpenters who will come around some day maybe, with executives whose minds are on the golf course, with teachers who demand a single salary schedule so that achievement cannot be rewarded nor poor work punished, with students who take cinch courses because the hard ones make them think, with spiritual delinquents of all kinds who have been triumphantly determined to enjoy what was known until the present crisis as "the new leisure." And the salesman who won't sell is only a part of this over-all mess.

A few months later, a Trendex poll was taken across the country to find out if Americans, as a whole, agreed with Mr. Brower. Here are the findings: Forty-eight per cent of those interviewed agreed that the statement was true. Ten per cent had no opinion. Forty-two per cent disagreed. As Mr. Brower later pointed out, "To have almost half of the people polled agree with such a statement is a phenomenal thing. Any candidate who went to the polls with that many of the people behind him would be almost certain of election!"

"Apparently," said Mr. Brower, "we recognize our national illness."

But recognizing a problem and being willing to do something about it are two different things. Thought leaders in this country are becoming increasingly disturbed by the deterioration of the traditional American "will to win." They are disturbed by the complacency, conformity, and want for security. Our people now have to relearn an old maxim if we are to muster the mental drive and creative support the country needs today: *Happiness is an idea—not a condition of living.* This problem is going to assume even greater importance in our national mental well-being in the years immediately ahead.

By 1975, according to most predictions, and even by 1965, according to others, most Americans will be working at their primary jobs only about thirty hours a week. Some authorities predict that annual four-week vacations will be universal. If such predictions come true, and there is every indication that they will, then the average American worker will find himself with up to 25 per cent more leisure time on his hands. The big question is, how will people use that time? The way the trend is right now, we are doomed to become a nation devoted to escapist recreation.

And what about the problems of doing business today? High taxes, high wages, and high materials costs, as well as the necessity of coping with the complications of ever-increasing technologies, are putting a real drain on the resources and resourcefulness of business executives. In many industries, profit margins are counted in pennies. And the pressures for more sales are tremendous, as are the pressures generated by competition.

Thirty-one per cent of America's top-brand consumer products in 1940 had lost their leadership by 1956. Roughly 23 per cent of this group lost their place because of competition from radically new products; 31 per cent because of improved competitive products; 25 per cent because competing products were able to provide new developments of enough interest to the consumer to cause a brand change; and 23 per cent were just outadvertised and outpromoted. So important has competitive selling become to our business picture that Dun & Bradstreet reports that of the 9,324 business failures in the United States in the first part of 1958, "Inadequate Sales" was the most frequent reason for failure (more than twice as much as any other cause), and "Competitive Weakness" was the strong second reason. Some of the problems that a business faces in selling at a profit in our economy today are these:

Leadership. We are short of the trained and experienced executives we need to cope with the complexities of modern marketing. This has been caused, at least in part, by overemphasis on specialization in the past. We find now that what we need are "generalists"—executives who can take a broad view of the business as a whole and who have the ability to handle a wide variety of problems and problem aspects.

Training. It is almost axiomatic in business operation that to increase profits, you must increase manpower efficiency. Executives and selling personnel must learn to make their business hours more productive. They must learn to study and analyze their operations and responsibilities in order to achieve greater efficiency. This takes education, and if a company wants the benefits of that education, it will have to assume the responsibility for providing it.

Marketing. The way a product was advertised and sold yesterday may be completely outmoded today. Just the change from urban to suburban living has greatly upset many traditional concepts of selling and distribution and will continue to do so as our pattern of population change keeps changing.

New Products. Here lies one of the greatest challenges of all for a business seeking sales. If products are practically identical to those of a competitor, a company's potential for profits may be nearly nonexistent today. And the company is in a dangerous way so far as the future is concerned.

One national marketing magazine made the editorial prediction that any company that didn't come out with a new product within the next ten years would be out of business by 1970. And they spelled this out: they said this couldn't be an old product with a new handle or an old product with a new style of trim on it; it would have to be a completely new product. And, to further compound the worries of their readers, they mentioned the fact that the chances of successfully introducing a new product these days are less than one in four!

Actually, when you study any report of new products or products under development, it is easy to see why businesses in all fields are under the gun to produce more new products. Many one-line or limited-line companies are faced with extinction by new—and, in some cases, as yet undeveloped—products that will be coming onto the market in the years ahead. As a cross-check on the predictions made by the twenty-four scientists reported earlier in this chapter, another group of twenty such men were asked this question: "What businesses in existence today do you think are likely to disappear within the next twenty years because of competitive innovations?"

Here are the replies from this group:

Wooden office furniture (replaced by metal, plastic)

Ordinary fountain pen and liquid ink (replaced by ball points and yet-to-be-developed permanent writing instruments)

Laundry starch (will be replaced by built-in plastics)

Laundry and hand soaps (replaced by detergents or to-be-developed electrostatic dirt precipitators)

Metal pipe (to be replaced by reinforced plastics)

Wool for fabrics (replaced by synthetics)

Dry cleaning (replaced by chemical pretreatment with dirt repellent)

Freezers and refrigerators and frozen foods (replaced by irradiated foods *)

Woven textiles (replaced by new "felted" or pressure-made fabrics)

Piloted military aircraft (replaced by missiles)

Solvent-base paints (replaced by rubber and other water-soluble products)

Lawnmowers (replaced by chemical grass inhibitors)

Piston engines (replaced by turbine or solar-powered electrical)

---

* Since this prediction was made, it was subsequently announced that irradiated foods which were already in distribution (mostly to the armed forces) were being withdrawn because it was found that present methods of irradiation also destroyed many important nutrients. This, however, is only a delay—not a prohibition of future development. The same type of situation existed when the milling industry first began to bleach flour to make it white. The solution in this case was to restore the vitamins and other nutrients lost in the bleaching process by means of chemical additives to the white flour.

All those predictions, of course, affect companies which make products. But they will also affect companies which service, distribute, advise, and finance. These predictions add up to a completely new and changing character for American business. It will not only be the manufacturers themselves who will be affected and have to make changes, but their attendant suppliers. And the successful adaptation to the changes will be in the hands of business executives. Right there, we have still another problem: although our total population is expected to grow by 25,000,000 by 1965, the best estimates indicate that our "future executive group"—men in the twenty-five- to forty-five-year age bracket—will decrease by 600,000. With expanding businesses to care for, the caretakers are going to be extremely shorthanded. And this will mean still more new problems in all areas of management: human relations, processing, marketing, labor relations, research and development, and personnel.

What all this adds up to is a crying need for more creativity from our business and government management. We need more men at executive and management levels who, instead of trying to "go by the book," have learned to use their imaginations to solve our problems. "The book" for the dynamic change years just ahead of us hasn't been written yet!

Now there has been, in recent years, an increasing amount of talk about the need for more creativity to help us cope with and solve the problems we have. Business, science, and government today need all the ideas they can get. This is usually admitted by even the most conservative managers. But very little observation of business is necessary to conclude that business, as yet, has done relatively little about getting anywhere near the full potential of creativity from either its leaders or its workers. As a matter of record, in the midst of the 1958 recession, when business was bad and businessmen *should* have been looking for new ideas and imaginative problem solutions, two major national conferences on creative thinking—aimed at the production of ideas—had to be canceled for lack of registrants. A third just barely made the minimum registration needed to break even! It seems to be a case of "After you, my dear Alphonse."

But in any business or other type organization, the creativity must come from the top. Top- and middle-management men must set the example. Or, if an executive does not have the inclination or the ability to become a top "idea man," he must at least acquire enough knowledge and understanding of the creative processes so that he can keep minds around him open to the rewards of creativity, and will not, himself, inadvertently block or discourage fresh or different kinds of thinking within his organization.

Creative thinking, in any circumstance, should be encouraged to the extent that it is a means to an end. It is never the end itself. No business executive should be expected to be interested in ideas for the sake of having ideas—not when he is trying to show a profit! The reason an executive should invest time and effort in improving his own creativity and in encouraging or assisting others to develop theirs is, from a strictly business point of view, that he will be able to solve more problems in more and better ways.

But no executive can inspire creativity if his own attitude toward it is skeptical. The first requirement for a creative leader is that he himself really wants new ideas and that he himself will have the capacity to change with the changes that new ideas require. This, in itself, means that an executive must at least familiarize himself with the creative processes, with the nature of ideas, with the techniques and methods of idea production. And he must also approach the subject with a certain attitude. He must have more than a little amount of faith.

After all, if we could learn creative thinking from a book or by listening to someone talk about it, we'd have no trouble at all in raising the nation's creative power. But creative thinking demands real application—and a positive attitude. You've got to believe in the power of ideas. You've got to believe in what you are trying to do. You've got to believe in yourself. And, in creativity, it isn't always easy, because often we are speculating about the unknown. No one knows with scientific accuracy just what creative thinking really is. We can point out symptoms and methods. But what really makes it, we don't know. Yet, if there is any one thing that today's business executive needs, it is a supreme confidence in the power of man to alter the events and circumstances of his environment through the application of his imagination.

2

What Is Creative?

Although there has been a growing awareness over the last few years that "this creative thinking bit" might be worth looking into by a company, actual knowledge of just what makes thinking "creative" lags somewhat behind. This is true not only in business, but in science, education, and even the arts that have always prided themselves on being "creative."

Because most people aren't too sure just what creativity really is, they use such terms as "original," "talented," and "imaginative" almost interchangeably with "creative." Of these, the most misused term is "creative."

We speak of a woman hobbyist who turns out copies of her evening-school art teacher's ceramic ash tray designs as "creative." Likewise, the husband who uses his basement workshop to make tables from mail-order patterns. Or the skilled cabinetmaker who faithfully reproduces exact copies of Chippendale or Sheraton pieces. We call "creative" the child prodigy who can play a Mozart piano sonata at ten years of age, and the television comic whose sense of timing lets him read his script-writer's gags with rib-splitting results. We call such people "creative" when what we really mean is "talented."

Now if our woman hobbyist eventually acquires the confidence to develop her own ceramic designs; or if the husband switches to planning his own furniture and using his own plans or begins to make original adaptations and changes from the mail-order plans; or if our cabinetmaker uses his years of skill and disciplined taste to develop a new family of fine furniture; or if the child prodigy begins to compose pleasing little tunes of his own; or if the comic assumes the leadership of his gag-writer's efforts—if any of these changes come about, then these people start to earn the right to be called "creative." But creativity is more than just talent.

We sometimes call a writer "creative" when what we mean is "clever" or even "perceptive." There has been a rash of what we now refer to as "social critics" writing of late. These people are highly skilled at pointing out the flaws and problems of whatever their field of the moment happens to be, and at presenting their discoveries in sharp and cutting and often amusing fashions. But merely pointing out problems does not complete the creative cycle—it only starts it. And much more of the credit for creativeness should go to the person who picks up the problem, develops the ideas to solve it, and puts the idea into action to effect the solution.

Please don't, at this point, begin to "write off" talent, originality, or imagination as requirements for creativity. As we shall see later, each of these attributes has a definite contribution to make to the creative process. But none of them alone earns a person the right to be called "creative."

Creativeness, in the best sense of the word, requires two things: an original concept, or "idea," and a benefit to someone. Now many people think up original concepts but fail to follow through on them, so that no benefit ever results. And many people think up original concepts that are more harmful than good (there have been many highly imaginative people on the FBI's "Ten Most Wanted" listings!). So to simplify the definition even more, we can say that *creativeness requires new and beneficial ideas put into action.*

(There are some people who feel very strongly that the word "creative" should never be applied to any efforts of man. It is a term they would rather have reserved to the works of God. To these, we can only point out that their Bible will tell them that man was created in the "image of God." It does not say that this "image" referred only to man's outward appearance to the exclusion of his mental abilities. In fact, it is doubtful whether even the most erudite Biblical scholar can say that the only God-image involved in man *isn't* his mind!)

What we will be concerned about in this book are the methods, techniques, and principles involved in developing new and different *concepts* and in putting those concepts into action. For the sake of familiarity, concepts will from now on be referred to as *ideas.*

Just what is an idea, anyway? It may be a *discovery*—the perception for the first time of something that has been in existence but not previously known. An idea may be an *innovation*—something new or novel applied to an existing way of doing something. An idea may be a new *synthesis*—a different mixture of known elements or parts to make a new whole. Or an idea may be a *mutation*—an alteration in the form or the qualities of an existing entity or concept. An idea may be any of these or a combination of any of them. Probably the quickest way to compare them is to look at a few ideas and analyze the differences.

A *discovery*, we said, usually involves the perception of something that no one has ever perceived before. Discoveries may come about as the result of an accident. Such an example that has become famous is Charles Goodyear's experience of accidentally dropping a ball of gum rubber he was experimenting with onto a hot stove. In scraping it off, he suddenly *discovered* that the gum had changed character; it had, in fact, become almost a new substance. This was one of the key points in his eventual development of rubber as we know it today.

Most worthwhile or important discoveries, however, are the result of long, careful, and painstaking study of cause and effect by a patient searcher. One of the most significant recent discoveries of our time involved the "repeal" of the "law of parity" in physics. This concerns the behavior of submicroscopic particles. Two Chinese-born physicists, Dr. T. D. Lee and Professor C. N. Yang of Columbia University, were conducting studies of such particles when they discovered that some of them weren't doing what the "natural laws" of physics said they should be doing. They then suggested some experiments to find out what was going on. Other experimenters followed through and found that, indeed, the two physicists had hit upon a discovery that opened new possibilities for the development of theories on subatomic particles.

Back before World War I, a similar observation of the defiance of generally accepted theories resulted in the discovery of the nucleus of the atom by Ernest Rutherford. At the time, he was experimenting with the newly developed "X rays," and found that alpha particles produced by the rays weren't behaving as they "should" when fired into a cloud chamber. His subsequent observations and deductions led him to the discovery that an atom was not, as was then thought, the smallest particle in existence —that the atom had within itself a still smaller particle that made its nucleus.

Before leaving the subject of discovery, we should probably take a look at two closely related factors, *chance* and *serendipity*.

Too many people are apt to write off the effects of "chance" on the development of an idea as just "good luck." They overlook the fact that the only people such "luck" seems to happen to with any regularity are those who have been searching for just such a break. For example, Charles Goodyear, mentioned earlier, had spent five years and every cent he could lay his hands on, even to the neglect of his family, experimenting with the crude rubber then available, trying to make it into a permanent substance. Without the benefit of the work and study he had put into the material before that stroke of "luck," it is doubtful that he would even have recognized the discovery of the new substance which resulted from the accidental burning on the stove. It is simply the old story that the best-coached team gets the breaks.

Serendipity is quite another matter. This is, basically, the discovery of one thing while you are looking for something else. For example, in attempting to perfect a new type of carbon copying paper, researchers of the National Cash Register Company developed a method of encapsulating microscopic droplets of ink in a gelatin solution. They suddenly discovered that their microscopic encapsulating process had literally thousands of other possibilities in fields quite far from typewriters and business machines. In fact, there is every possibility that some of the other uses—in photography, medicine, electronics, and even cosmetics—may prove to be more profitable than the original carbon-paper business.

Probably the chief distinction between "chance" and serendipity is that the "serendipist" is usually looking for "something." He may not be sure just what that "something" is, therefore he is alert to almost anything that comes along. In fact, he may even be hypersensitized to the appearance of anything new or different. Therefore, while his discovery may also appear to be "luck," in the sense that this wasn't what he was really searching for, it is not so much luck when you consider that he was really searching for *anything* new. As the Greek philosopher, Heraclitus, said, "You will never find the unexpected unless you are looking for it."

Serendipity also explains another phenomenon that has vexed inventors in many fields throughout history: simultaneous discovery. At any given time, there is always a great body of unresolved knowledge to contend with—bits and pieces that only wait for some mind somewhere to pull them together. There is also a unity in scientific thinking that overrides any tendencies to isolate those bits and pieces into special fields or separate spheres. Therefore, no matter what field the scientist or specialist is working in—no matter what country he lives in or what language he speaks—if he has sufficient background in his field, he will be cognizant of this body of knowledge and will approach it in the same ways that his contemporaries in other fields and even other parts of the world will. The bits and pieces he is working with are truths (else they would not be knowledge), and if he asks the same questions that others are asking, he is bound to come up with the same answers. This has often, in history, led to the simultaneous discovery of new truths by different scientists in different fields. As examples:

Newton and Hooke independently arrived at theories of gravity at the same time.

Henry and Faraday both hit on the principle of magnetic induction of electric current at practically the same time.

Darwin and Wallace both proposed theories of natural selection within a short period of time—so short that neither could have "stolen" from the other in time to formulate and propose his independent theory.

Unfortunately, history is apt to deal harshly with such coincidental discoveries: usually one man is given the full credit and the other is accused of being an idea thief. But both men were working from the same body of unresolved truths; both asked the same questions; both could only get the same answers; and, logically, both should be credited with the new discovery.

Today, of course, that cloud of unresolved knowledge hangs heavier than ever. Somewhere, among the bits and pieces, are the answers we need to get us to outer space and back again— or to permanent world peace—or to economic security—or to wherever we want to go. These answers can take Russia or any other country in the world to all those places also. The big question confronting us today is not who is going to pull the answers together, but who is going to pull them together first.

Innovation, another form of idea production, is less complex in its definition and application. In fact, almost any product you can buy that has been on the market for more than two or three years is probably the result of progressive innovations in its design. Innovation is simply the introduction of change by adding something new or changing something in a new way. Just by considering the ordinary automobile we get a quick listing of innovations:

The introduction of the gasoline engine; the self-starter; hydraulic brakes and four-wheel brakes; automatic transmissions; power brakes and power steering; curved windshields for greater visibility; torsion-bar suspension. Each of these new features, the first time it was applied, was an innovation. And, not to complicate the explanation, it should probably be noted that each of these particular innovations undoubtedly called for the development of hundreds of separate ideas, and many of these ideas were probably innovations in themselves!

Synthesis, the bringing together of apparently unrelated items to make a new whole, is one of the most common idea-producing methods. Charles Duryea, the automotive engineer, was watching his wife spray perfume on herself with an atomizer. At that time, he was looking for a way to "break up" gasoline so it would burn better in the automobile engine he was developing. His imagination enabled him to synthesize the two ideas, and he developed the first practical carburetor. Cyrus McCormick became interested in the action of the barber's clippers while having his hair cut one day. He realized that this particular cutting action could be used in more ways than just on hair, and from that realization eventually came his idea for the farm reaper. A more recent example of commercial synthesis was made by the Corning Glass Works when it combined the famous "Pyrex" brand cooking utensils with the material used in the Pyroceram nose cones the company had developed for guided missiles. The result was a set of glass cooking ware that looks like china, but can go from the freezer to a red-hot burner without cracking. Another example of a modern-day synthesis is the plastic "squeeze" bottles which have become so popular for toothpaste. They resulted from an observation of a mustard dispenser bottle at a Coney Island hot dog stand!

Closely allied to synthesis is the idea-producing technique of *mutation*. This is usually a simple alteration in the form or quality of a material to adapt it to a new use, the way Eberhard Faber got the idea of putting an eraser on his pencils after watching a servant clean wallpaper with a piece of sponge rubber. Or the army man who simply switched the principle of the repeating rifle to make a new cartridge-loading razor for shaving. A more exotic example of a mutation is the use of powdered metal, pressed under weight and baked in an oven, to make gears and other intricately shaped metal parts. This was first used by the Egyptians before the time of Christ. The mutation consists only in adapting the method to modern-day production methods.

These have all been examples of ways in which ideas can come into being. But, as mentioned, for an idea to be considered creative, it must also be of benefit to someone. All of the ideas mentioned, of course, pass that test because, if nothing else, they contributed to the basic knowledge of our world. But, at the same time, they also destroyed. And this brings up a new characteristic of creativity that must be understood, for it is basic to the entire development of your own ability to create.

Creativeness, or an idea, has a dual nature: it is both constructive and destructive. An idea can give us a new way of doing something or a new approach to thinking—but only at the expense of giving up an old way of doing something or an old way of thinking. And we are not, remember, referring to the ideas which have destruction as their only objective. We are concerned solely with that creativity which does meet our test of bringing a benefit with its change.

It has been said that the creativeness of American business is almost wholly responsible for the tremendous growth and industrial strength of our country today. But, at the same time, this beneficial creativeness is one of the most destructive forces an industrial era has ever known. Just consider:

Any new product introduced on the market can win acceptance only if the public at large is willing to abandon an old way of satisfying the same need. Every new production method adopted means the end of a former way of doing something. Every new material designed into a product means that a former material has lost a use.

One of the relatively unknown great dramas of American industry centered around the progressiveness of a new idea battling the old established way: In 1882, a young man named Nikola Tesla invented an electric generator for producing alternating current—the type of current that supplies the electrical needs of most of the world today. But in 1882, the only electric power in general use was direct current produced by the generators invented by Thomas A. Edison. This system was costly to install —requiring an expensive generator for about every 2 square miles. And it was costly to operate. But it was also highly profitable. And the people who were realizing those profits weren't about to give them up easily. So Tesla found that none of the established companies in the field would handle his new system. It was not until several years later, when Tesla was discovered by George Westinghouse, that he was able to get the financial and production backing to put his alternating current generators into use. The rest, of course, is electrical history.

An example of how a creative insight can destroy years of preconceived notions is observed in the discovery back in 1910, by Dr. Francis Peyton Rous of the Rockefeller Institute for Medical Research, that a certain type of animal cancer was caused by a filterable virus. This challenged the one basic thing that all medical researchers knew—or thought they knew—about cancer: it was not an infectious disease, which it would have to be if it were caused by a virus. Many respected researchers of the day flatly refused to believe that Rous was right, even after he went on to find other types of animal cancers that were also caused by viruses. Today, of course, no line of investigation into the origins of cancer is being pursued more vigorously than the one aimed at finding virus causes. But several generations of thinking had to be changed before this hopeful situation came about.

So it is a natural condition of all creative advances—all worthwhile new ideas—that they will have to overcome previous thought patterns, habits, and accepted ways before they can enjoy the success of their own acceptance. Some ideas are so obviously good that they win acceptance easily. But even many ideas which are obviously good to many people do not win general acceptance purely because of the natural resistance people have to giving up a familiar or understood way of doing things in favor of a somewhat uncertain new way. The job of winning acceptance for a new idea may require more creativeness than did getting the original idea.

Once acceptance is gained, however, it may be the beginning of a period of rapid advancement in commercial adaptation and refinement of the new idea. The history of ideas shows that most long-term developments and expansions occur in "spurts" —rapid progress, followed by "breath-catching" slower periods when we search out weaknesses which indicate new directions to research. Following these new directions can, in turn, result in our discovery of still another new fundamental which, in its turn, will touch off another spurt.

After all, human knowledge is just an accumulation of small facts and assumed facts. As the experience of generation after generation successively confirms or denies those facts, we build them into our knowledge. And it is the same with ideas: one leads to another, and the growth of human progress in every field—the arts, business, science, medicine, or human relations —is based on the progressive addition of one new idea to another, or to another group of ideas, to form a new entity that is a creative whole in itself. Two examples, one from science and one from industry, will serve to show this progression from one idea to another and the pyramiding effects this progression can have on humanity:

We have already mentioned the discovery of the nucleus of the atom by Ernest Rutherford just before World War I. Rutherford continued his experiments in bombarding substances with alpha rays from radium. When he tried nitrogen, he found that it broke down into hydrogen and oxygen. This, he realized, meant he was actually breaking up the nucleus of the atom. The year of this discovery was 1918—right in the midst of World War I. This was a key discovery which unlocked a chain of subsequent research and discoveries.

Two of Rutherford's co-workers, Mssrs. Cockcroft and Walton, were able to duplicate his results by using artificially accelerated ions rather than the natural alpha particles of radium. Next, James Chadwick found that when certain substances were hit by alpha rays, a new kind of particle was emitted—the neutron. Then, Enrico Fermi, working in Rome, found that if the target were surrounded by paraffin, to slow down the neutrons, isotopes could be produced. As a result of Fermi's experiments, other scientists carried out further studies that resulted in the discovery that the uranium nucleus could be split into parts—the first proof of the possibility of uranium fission.

Meanwhile, Fermi had moved to the United States and was working at Columbia University. In his experiments there, he discovered that neutrons are emitted when the uranium nucleus breaks apart. This was another major breakthrough in knowledge. *At that stage physicists all over the world knew that a chain reaction could be set up.* The only questions from then on were when and under what conditions.

The basic research then went into a relatively fallow stage until the beginning of World War II, when Ernest Lawrence saw the possibility that this chain-reaction effect could be of importance as a military development. Lawrence, while at the University of California, had developed the first practical cyclotron. It was suggested to Lawrence that this chain reaction might be accomplished with uranium-235. Then, in Lawrence's laboratory, three assistants, Glen Seaburg, Joe Kennedy, and Arthur Wall, found that a new element could be produced by bombarding uranium with neutrons. This new element we now call plutonium. And they discovered that plutonium would not only undergo fission like uranium-235, but could also be separated chemically from the U-235 to offer important production and performance advantages. Lawrence then contacted Dr. James B. Conant and Dr. Arthur Holly Compton in Chicago to propose the use of uranium-235 to get the chemical plutonium for making an atomic bomb. Out of this meeting came the real start of the atomic project as a war program.

It is clear from this history that the building up of discoveries, with one leading to another, may go on for years before an ultimate product or final theory can result. And, of course, the atomic bomb was by no means the "ultimate" result of all this research. We are just beginning to realize the commercial, medical, and technological by-products of this early atomic research, and there is no measuring at this time what the ultimate results will be.

In his fascinating book, *Machines That Built America*, Roger Burlingame traces the effects that one idea had on the industrial course of the United States and the world. The idea itself was for a pneumatic tire patented in 1888 by John Boyd Dunlop, an Irish veterinary.

When the tire was applied to bicycles, which had been invented eighteen years before, the bicycle changed its shape and became a world-wide fad. Until then, bicycles had been trick machines, with one wheel over 4 feet high and a very small wheel in the rear. But with the possibilities in the pneumatic tire, inventive minds began to move quickly:

They equalized the diameters of the wheels; devised a chain-and-sprocket mechanism to put the driving force into the rear wheel, and, by a proper ratio of diameters and sprockets, reduced the rider's effort. These things were not, of themselves, new. Gearing was ancient. Rear-wheel drive had been used on locomotives. The really new idea was that of making contact with the earth's surface by means of the new substance of rubber. And the bicycle, in America, became a twenty-year fad. Before the fad had run its course, it had completely changed our private and industrial outlook. Here are some of the results of that particular combination of ideas:

Women changed to shorter skirts—from the cumbersome dust-gathering dress of that late Victorian era.

Repair shops sprang up all over the country. But no shop could be expected to carry different pedals, handle bars, sprockets, etc. for the different makes of bicycles, so the idea that machined parts must be standardized and interchangeable began to spread.

Workers in small-town machine shops, small bicycle factories, even tiny village repair shops learned skills and techniques which would make the more complex adjustments on still-to-come automobile motors and transmissions easier. (Two such small-town bicycle mechanics later used their skills to invent the airplane!)

Steel formulas had to be improved because new steels were needed for a light machine that would stand hard usage. New steel alloys for durable moving parts came in with the bicycle.

Sheet steel and steel die presses were needed for mudguards and chain housings. Small accessories like lamps, bells, brakes, tool kits, and pumps helped spur new arts in gadgetry. And the movement to get better roads on which people could ride their bikes advanced to the point where the Massachusetts Institute of Technology introduced a course in road engineering. This movement gained enough momentum to carry on when the mass production of motor cars made it a necessity.*

Thus one simple combination of ideas was enough to completely change dozens of industrial fates through the multiplying effects of its benefits. Is it any wonder then that there should be such a growing realization of the power of ideas? And such a demand for new and different ideas to meet the compounding problems

* Condensed from *Machines That Built America,* copyright, 1953 by Roger Burlingame. Used by permission of Harcourt, Brace and Company, Inc., New York.

that business, humanity, and the world itself all face today? With this realization of the power and need of ideas has come the growing interest in a new art: that of *deliberate* creativity—the utilization of the principles, methods, and techniques we learn from studying highly creative people to try to develop new ideas almost "to order."

Probably the person who should be credited most with stirring up interest in this new art is advertising man Alex F. Osborn. Others had also realized that there were similarities in creative processes and that our highly creative people seem to exhibit some personal characteristics in common. But when Mr. Osborn became interested in the subject, he had the promotional experience and ability to interest others in what has since become a rapidly growing movement throughout business, industry, education, government, and social organizations.

A prime example of how creativity is deliberately being fostered in more progressive organizations is the "Value Analysis" service of the General Electric Company. The aim of Value Analysis at G.E. is to relate the cost of any item to the function, service, or operation purchased by that cost. The value analysts are engineers trained in deliberate problem-solving methods. They are taught, for instance, to challenge systematically anything that "seems" to be obvious. For example, one department recorded all important changes made in the major components of a product. If it developed that a component had not had a major change in five years or more, value analysts were put to work with the object of removing 50 per cent of the cost from that component. Even though it was apparently satisfactory and still a good design, the engineers knew that changes in methods, materials, and production alone take place so rapidly that in five years' time it is quite possible that a 50 per cent cost reduction could be obtained. Another G.E. example: a new industrial X-ray installation was being contemplated. The drawings called for a ring of concrete 12 feet high and 7 feet thick around the installation to stop the X-rays. A value analyst began to ask questions: A wall so large!

What would they do with it after they were through with the X-rays? Was there another material that would also stop X-rays?

He was told that lead would do it, but would cost even more than the concrete. "Well," he asked, "how about dirt? Won't dirt stop X-rays?" This was one the experts hadn't thought of —they had to look it up. "Yes," they reported, "two feet of dirt is equivalent to one foot of concrete when it comes to stopping X-rays." This resulted in a wall made of $5,000 worth of dirt instead of $50,000 worth of concrete—all because a man had been trained to ask questions and look for alternatives.

There are some people who still doubt that the ability to generate creative ideas at will can really be "learned." Or they wonder if ideas produced through such "forced" methods can be as good as ideas produced through inspiration or some other occult and unknown method. "Primary creativeness," they say, "comes out of the unconscious—it involves a leap into the dark. Anything conscious, logical, sensible, realistic, or learned could only be secondary creativity."

However, recent research tends to demonstrate that if people will practice—diligently—the "secondary" techniques, they will, in time, begin to develop signs of the "primary" techniques. Furthermore, even the ideas produced by the so-called "secondary" creativity can be of far more value to a businessman than no ideas at all.

No one seriously claims that creative thinking is becoming a science or that there is any intention of making it a science. There are far too many human variables involved for anyone to be able to locate a specific "imagination button" which can be pushed to turn on the creativity. By the same token, however, no one has yet found the "music button" that makes a musician, or the "painting button" that makes an artist, or the "write button" that makes a novelist. And yet we do have trained musicians, schooled artists, and taught writers. And some of these trained, schooled, and taught people, once they acquired the basic foundations of their arts, have gone on to creativeness in its true sense.

And no one has as yet produced any evidence that a businessman, seeking to cope with his problems and improve his creative output of ideas, cannot, by grounding himself in basic principles and techniques that have worked for other people, go on to become a more creative force in his company or industry.

Now the use of words like "principles," "techniques," or "methods" requires a further caution: creative thinking is not a gimmick. It is not a stunt. It is something that can encompass your whole range of living—from your job and company needs, on out to the kind of parent you are. But sticking strictly to business, we should remember that we are interested in getting ideas, not just for the sake of ideas, but for solving problems. This cannot be overemphasized. And we should begin early in our study of ideas to learn the difference between an idea that is *important* and an idea that is just an idea.

Only by setting our standards high and insisting on meeting them will we be able to reach up to true creativity—deliberately!

3

Characteristics of
Creative People

What makes a man creative? Is it something in his education, or his upbringing, or his physical make-up? Was it where he went to school? Or the books he read while growing up? Is it his intelligence? Is it the kind of job he has? Or the problems he has had to overcome merely to stay alive?

Actually, all of these factors may have some bearing on any individual's creativeness. But not necessarily. In studying the great creative thinkers of the past, we find that they came from all walks of life; were in all kinds of businesses. They had varied interests, beliefs, educations, and temperaments. And the same thing holds true for the creative people we have been able to study in our own time.

Current studies of what makes a person creative are far from complete. But preliminary findings, from independently conducted studies, are so closely in agreement that we think we can now predict what characteristics will indicate at least a *potential*

31

for creativeness. The most comprehensive research effort in this field is probably that of Dr. J. P. Guilford at the University of Southern California. A similar type of study, with almost identical preliminary findings, has been initiated at Penn State College, Pennsylvania, by Dr. Viktor Lowenfeld. Industrial companies have also been studying their personnel assigned to creative activities with similar confirming results. Among the leaders in this are such firms as the AC Spark Plug Division of General Motors; the General Electric Company; and RCA–Victor's Television Engineering Department. We shall expand on the findings of these business concerns in Chapter 14. For now, however, it is important only to note that their researching has, to a large extent, given some practical, dollars-and-cents support to the more academic and scientific studies made by Drs. Guilford and Lowenfeld.

There are at least five primary characteristics common to highly creative people: *problem sensitivity; idea fluency; originality; flexibility;* and *drive.* There are a few other secondary characteristics which, though they may be subdivisions of the first four, are in other ways unique to the point of meriting special mention: redefinition skill; abstracting ability; synthesizing ability; and organizational ability.

Before going into these characteristics in detail, a few qualifications should be made. The first is that no one of these characteristics, by itself, necessarily makes a person creative. All of them together indicate only a *potential* for creativeness. Next, probably no one person would ever possess all of these characteristics to the same degree. They are parts of a whole, however, and though a person may be stronger in one than in the others, he will probably possess at least some ability to manifest the others in his thinking. Finally, it is possible for a person to strengthen his ability in any of these specific areas. This means that it is also possible for a person to effect an over-all improvement in all of them through conscious effort to cultivate these characteristics.

1 · Problem Sensitivity

Basically, problem sensitivity is the ability to recognize that a problem exists. It is also the ability to cut through misunderstandings, misconceptions, lack of facts, or other obscuring handicaps, to recognize the real problem in an apparent situation. Problem sensitivity is vital to creativity, because you can't solve a problem until you know what the problem is, or at least know that you have a problem.

Problem sensitivity, in an individual, manifests itself in many ways. For example, a person seems to be highly aware of the difficulties, needs, and feelings of other people. He is quick to catch anything out of the ordinary or odd or unusual in any situation in which he may find himself. He has the ability to see possibilities that other people miss in situations, people, or materials. As examples:

Howard W. Sams, sales manager of an electronics firm in Indianapolis, quit his job in 1946 to go into business for himself producing service manuals for radio-TV repairmen. There were manuals on the market at that time, but they were poorly organized, nonstandardized hodgepodges of information—highly unsatisfactory to use. Sams also sensed that the TV industry, which was just coming into being, was going to mushroom. And with the industry growth, would come a growing need for more servicemen who would have to absorb thousands of new facts and bits of electronic information in far too little time, if the repair business were to keep pace with the demand. Out of all this came the idea for his simplified servicing manuals which he called "Photofact Folders" for radio-TV repairmen. These folders include complete measurements of every TV model; photographs of the models inside and out; and, where necessary, "explosion" diagrams showing how every part is assembled. Almost overnight, Howard Sams' repair manuals became the "bibles" of servicemen across the country. In less than eight years, Sams' sales soared from $430,000 to well over $3-million!

Donald Brann, of Pleasantville, New York, exhibited problem sensitivity when he related his previous experience selling dress patterns to some carpentry work he was doing in a new home at the request of his wife. His idea was to sell woodworking patterns to the growing army of do-it-yourself homeowners. Selling the patterns was difficult, at first, until Brann realized that his best outlet would be lumberyards and hardware stores. He was able to get his "Easi-Bild" Patterns into these outlets through the simple approach of convincing these dealers that his patterns would help their sales on other products. Today his gross sales are in excess of $1-million a year.

One of the largest and most important corporations in the United States today is General Dynamics. This giant of defense-production industries came into being largely as the result of the problem sensitivity of one man: John Jay Hopkins. In 1945, at the end of World War II, General Dynamics consisted of only the small, but *financially* sound, Electric Boat Company, which had produced, under Hopkins' leadership, seventy-two submarines for the Navy during the war. By 1945 the company had plenty of cash, but very few orders for future business. It was a time when everyone else was talking disarmament and "get the boys home." Hopkins, however, with his far-reaching mind, was able to foresee the problems ahead for the world and realize that the United States was in for a cold war on a more or less permanent basis. Furthermore, he was able to see that the United States was going to need a new kind of defense company to bolster its position in this war: a company capable of producing complete weapons systems, rather than isolated specialties like tanks, guns, planes, or boats. Using his Electric Boat Company as the nucleus, he was able to plan a careful program of acquisition of other companies and to integrate them into a well-managed, soundly financed whole. John Jay Hopkins' death in 1957 robbed American industry of one of its most powerful future-oriented minds.

It is highly significant that in each of these examples the person who anticipated a growing "problem" did not regard it as a problem at all. In each case, his approach was to capitalize on an *opportunity*. This attitude toward problems is probably the chief distinguishing attribute which differentiates the problem-sensitive person from what, for lack of any better term, we could call the "career critic." The world often seems to be filled with people who are only too happy to tell you what is wrong with the world or you or your ideas or your environment or anything else. Some of these are also very brilliant people. And, in a sense, they serve a purpose. They do point out our faults. And, occasionally, with hindsight, they tell us how we could have done better. But strangely enough, these people contribute very little to making the world a better place. It may be that they are so busy waiting for other people to make mistakes that can be pounced on and loudly denounced that they just don't have time to contribute anything constructive themselves.

But the creative person—one who exhibits true problem sensitivity—is more positively oriented. He looks upon a problem as an opportunity. And his deep conviction is that any problem can be solved if the right idea can be found to unlock it. Creative people are positive people. Creative people are confident people. They know that nothing is ever done finally and that everything that has been done in our world can be done over and done better. And they use their sensitivity to people, situations, environment, and the future to find opportunities for contributing their own ideas and effort.

In this basic attitude of a creative person lies your best opportunity to strengthen or develop your own faculty for problem identification. Keep in mind that nothing is ever as well done as it could be. Every man-made article, every business operation, every human-relations technique can be improved and someday will be. In every situation you encounter as an executive, no matter how many times you have met and handled it before, there exists an opportunity to find a better way.

And, as the eminent business statesman, Bruce Barton, once

said, "Don't complain about your troubles. They're responsible for 90 per cent of your income!"

2 · Idea Fluency

The term *idea fluency* simply means that a person has the ability to think up quantities of ideas against a given problem. The value of fluency lies in the fact that the more ideas you have for solving a problem, the greater will be the chances that you will find a really new idea, or at least an idea that is better than anything now in existence.

This, in a way, is just common sense. The human mind, even an ambitious one, is apt to be lazy at times. When it works out one solution to a problem, it is tempted to slip into neutral. That particular problem is "solved." But the best that can be said, ordinarily, is that one solution has been found. It is not necessarily the best solution, or even the "right" one. If you can think of two ways in which the problem might possibly be solved, then the chances are that one of them will be better than the other. If you start out with ten or twenty or a hundred possible ideas, you may easily find that your biggest problem is how to pick the best one.

In the strict sense of the word, *fluency* means that a person not only produces a quantity of ideas, but he also produces them rapidly. You probably know someone among your acquaintances who does this at the drop of a question: you mention some problem you have, and he immediately begins to throw out ideas— all kinds of ideas. Not all of them are good, of course, but at least he is turning his imagination loose to think up possibilities. And this is the key to developing your own fluency: you learn to shift your mental gears into "free-wheeling"—you give your own mind the freedom it needs to produce a chain reaction of thoughts on your problem. In Chapter 8, you'll get some specific tips and devices that should help you improve your own ability to be fluent in ideas.

3 · Originality

Originality is the ability to find a new or different way of solving a problem. It is a measure of uniqueness. And, in creative problem-solving, it comes in all shapes and sizes and degrees. Ideas can range in value from the completely new abstract mathematical theory, which will affect the thinking of scientists for generations, down to a way to save 10 cents a day in your mailroom. In practical, everyday business problem-solving, complete newness, or pure originality, is usually not what is needed. In fact, it may not even be wanted! The originality required of the business executive is more apt to be that of finding new ways to vary existing conditions, or new ways to adapt existing ideas to new conditions, or a new modification of something that will fit in with an existing condition. And the difference between a great business executive and an ordinary one is often the ability to produce these "original" variations to meet new or existing conditions.

The 1958–1959 "nervous period" in American business produced several examples of the type of original thinking that can pay off in everyday problem-solving for an executive:

Sylvania Electric demonstrated a new approach to an existing condition this way: One of their lighting products had 15 per cent of the national market. The company wasn't trying to get more than this, because there were just too many competitors scrambling for that particular business. But when their sales in other lines began to decline, they took a new look at the problem. They finally decided to mechanize the whole production of that product. This resulted in their being able to cut costs and increase production to the point where they went way ahead of competition and actually cornered 60 per cent of the market in the midst of the bad business times.

Reynolds Metals decided to adapt some of their existing ideas to the new conditions of selling caused by the recession. They began a rapid diversification into new markets with aluminum swimming pools, auto parts, boats, and cans. A vice president of the company, John Blomquist, said at the time, "We had all these programs before, but now that business is tough, we're moving a lot faster in these development areas."

California's Consolidated Electrodynamics showed real originality by coming up with a new modification of the duties of their top-management personnel to fit the existing conditions of tougher business: their president stepped down to become an operating man again as senior vice president in charge of four of their fast-growing, but troublesome, divisions; their chairman of the board took over the president's duties.

These, of course, sound like obvious solutions to such problems. And, like most original solutions, they are obvious—once someone else has used them. But the first time they were used, they were *original.*

Of course some degrees of originality rate higher than others: that which rates highest calls for throwing out all the "accepted" or "ordinary" concepts and striking out in a bold new direction. For many of our national and social and civic problems, this type of originality seems to offer the only hope of permanent solutions. Fortunately, on some of these problems, some original thinking is being done—or at least started. Because it does strike at the very roots of traditional ways, it is meeting the resistance that all such bold new concepts meet when they are first launched. Nevertheless, in at least two fields, enough progress has been made to provide hope that new solutions will be forthcoming. Those two fields are education and medicine.

The new experiment in education is that of "tape teaching." The first electronics school has been established in the St. Scholastica Convent School in Covington, Louisiana. This school originated the idea and later received assistance and support from the Fund for the Advancement of Education. St. Scholastica, by an imaginative use of audio-visual devices, has actually managed to reintroduce to its classrooms both individual attention to students in oversize classes, and the demand that the student develop the capacity to think for himself. You can expect to see national attention focused on this technique in the future. It is original—it is different—and, best of all, it seems to work.

In medicine, one of the critical problems today is a constantly growing shortage of hospital beds due to the rapid expansion of our population. Expenditures on new hospital "plants" and new patient treatment facilities have not been able to keep up. Meanwhile, the daily cost of patient care has kept rising. Where an occasional community, in a burst of civic consciousness, has gathered together support for hospital expansion and improvement, the inclination has been to follow tradition in the new façades and floor plans, and thus to perpetuate the mistakes of the past without ever challenging the old ideas of hospital design and patient care to see if they are still the best ways. By the time the funds are raised and the new buildings are put up and equipped, the community usually finds that it is still short of hospital beds, and that the costs of hospital operations have risen to the point where the hospital still can't afford to finance itself.

But in February, 1958, a new look at the job of the medical profession and the hospitals was taken at a special symposium held at the Air University, Montgomery, Alabama. This new look consisted of a completely original approach to the problem: medicine and hospitals should be more than a means to repair damaged health; they should be considered a means to *preserve* good health in the first place. Out of this approach came a recommendation for a completely new type of hospital—one constructed, equipped, and staffed to take advantage of every technical, material, and communications advance of this atomic age. It is called the "Atomedic Hospital." This new idea incorporates sweeping changes in every phase of hospital design, operation, and administration. Such a hospital could provide far better patient care, at much lower cost, for a greater number of people than any conventional hospital. Fortunately, the representatives attending the symposium are practical enough to realize the resistance they are up against in winning acceptance for this new idea, and they are moving in carefully planned steps to overcome it. But this highly unique and original idea may be the answer to medical-care problems Americans will face fifty years from now —which is more than the present methods of constructing and building hospitals can even hope to promise!

Needless to say, the greater the degree of orginality called for to solve a particular problem, the more difficult it is to get that originality. Only through extra effort can you hope to break the boundaries of routine, ordinary, everyday thinking patterns and come up with ideas that are not only usable, but also unique and different.

4 · Flexibility

Creative flexibility is a willingness to consider a wide variety of approaches to a problem. Instead of obstinately freezing onto one particular idea or approach, the flexible person starts out by remembering that if his first solution won't work, he can always back off and approach the problem from another angle.

Flexibility also helps the creative person "roll with the punches" in the development of his idea. In this sense, it has been compared to the "change of pace" used by an athlete. A businessman may be doing a good business on a particular line, with his production, selling, and costs all in a neat ratio, when a sudden shift in public tastes causes an increased demand for the product. A nonflexible mind might hit the panic button in attempts to cope with the upset in the nicely balanced and controlled ratio. A flexible person moves swiftly to switch his thinking into a new gear to accommodate the changes.

Flexibility is also what gives researchers and others that ability to capitalize on the "accidents" we considered in Chapter 2. Since they are flexible in their thinking, they are able to switch their efforts to a more promising discovery if what they are actually looking for continues to be elusive.

Flexibility, of course, is invaluable to the businessman. The administrative executive is not a scientist working in a laboratory with precisely controlled ingredients which he can vary at will in exactly the desired quantities. The businessman is dealing always with people—either the people in his plant, or the people he is dependent upon to sell his product or service, or the people he is counting on to buy his product. And people are not precisely measurable and predictable quantities. Nor are the economic conditions under which he must operate his business or his department. Therefore, the business executive lives in an unpredictable world, where his best-laid plans may be upset by a newspaper headline, a sudden change in the weather, or a line foreman who lost his temper and caused a wildcat strike on the production line.

The symptoms of flexibility are usually easy to observe in others. The quality may be difficult to acquire in your own thinking. The man who sits in a conference or meeting, listening to others "kick a problem around" and sell themselves on what was perhaps the only idea to be produced, and then upsets all the thinking by asking, "Well, what else could we do?" is at least manifesting an inclination toward flexibility.

On the other hand, the person who early in a problem or meeting proposes one idea and one idea alone, and then "fights for it" right down the line, without giving an inch—sometimes, even after it has been conclusively demonstrated that his idea won't work!—is manifesting an unfortunate lack of flexibility.

The person who can seriously consider several possible approaches to a problem solution, each probably being "sold" by its originator, and then, and seemingly out of the blue, propose still another approach that none of the others had even thought of, is exhibiting flexibility.

Actually, flexibility may be closely related to fluency of ideas, in so far as the ability to think up different approaches is concerned. It is certain that the person who contributes twenty or thirty ideas as possibilities will have a better chance of having at least two or three basic approaches in his list than will the person who produces only two or three ideas in the first place. In trying to develop or improve your own flexibility, this fact may give you some help. By deliberately searching out different directions or approaches to your problem solution, and setting some sort of quantity goal for each, chances are you will be able to acquire the habit of starting to think "around" any problem when it first presents itself.

5 · Drive

Drive is possibly the most important characteristic of all for anyone who wants to make himself more creative. If there is enough drive—enough ambition—present, it will go a long way toward overcoming even major deficiencies in some of the other characteristics.

After all, everyone has imagination to some degree—they were born with it. The average person has more imagination than he would ever need to solve any problems he meets up with in his entire lifetime. But when a problem that calls for extra thinking effort presents itself, it is *easier* to pass it by by ignoring it, or to mentally disqualify yourself on the ground that you don't know enough about it, or to hope the problem just goes away by refusing to think about it. But if you would be a creative person, then you need *drive*—and the ability to channel that drive into carrying your ideas through to tangible results in spite of the disappointments, frustrations, obstructions, and blind alleys that are normal, everyday occurrences to the person who innovates and creates.

It is an attitude that has been described as *want to*. If a man *wants* to be creative badly enough, he will find a way. We know from observation that the really creative people, in any field, feel an intense and driving interest in the work they are doing. They have a single-minded approach that other people just do not have. It makes little difference what the creative person is working on; his basic motivation is this driving desire to experience the excitement and pleasure of developing his own ideas. There is nothing "eager" or "put on" about this attitude. The creative man is not driving for his own glorification or power. It is an honest, sincere approach. *It is the love of the work itself.*

This characteristic of drive shows itself in many ways. For example, it makes the person who has it seem able to accomplish much more with his talents or abilities than another person, equally gifted, who does not have this spark. This is because the driving person has learned to concentrate and channel his abilities toward a specific goal: the solution of a problem.

Drive increases the efficiency and productivity of a person. He is not distracted by "little" things or unimportant details. He is, psychologically speaking, a much "healthier" person because unimportant irritations do not have a chance to build up and multiply in his mind—his mind is busy with more important things. The driving person is not afraid to express himself—he doesn't worry about ridicule. He is in a way much less dependent upon other people. In fact, he may frequently feel that other people hamper and handicap him in his efforts. He will probably be much closer to the real world of nature; he will not be too patient with abstract thoughts and fuzzy concepts; he would rather *do* than talk about. He will probably be a relatively happy person because one of his motivating forces is the feeling of accomplishment—the knowledge that he is making progressive contributions and using his natural abilities and talents to the utmost. And, because he does not exercise his drive without direction, he will probably be much more interested in the future than in the past or even the present.

The president of one of our major companies summed up his feelings about people with drive this way: "If I am trying to decide between two men of fairly equal ability, I know that the one with the more enthusiasm will go further than the other because enthusiasm acts as a self-releasing power and helps focus the entire force of personality on any matter at hand. Enthusiasm is infectious; it carries all before it."

Now how do you develop this drive? This, unfortunately, is a question no one is really prepared to answer or even give very firm opinions on. We do know that there seems to be a correlation between general creativeness and drive. People who have taken courses in creative methods and who, according to tests, have shown an increase in their abilities to produce ideas have also shown an increase in what the psychologists call "dominance" —a manifestation, at least, of drive.

It may only be that it was the exercise of will power to complete the course that improved the drive. After all, will power can be developed by practice. Every time you exert your will to make yourself complete a difficult, complicated, or unpleasant task, you make it that much easier to do that same type of task the next time. Your self-confidence gets a boost. And will power, we know, is an important part of drive.

Will power, for instance, helped a young lawyer, Fidel Castro, overthrow a powerful dictator and become the master of Cuba. When Castro first began his revolution, he had only a few followers, and no one paid any attention to him or gave him any chance to win.

Will power carried Dr. Wilder Penfield to world honors as a neurosurgeon in the field of epilepsy. In his trail-blazing days in this exceptionally difficult specialty he was, at times, regarded with actual pity by his contemporaries. A famous British surgeon, commenting on Penfield's accomplishments, said: "Penfield devoted his life to epilepsy research at a time when the subject was regarded by the medical profession as fruitless. He persevered for twenty years in a medical desert, in the face of every kind of discouragement."

And it was sheer will power that kept the brilliant mathematician, Dr. John Von Neumann, going when he knew beyond a doubt that he was dying of cancer. Even when his illness was far advanced, he continued to serve as a member of the Atomic Energy Commission. U.S. Cabinet members and Air Force and other top military officials consulted with him almost daily up to the time of his death. And Von Neumann insisted that it be this way.

Perhaps we can sum up the importance of drive to a creative person with this quotation, author unknown: "Nothing in the world can take the place of persistence. Talent will not; nothing is more common than unsuccessful men with talent. Genius will not; unrewarded genius is almost a proverb. Education will not; the world is full of educated derelicts. Persistence and determination are omnipotent."

6 · Other Characteristics

In addition to the five basic qualities, researchers have also been able to define a few secondary characteristics that are significant to business executives:

Redefinition Skill. This is the ability to shift ideas, conceptions, objects, or people—to use them in new ways. It is important because all creativity does not call for the invention of new or original problem solutions. Much of it, particularly in business, calls for an imaginative use of old ideas or things in a new setting or situation.

Abstracting Ability. This is an analytical ability, which shows up in the capacity to break down complex or difficult problems into their more easily handled components, while, at the same time, keeping track of the interrelationships of the parts. The presence of this ability may, by itself, be a strong indicator of creative potential. When a noncreative person is given a complicated problem, he tends to become bewildered or confused by the whole big mess—he often wastes a great deal of time just trying to figure out where to start. But a more creative person will start wherever he can by biting off any convenient-size chunk and going to work on it.

Synthesizing Ability. This characteristic is the ability to pull seemingly unrelated ideas or objects into a working whole. As we have already seen, synthesized ideas may make up the bulk of the ideas used and needed in business. And this ability to see through the appearances of ideas or objects, which simply confuse or mislead less creative minds, and to see true relationships and possibilities for combinations, is invaluable to an idea man.

Organizational Ability. The popular conception of highly creative people is that they are, if anything, slightly *dis*organized in their thinking. Actually, while this may be true in relation to their personal lives, modes of dress, eating habits, and other surface signs, which the person intent upon more important things may not even be conscious of, it is not true in their thinking patterns on the problems they are trying to solve. This ability shows itself strongly in the way such people can organize a problem; find the place to start; drive themselves into idea production; and then follow through completely and without waste motion to a successful conclusion of their efforts.

So these, in broadly generalized descriptions, are the things we know about creative people. These are the qualities you should strive to develop or improve in your own thinking if you really want to improve your own imaginative output. But remember that possession of these traits alone cannot make you a creative person. They will merely give you the capabilities toward that end.

You can draw an analogy by considering an automobile driver. The good driver knows that for safe driving he needs good tires, good brakes, good eyesight, a steering wheel, and a knowledge of driving laws. But he also knows that all these things will not necessarily make him a safe driver. He also needs a proper attitude —a way of driving to make himself a careful driver. And it is the same with creativity. Mere knowledge of the principles underlying creative thought or creative personalities, and a familiarity with techniques and methods used by other idea men, will not make you a creative person. You also need the attitude.

Blocks to Creativeness

The positive characteristics covered in the preceding chapter represent the *potential* any person has to be creative. But there are also negative forces at work within any personality which can inhibit new or novel ideas. These we can term *mental blocks*. They are, in a way, mental short circuits which literally block off parts of our memory or imagination to keep them from coming into play when we need them. As a corollary effect, they often cause our thinking to be sidetracked into completely unproductive directions so far as solving the problem at hand is concerned.

If not subdued, controlled, or otherwise compensated for, these blocks can win out over our positive characteristics and prevent us from fully utilizing our imaginative powers. Like the positive characteristics, these deterring factors will probably never occur to the same degree throughout the mental make-up of any one individual (he would certainly be a most unpleasant person if they did!). It is, therefore, possible for a person to have a strong mental block, or "set," in one category or direction, and be completely free of inhibitions in others. The average person, and also those who have demonstrated themselves to be highly creative, may

suffer from all the different types of blocks in greater and
lesser degrees. How well they can control or outwit them
determines their final and total creative potential.

Although psychologists can give us many mental "set" descriptions, for all practical purposes they can be generalized and
grouped into three major types: *Perceptual* blocks—the way we
see things; *Cultural* blocks—the way we think we should think
about things; and *Emotional* blocks—the way we feel about
things. There is a fourth category that is probably just a combination of the first three, but for purposes of examination we shall set
it out as a separate type: *Habits*—the automatic thinking processes
that govern so much of what we do.

1 · Perceptual Blocks

A perceptual block is caused by the mind's tendency to short-
circuit and jump to a conclusion too rapidly. We look at something, and what we see appears to be all there is. (The way the
human male can look at a well-endowed young female, and immediately overestimate all her other attributes.) However, *perception*, as we are using it here, is not limited to the physical act
of seeing. It also includes the mental act of synthesizing facts or
observations into a whole. This manifests itself frequently when
we are given a new problem to work on, with an incomplete
background of facts. We jump to a conclusion on the basis of
the facts we have, and then put our minds to work trying to
justify that conclusion. Actually we frequently block ourselves
from ever solving the problem satisfactorily because the jump
carried us to the *wrong* conclusion.

A glance at the drawing on the next page will probably give you
a firsthand demonstration of a perceptual block in action. What
did you see when you first looked at it?—a wineglass?—or two
faces looking at each other?

If you saw the wineglass, you saw a white object in front of
a black background. If you first saw the faces, you saw black

objects in front of a white background. By now, of course, you should be able to see *both* pictures—*but only one at a time.* Although it is possible to make an instantaneous mental shift back and forth, you cannot see both pictures at one and the same time. Therefore, if, when you first looked at the drawing, your mind stopped with a single impression—either the wineglass or the faces—and did not go on to see the other, you were being restricted by a perceptual block.

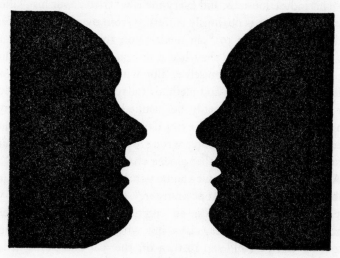

Fig. 1

Now let's translate that into a very common business problem with a salesman as an example: This salesman is on his way into a plant to call on the purchasing agent. In his hand is a briefcase containing a catalogue describing a whole line of products his company has to sell. But this salesman is calling on that purchasing agent to sell him one item he thinks the man might be interested in buying. He either makes the sale or he doesn't, and then he leaves. On the way in, and on the way out, he passed right by a dozen opportunities to sell other products he had right in that catalogue right in the briefcase, right in his hand. But he never even saw these opportunities because his perception was limited to that one opportunity he had in mind when he entered the plant. This is the kind of perceptual block that hurts—it costs money!

Another example: we watch a fellow-executive or co-worker who seems to be the most industrious man in the company. He works nearly every night and at least one day every weekend, in addition to his daily schedule on the job. Everyone is impressed with his industriousness, and everyone is worried about his "killing pace," because he is obviously suffering from overwork. It is easy and all too common to "pin medals" on this man. Chances are his management wishes they had a dozen more like him so they could take life easier themselves. But with what we know about efficient working habits and methods today, such a work schedule for any man cannot possibly be justified. If a man has to work long hours of overtime and extra days a week to handle his job, then there is either something wrong with the man or something wrong with the job. In either case, a change is called for.

Another way in which we can be perceptually blocked is in our inability to carry over, or "transfer," the creative abilities we already have. As examples: an engineer who solves problems wholesale on his job every day—but who has to use brute force to get his ten-year-old son to turn off the TV and go to bed at ten o'clock. Or a highly talented designer who can't solve simple problems of personal finance and money management and so has to spend his time both in and out of the office dodging collection agencies. Or the do-it-yourself home hobbyist who spends every spare hour creating beautiful pieces of furniture—starting with orange crates—but who treats his job as a dull routine, to be gotten through with in the easiest possible way every day, when actually any job presents the same kind of creative challenge he enjoys in his basement workshop. All these people are blocked from using their imaginations because they do not see, or do not realize, that the same methods, the same attitudes, and the same approaches that they use so successfully in one field can also be applied to solving their personal problems or job problems of other types.

Perceptual blocks, then, are all those factors that prevent us from getting a complete, accurate, and pertinent picture of the world around us. If you do not know with accuracy what your world or your problems really consist of, you will find it extremely difficult, and perhaps impossible, to be creative.

2 · Cultural Blocks

Cultural blocks represent all the effects of society on the individual. These are the forces that tear down our individuality— that shove us into accepted grooves in our thinking. Cultural blocks make us conformists. And the pressures to conform in our society today often seem so overwhelming that they may also seem irresistible. A great part of this pressure comes from our natural election to live, work, and participate in groups. By electing to be a member of a group, we feel that in one way or another we should change. We find ourselves beginning to behave in a group as though certain things were expected of us, even though the other members of the group would probably deny that they had ever attempted to "set us straight." Even a group with the attitude of do-nothing and care-nothing tends to exert an influence on a member. As an example, the so-called "beat" set. Whether we like it or not, a group tends to make its members over into a group image. And whether we like it or not, a company or business organization is a group, and unless we want to leave civilization and become beachcombers or hermits, we have to learn to live with groups. But we do not have to become *blind* conformists to any group's ways of thinking, acting, or behaving.

Let's examine a few of the reasons why we feel we are under pressure to conform to a group image:

To start with, inclinations to conform begin early in childhood. The child learns to conform to family standards, because when he tries to ignore those standards, he is punished for it—or, when he is older, he runs the risk of being criticized for his actions and, according to the standards, criticism is bad. Now when this child grows to be a man and joins a business organization, his first inclination is to look for the standards. Every organization which has been in existence for any time at all will have certain traditions, values, and standards which have become "accepted" as the way things are done. The newcomer, just joining such an organization, quickly learns that certain kinds of behavior are approved, while others are definitely frowned upon.

Some of these standards and values are never written into company policy. They are sometimes never even talked about. And yet they seem to exist—"seem" because often no one has ever had the courage to challenge them and find out if they really do exist! Not all of these standards are based on the best of motives, and some may, in actuality, be bad for the welfare of a company. Some such standards are relative to the various levels of a company. For instance, an ambitious and talented young man may find that other employees of his age group or position have set up an implied restriction which requires him to limit his ambition and the use of his talent. The motive behind this may be nothing more than pure envy. If he does not conform and if, in spite of the group's disapproval, he continues to exercise his ambition and display his resourcefulness to the point where he attracts management's attention and support, he will find himself becoming a lonely person. His group, and its individual members, will tend to expel him. If his character is strong and his perception great enough to realize what is happening, the individual will stand up to the group and continue to go his own way. But "no man is an island," and few individuals can stand to be ostracized by their fellows. Therefore, the odds are probably greater that the ambitious young man will take the edge off his ambitions and slow down his efforts in order to stay in the good graces of his group.

(This type of group pressure is certainly not confined to the business world. It is demonstrated in *every* group in one way or another: community, social, civic, church, or educational classroom. In fact, some of these may affect an individual's outlook and approach to life to a far greater extent than does his business or work group.)

Actually, a certain amount of conformity is a very necessary thing. Without it, we'd have no civilization. And the lifetime conformists in our population are, in one way, society's stabilizing elements. The conformists are the ones who remind us to "Take it easy—Rome wasn't built in a day" (ignoring, of course, the fact that it was destroyed in a night!). The conformists say, "Understand your neighbor—be tolerant of him" (without understanding that tolerance is no virtue at all unless what you are tolerating is worthwhile). But when conformity assumes such importance that it begins to interfere with free and original and different thinking, it begins to stifle individual initiative. And this is where the danger lies.

The person who goes out of his way to refuse to conform, however, is, in his way, just as much a conformist as any "group-think" advocate. If he is taking a negative attitude toward everything, just to avoid conformity or just to oppose the group, he has also surrendered his freedom of thought and action. He just says "no" to everything, and you can depend on it.

Fortunately it is not necessary to adopt such an extreme in order to retain or regain your own freedom of thought. Many of the social or implied pressures to conform are not really pressures at all. They don't exist anywhere except in the minds of the individuals who think they exist. To take just one fairly common business situation, let's consider the age-old institutions of the office party and the company picnic.

There are four types of people who attend such company gatherings: The boss, who feels he should at least put in an appearance, since it is an opportunity for him to demonstrate his interest in his workers. This may be the only time in the year that he does demonstrate an interest in his workers, or it may not.

But since he is really responsible for the whole thing in the first place, he feels he should be there. And he probably should. The second type are those who honestly enjoy such affairs, and they certainly should not be reproached for attending. Then there are those who are "on the fence"—when they go, they have a good time, but they wouldn't feel any great loss if the whole benevolent practice were discontinued. But there is a fourth type who attend and shouldn't. These are the people who dislike such affairs from beginning to end, but who attend purely out of fear. They are afraid that if they do not show up, the group will censure them. Or they are afraid the boss will take it as a sign of disloyalty or disinterest if they do not support the regimented "fun" the company is supplying. Both of these fears are usually groundless, and giving in to them means a sacrifice of integrity and moral values for the person who gives in. And just as you can build up your mental abilities and character by practicing them, so you can tear down your individuality by chipping it away. Let's examine those two fears to see how much real danger there is if a person refuses to "go along with the crowd":

First, the fear that he will be censured by his co-workers if he does not show up at the party or picnic: He may receive a few snide remarks from other members of his group—but they will be in the fourth class of people. Their remarks will probably be made out of envy that they themselves didn't have the courage to avoid what they also considered an unpleasant "duty." The majority of his co-workers—if they even noticed his absence—probably won't say anything at all or have their feelings about this individual changed one bit. On the contrary, those who really enjoyed themselves at the outing or whatever may feel rather sympathetic toward the person who didn't attend because "He missed such a good time!"

And what about the boss? How will he take it if the man is truant? That will depend, to a large extent, on the man. In this day of penny-profits and cut-throat competition, no manager is ever going to fire a good worker or able executive simply because this person felt he had better things to do than attend a picnic. If a man has consistently demonstrated his ability to think for himself and act on his own values, chances are he is enjoying whatever job or position he has because of those attributes, and the boss could even *expect* him to be independent in deciding his amusements.

So, generally, what all these fears of nonconformity come down to is a fear of being "different." We have been taught, since childhood, that to be different is to be wrong. Unfortunately, we weren't given any scales to measure the degrees of difference. We have learned only that to be different at all is to be wrong. But today, in business or any other field you choose to examine, the need is for *individualists*—people who can be above average in their thinking and in their job performance and who are, just by virtue of being above average, *different*.

Any fear of being different can quickly disappear if you take a cold, objective look at it and the possible outcomes of practicing it. We should realize and admit at the outset that much of the fear is simply *ego involvement*—we are so wrapped up in ourselves, and in preserving what we think other people think about ourselves, that we don't realize that these people are just as wrapped up in themselves and probably won't even notice if we begin to exercise some independence and individuality in our thinking and actions.

Of course, one must use caution in being different. You have no right to let your differing interfere with the rights of others. People won't mind your being independent and freethinking as long as you don't adopt an attitude of superiority about it. Chances are that if you can just learn to tolerate other people and their differences—granting them, in your own mind, the right to be different—you will have made a better start on individuality than most people accomplish in their entire lifetime!

Now we have said that some conformity is good and even necessary. So to put a proper perspective on when you should and when you shouldn't, and when you need to and when you don't, let's take a look at the "big" picture of a modern man in his *total* environment.

Imagine a large circle. In the very center of the circle, put a small dot. This dot is a modern man and the circle is the environment in which he lives. By a "modern" man we mean you—or any other person you care to think of. This is not a cave man wresting a bare existence out of his prowess as a hunter; it is not a medieval serf working in lifetime servitude for his lord and master; it is not a pioneer American carving a new country out of the wilderness. It is you and the way you live today.

Now divide that mental circle into three parts. One part we label "WORK." The second we label "OTHERS." The third, we label "SELF." Together, they make up the three basic relationships a man has to consider in his living. The lines between the segments represent opportunities to compartmentalize your thinking. Let's start by considering the thinking needed for the part of your life reserved for WORK:

We use the term WORK, rather than job, to make it as all-inclusive as possible. After all, the job you have today may not be the job you will have tomorrow. But the same mental approach will have to be used. Now any kind of work demands a certain amount of standardization just for efficiency and quality. This is why we have organizational charts and job descriptions in business. Even a medical doctor, who may consider himself the most free of men, will follow certain procedures in an operating room and insist on certain standards of purity in the medicines he prescribes. And, to carry out this standardization in our work, it may even be necessary for us to learn to think in terms of standardization and set patterns. But carrying on our day-to-day standardized routines does not require us to standardize our thinking toward the larger pattern of our WORK. Nor does it mean that we have to carry production-type thinking over the boundary on either side of WORK so that it creeps into our relationships with either OTHERS or SELF.

In deciding just how much "creep-over" we will allow in our three areas, we have to exercise some judgment. We have to decide just what kind of life it is we *want* to lead.

If our social life—away from our *official* WORK area—includes mostly people and friends with whom we work all day, then we have removed, or at least punctured, the barrier between the areas of WORK and OTHERS.

If we become so dependent upon a group to think or decide for us that we cannot think or make a simple decision contrary to the group opinion, then we have destroyed the barrier between OTHERS and SELF.

Actually these barriers do exist, or can exist, for any man. In exercising independence of thought and action, it is completely possible for a man to move freely and without harming others if he just remembers that the barriers are there, and that it is on his own volition that he crosses them. There is no social pressure that can force a man to lower or destroy the barrier between his inner SELF and the outside world of OTHERS. There is no job or business pressure that can force a man to sacrifice the integrity felt by his inner SELF for the expediencies of WORK. If any such sacrifices, or giving in to conformity, do occur, they will only happen if the individual himself decides to allow them to happen.

Conformity, then, is a voluntary thing. And it can be voluntary to almost any degree in different areas of environment. The important thing is to make certain that you do not let conforming to someone else's way of doing something rob you of your own initiative to think independently wherever and whenever you are in control of the situation. The big danger in conforming to a pattern is that we don't question why the accepted pattern is accepted, or by whom it was accepted in the first place, or whether the original conditions of acceptance still prevail. It is not a crime, or even morally wrong, to conform—but to sacrifice your independence to decide whether or not you will conform is.

3 · Emotional Blocks

Emotional blocks to creativity are those caused by anger, envy, fear, dread, hate, greed, love, lust, and so forth. They are, principally, divided into two major types: the *transient* blocks which come and go from day to day or week to week, and the *permanent* ones which were built into our personalities early in life and which probably underlie nearly everything we do for the rest of our lives. Both types interfere with our thinking because they rob us of our concentration, mental energy, and initiative by making us squander ourselves on worries, anxieties, and phantasies over what might occur should our worries and anxieties be realized.

Transient blocks are the lesser of the two types so far as permanently hampering the imaginative abilities. These can be caused by temporary financial difficulties, problems with children, an argument with your wife, a lack of recognition at work, worry about the outcome of a decision, and so forth. Finding yourself forced to work with an incompatible personality on your job may cause you to suffer from a temporary overloading of your emotional resources.

When you are suffering from a temporary emotional block, your mental efficiency and freedom are impaired. It can happen as simply as this:

Every morning when the boss comes in, he greets you with "Hi, Bill, how're tricks?" But one morning he comes in, and as he passes by your desk he says, "Hello, Bill, what are you up to today?"

Immediately your mind short-circuits: "What does he mean, what am I up to? Do you suppose someone has been talking to him about me? I haven't done anything to make anyone suspicious ... who do you suppose has been in there lying to him?"

And from there on, your train of thought leads you to suspect everyone in the office of trying to "get" you, and your mind is completely lost so far as productive thinking is concerned. Worry and fear take over, and frustration at an imagined situation simply freezes the gears for any normal thinking. It isn't until you can invent an excuse to get in to see the boss and make sure that your relationship is still "safe," or until the next morning when he comes by again and says, "Hi, Bill, how're tricks?" that your mind will calm down and permit you to think normally once more. And, chances are, during this period of mental anguish, you yourself may never have realized that you weren't thinking in your usual normal productive way.

Pressure, in the sense of a very real pressure originating outside yourself, is something else that can emotionally block you from finding creative solutions to problems. There are people who believe that pressure is the key to getting more work out of others; there are whole businesses where *fear* is the prod to production. Like the manager who brags, "My men don't give me ulcers—*I* give *them* ulcers!"

What actually happens is that under pressure your mind sets up a feedback effect: your thoughts begin to go round and round in a tight, closed circuit—nothing new or different can get in; nothing unusual or original can get out. What you do then is to strike blindly for the easy way out: the simplest, most logical solution to the problem you can find—one that is safe, tried, and true, and that you will be able to defend against all challenges. In a pressure situation, there will be challenges—you know that before you start. And it is almost certain that any answer or idea that is safe, tried, and true will *not* be original, creative, or even worth the time it took you to get it!

Other causes of temporary emotional blocks can be laid to such factors as health and personal habits. If you are overly tired, or have to put up with the prolonged mental drain of a serious family illness, or are physically ill yourself, your own mental nervous system begins to feel the drain of the static. Your ability to organize thoughts and problem parts into logical patterns or theories begins to be affected. This, in turn, may cause a subconscious frustration which, in its turn, adds still more confusion to the nervous system. Finding the cure for this type of emotional upset, of course, requires getting at the causes. Physical and emotional health and well-being are prerequisites to maximum mental efficiency.

Of the more permanent types of emotional blocks, the kind we acquire early in life and carry with us ever after, probably the two most important are the *fear of failure* and the *fear of ridicule*. We manage to learn early in life that "nothing succeeds like success" and, its companion adage, "nothing fails like failure." And so we go through life doing everything we can to avoid making mistakes—"it's better to be safe than sorry."

One of the dangers of this attitude is that we can rationalize it to ourselves so that we don't even realize this *is* our governing attitude. For instance, on our jobs, we tell ourselves that the reason we don't openly disagree with some idea of management, or try to promote an idea of our own that would be contrary to current management thinking, is that this would be "disloyal"—and we are very loyal to our boss and our company! So we avoid the disagreement. Not to belittle loyalty in any way, but a very sharp manager once remarked that "When two men in an organization think exactly alike, you can usually fire one of them—and maybe both of them!"

One of the things we forget in "playing it safe" is that one can usually *learn* more from a mistake than from a success. Failure teaches us what we don't know and what we need to know about ourselves. And this is the key to your own progress and development.

Sometimes we hold off taking any action because we are afraid we don't know enough. But this can often be a help, rather than a hindrance. Consider Henry Ford. There are many men in business today who, had they been around at the time, would have advised Henry Ford against going into production on his

Model T. They would have suggested that he hold off until marketing research could find out if there really was a market for such a thing as an "automobile." They would have wanted to test the "price structure" to see if people would pay $300 or $400 or $500 for such a thing. They would have wanted him to find out if people would consider this automobile better than a horse, streetcar, or bicycle. And they certainly would have insisted that he find out what colors people preferred, instead of just going ahead with black. But "poor" Henry Ford didn't have any of these people around to advise him, and he didn't know the answers himself, so all he could do was to take the risk of failure and go ahead and make a few million dollars for himself!

Another strong emotional deterrent to creative thought, which may usually be classed as a "permanent" type of block, is the fear of ridicule. This is ingrained in most people through having had their ideas laughed at or ignored at some time in the past. It may have been an idea that the person was particularly proud of; or it may have been a succession of criticisms which gradually wore away his confidence and sense of daring.

Even in this day of scientific and social achievement, where things that were only dreamed of yesterday are realities today, it is still common for people to laugh at or criticize any unusual or different ideas before they've taken the time to really think them through and determine whether they have possibilities. It may be of some comfort to you to realize that almost every great idea was laughed at when it was first proposed—and usually, the greater the idea, the louder the laughter.

There is actually a sound psychological explanation of why people, including yourself, are apt to laugh at a new or novel idea: it is a natural reaction caused by your inborn instinct for self-preservation.

A new idea sounds an alarm to your psyche of a "change" coming. Immediately, your instinctive reaction is to come to full nervous alert in response to a need for possible action. This is pure instinct and you can no more prevent it than you can prevent tensing up at a sudden strange or new noise until you have identified the noise as friendly or unfriendly.

In the case of the new idea, however, your mind immediately recognizes it for what it is, and the next psychological reaction, again purely instinctive, is to seek a release of the nervous tension that has been built up. Laughter is an automatic form of release —it comes out spontaneously and often uncontrollably in response to your nervous system's demand for relaxation.

In this respect, the act of laughing at a new idea is not bad. The danger is in the effect that the laughter may have on the confidence of the idea's creator, because fear of ridicule, in any form, is a deterrent to creative effort.

The *fear* of ridicule is probably closely allied with the basic fear of failure we carry with us. If an idea is so new or so novel or so striking that it seems to go against "common sense," then there is at least an implied danger of its failing. But common sense is not always right—and it is not really so common or so sensible as its advocates like to think. The late Albert Einstein, who probably contributed as much as any other human being to laying the groundwork for truth in science, once made the observation that "Common sense is nothing but a deposit of prejudices laid down in the mind prior to the age of eighteen."

Timidity can also kill off creativity. The timid person lacks the self-confidence to venture into new and daring directions. Frequently, the cause of such timidity is merely lack of opportunity or failure to recognize opportunity. Self-confidence comes from repeated successes and the gradual realization of ability which the truly confident person has. A confident person feels more daring and thinks more daringly because he has the backing of previous successes. This may be the basis of that old half-truth that "nothing succeeds like success." On the other hand, the timid person might want to consider for a moment that the person best able to take a chance on a new or different venture is the person with the *least* to lose.

Two other fairly common blocks to creativity are those of *self-satisfaction* and *superperfectionism*. Self-satisfaction may, of course, be the quality of self-confidence that has gone to a person's head. But when we become so convinced of our innate abilities that we become smug about them, we lose sight of opportunities for improvement. Everything that has been done remains to be done over—even if we ourselves did it.

Superperfectionism has killed off many worthwhile ideas and kept them from coming into being simply because the perfectionist kept searching for the ultimate—a point which is never reached. If you have an idea, and your idea is better than anything in existence at the time, then you should put it to work. You can get rid of the "bugs" or drawbacks later on. But first, get your idea going for the good of everyone concerned.

We cannot drop the subject of emotional blocks without some attention to another phenomenon that seems peculiarly American: the "happiness" seekers. People have begun to run from crises that are only normal problems of living normally. It is not true that a complete freedom from either fear or anxiety is a "healthy" state of mind. Both fear and anxiety are normal attributes that serve helpful purposes by keeping us at our best. Fear makes us uncomfortable, certainly. But the reason we feel fear at all is that it is basic to self-preservation. Anxiety tenses us and may cause all sorts of minor physical side effects. But the fact that it can tense you up makes it helpful. It keeps you doing your best and it helps you anticipate problems well in advance. If you aren't anxious, you will dull such anticipation. The act of swallowing some pill to make fear and normal anxiety go away is a complete chimera: when the effects of the pill have worn off, the causes of anxiety and fear will still be there. And trouble has a way of getting worse if left to its own devices even for the time it takes to digest and assimilate a small pill.

So how do you live with fears, tensions, and anxieties? It may sound oversimplified, but it is the truth: you take advantage of them. Learn to make your tensions work for you.

Realize first that tension is normal. So is fear. So is anxiety. Usually, if you face up to a fear, you can trace it in your own mind to what is causing it. This may actually be the means of sensitizing yourself to a problem. Once you have faced your problem squarely, then you can reduce it to an academic problem: work on ways to solve it. This is far different from worrying about it. Worry, of course, is fruitless. It is much better to imagine all the possible consequences of your trouble, even the worst possible thing that could happen, and then figure out what you will do if that does happen. In this way, you will gradually begin to build your self-confidence to the point where it will take more than a minor tension to upset you. Tension may spell trouble—but trouble can spell opportunity.

4 · Habits

To a great extent, any person's personality consists of his own individual pattern of actions, thoughts, and habits. And much of what we do every day is determined by a carefully conditioned and developed pattern of habits.

These habits are useful to us in many ways. They consist, of course, of successful solutions to problems that we have met up with and faced before. And, because so many of the "problems" that we face every day are of a repetitious nature, we can use these previously successful solutions over and over again. In one way this is all to the good because it frees our minds to think about more important things. The big danger of habitual living is that our habit of using past problem solutions often prevents us from seeing a better solution. And, of course, we eventually lose the very worthwhile habit of actually *looking* for new solutions to problems.

In our work, habits of certain kinds are a necessity. As business becomes larger and more complex, companies must reduce more and more of their operations to standardized procedures—or habits. We are forced to accept certain "habits" in our day-to-day working. But here, too, it is easy to get the habit of accepting habit without challenge. We do many things because someone has said, "That's company policy." Habit may make us accept this without questioning whether or not the whole thing makes sense. But if something doesn't make sense, then the chances are it is *not* company policy—unless the company is intentionally heading into bankruptcy.

There are times when we do find something that doesn't make sense, but does indeed seem to be company policy. Often this will turn out to be a policy that started out as expediency. One business consultant put it this way: "I often get the impression that 'the way we do things around here' developed back in the early days of the company when some overworked executive was tossed a problem. He made a snap decision as to how it could be handled and, fortunately, it worked. Later, someone wrote this into a manual and permanently froze the thinking on it. Ever since, 'that is the way we do it.' No one else ever had the guts to challenge the old way by proposing a new way. Consequently, these 'standard procedures' are costing American business millions of dollars a year!"

The difficulty with overcoming bad habits lies in the fact that people are usually not aware of the extent to which habit has taken over their thinking. Habits in our day-to-day living, and in our daily working, can develop into a fixed pattern that seems "normal." For this reason, we find it difficult to see that it is our own complacency that has dug us deep into a habit groove. We prefer to blame others or outside conditions: our boss, our wife, our office location, our children—in fact, anyone or anything but ourselves.

Furthermore, getting out of a mental rut requires real effort. Creative thinking entails the hardest kind of mental discipline and effort. Unless there is some great incentive, and money is often not enough, people prefer the *status quo*. Life is so much simpler that way. But before you can begin to overcome noncreative habits, you must first face up to them in yourself. After all, the devil you know is a lot friendlier than the devil you don't. But first you have to recognize the devil for what he is!

Now it is obvious that if habits aren't actually caused by some of the primary types of mental blocks, all blocks are, in a way, also habits. The difficulty is that we have allowed ourselves to become so absorbed in routine matters, routine ways of thinking, and routine reactions to situations that we seldom use our senses to help us break the routines. Routine seems normal—it is a self-perpetuating circle. But the way to overcome mental-blocking patterns is the same way you overcome bad habits. By changing one set of creative inhibitors, you will also probably change the other.

Now the best way to "change" any bad habit is to *replace* it with a *good* habit. Sometimes, in the case of mental habits, something as simple as dressing differently can help you. If you've always worn dark blue suits, get a brown one. If you've always worn four-in-hand ties, live a little—get a bow tie!

Deliberately vary your living routine. Try driving to work or driving home a different way—even a different way every day for a week. Try changing your meals around—try soup for breakfast some morning. (It actually makes a very good breakfast!)

Give your mind some thinking to do that is different from what it is normally called upon to do. Read books that make you think. These don't have to be "great" literature—even a 25-cent detective story can do it: stick with the story until you've got all the clues that Inspector Bloodstone has, then close the book; analyze the case; and imagine an ending yourself.

Begin associating with people who make you think. These won't necessarily be people who always agree with you—in fact, you may find yourself disagreeing with them most of the time. But make sure it is not *blind* disagreement. Really try to understand them and why they think as they do. This will help you understand yourself better.

A change of pace can help you avoid getting into a mental rut on your job. If you've been sticking at one type of work for some time—say two or three hours—put it aside and do something else. Something completely different. One executive reported that his formula is "to slip over into the park and just relax. It's the quickest way I know to snap myself out of a mental roadblock."

The key to getting out of a rut—or avoiding one in the first place—seems to be to do something completely out of your regular routine, rather than to continue the fight to get ahead by means of your regular routine.

And as you go after these new experiences, practice the art of relating them to you, your job, and your problems. Learn to look around you—at everything. And as you observe, ask questions about what you see. Ask yourself: Why was this made this way? Why was this done like this? Is this object really necessary? What would happen to the whole if this detail were eliminated? How can this be improved? Don't let your own habits or conformity to other people's thinking stop you. There's a better way to do anything, and if you ask enough questions you will begin to find the better ways!

5

The Nature of
Creative Thought

There is not a great deal of difference in the mental processes of creative minds, whether the minds belong to artists, writers, scientists, musicians, medical researchers, or business executives.

Some individuals may take exception to this, feeling that their problems are so "different" that their mental processes must also be different. But their problems, as we shall see in the next chapter, aren't really so different after all. And their mental processes are really quite similar, as we shall try to demonstrate in this chapter.

The difficulty is one of perception. It is difficult to see the similarities because of the surface appearances. The artist, writer, scientist, and business executive do move in different "thought worlds" in that the words, or "symbols" of thought, are somewhat different. Then, too, very real differences in talents and aptitudes are called for. And it is the exercise and domination of these that determine whether a creative mind will initially turn toward art, music, science, or business as an outlet.

Ben Hecht, the successful author of many books, articles, and short stories, in addition to more than seventy motion-picture screen plays, pointed out the ways in which writers differ from other types of creative workers in an article in the February, 1959, *Esquire:*

> The writer is a definite human phenomenon. He is almost a type— as pugilists are a type. He may be a bad writer—an insipid one or a clumsy one—but there is a bug in him that keeps spinning yarns; and that bulges his brow a bit, narrows his jaws, weakens his eyes, and gives him girl children instead of boys. Nobody but a writer can write. People who hang around writers for years... who are much smarter and have much better taste, never learn to write.
>
> ... The writer, put in any active group of men, will always collapse as a dominant. He will be the least listened to in any mixed company. Even other writers shy at hearing a writer sound off.
>
> The reason is sort of biologic. A writer's ego goes into the game of solitaire he plays with plot turns and speeches. He has, usually, little left over for the domination of the realities around him. A long-suffering wife or an aging concubine are usually the only human beings before whom he can strut successfully.*

Similar descriptions of the surface changes brought about by years of specialized thinking patterns can be, and have been, made for artists, scientists, musicians, and other types of creative personalities. But these do not adequately picture the creative minds in action. There are people who resist any attempts to paint such basic pictures. They feel that creativity must have a certain "mystery" to be truly creative. They use such words as aesthetic, phantasy, intuition, fancy, and vision in trying to describe it themselves. And they may be partly right.

But the fact that the great creative men of the past practiced idea production by intuition, does not mean that the art or science or procedures or whatever you choose to call them cannot be learned. If a young man does not happen to have been born with the intuitive sense of a Marconi, there is still no reason why

* © 1959 by Esquire, Inc.

he cannot study the science of ether waves and make himself proficient in communications electronics. And the same holds true of creative thought processes in general: it is possible to point out similarities and generalizations in the way creative minds work, and there is no reason why someone else cannot study these and try to adapt or adopt them in solving his own problems.

As a generalization, we can say that almost any creative worker will proceed through these stages in his idea production:

He starts with an interest, which may stem from talent or aptitude, or which may be acquired out of some form of "hero worship"—of a father, a teacher, uncle, friend. Whatever the source, his interest causes him to become familiar with some particular field. This is the *learning* period where he gets his fundamentals.

As he becomes more familiar with the field, he becomes aware of specific needs and deficiencies of various kinds. And, the more he learns about it, the more such problems he becomes aware of.

At some stage, one of these problems will become important enough to stand out and present a personal challenge to a creative mind. Then begins a struggle, because a creative mind will literally "force" itself to attack that particular problem. This is the *drive* manifesting itself. *The lack of this feeling of challenge and determination to master the problem is largely what distinguishes the noncreative person from the creative.*

As the creative mind struggles with this problem, it will usually alternate between the "battle" and a less-intensive "relaxation." This activity usually ends with a sudden sense of illumination— the person literally "sees the light."

At this point, his whole energy will begin to storm toward a solution—he quickly throws all his mental powers into the successful conclusion of all his previous struggling and effort.

The final stage is the perfecting of his idea—the careful polishing and adjusting to "get the bugs out" and produce a finished product from his imagination.

Now are these steps so intuitive, or instinctive, that the people following them must be completely unaware of their existence?

The answer seems to be a definite "No." Just as the machinist or carpenter knows that for his best work he must develop skills and techniques through practice and analysis, the really productive creative workers seem to realize that the only way to make efficient use of *their* tools—mental skills and imagination—is through awareness of them and a conscious effort to improve their use.

At a special symposium on Creative Thinking, sponsored by the Industrial Research Institute, three artists—a painter, a musician, and a poet—were asked to describe, as aptly as possible, what they went through in producing a new piece of work.* Their descriptions show not only great awareness of their own mental patterns, but also great similarities—even though they work in different fields, using different materials and thought symbols:

Mr. John Ferren, of New York, the painter, analyzed the process this way:

> Creative thinking, in my personal experience, divides into three phases, of which the middle only contains the essential act of perceiving structure. The first phase, I would call the intellectual sensibility phase. To the scientist it is the collection of data, the period of observation, of speculative thought, of curiosity, of prodding into weak spots, and apparent dead ends. Ideally, all possible knowledge on the particular subject should be covered and exhausted. With the artist, the process is very much the same. The storehouse of visual memory is racked over, the work of other artists is regarded, accepted, or rejected. The errors of the artist's past work are considered and meditated on. New visual experiences are catalogued and correlations attempted in painting terms. Certainly some philosophical considerations, ultimate goods, purposes, and so forth cross his mind—psychological ones too. In this phase, the modern artist has widely used automatism, which is a deliberate playing with the brush with no idea in mind, akin to the telephone doodle.
>
> ...In sum, this period is that of the accumulation of source material...it may be plodding and passive, or playful and speculative

* A monograph titled "The Nature of Creative Thinking" reports this symposium in its entirety. It is published by, and is available from, The New York University Press, Washington Square, New York 3, N. Y.

or intense and anguished. Its essential character is complexity and diffuseness.

The pinpointing comes with the creative act, and I believe that the occasional intensity and drama of the first and last phases of creative thinking have clouded the true nature of the moment of perception. The *effect* of an insight may be that of the proverbial clap of thunder, but the immediate *cause* of insight is to me calm and quiet.

... The moment of insight is nearly always brief, and cannot be long sustained or cultivated, but passes rapidly into the third phase where the insight releases the energy necessary to implement itself and give it flesh. It is in this third period that occurs the conventional white heat of inspiration which is, actually, the mad scramble to fit all the little pieces together in their new order.

The musician was the composer, Mr. Ernst Krenek, of Los Angeles. He agreed, almost without exception, with Ferren's remarks, and then added these specific observations on his own art:

The writing down of music, the creative act, is a very complicated technical procedure. You can't improvise that. The man who wants to write music has to learn a great deal, he also has to learn a whole set of special symbols in order to produce musical form. I think it is for this reason that the creation of music is really a very highly intellectual activity.

... In fact, the professional composer is extremely doubtful of persons who compose at the piano, which most amateurs do. They let their fingers run over the keyboard and wait for something to happen. When they hear it, they think "Oh, that's perhaps it; no, let's see what was it now," and try to write it down, and then reject it again, and start playing around a little more. The real composer does not believe in this kind of preparation because he feels that it entails a great waste of energy and that the person rather confuses the creative intellect instead of stimulating it.

Richard Wilbur, of the Department of English, Harvard University, traced through the development of a piece of poetry:

A poem begins with a feeling of inadequacy. That's the preparation stage, or part of it, anyway. The preparation for a poem may also include the development of some very slight notion as to what elements the coming poem may contain. But at this point, these elements will be completely awash and unrelated in the mind. It's important that they be unrelated. The incubation period of a poem may be short or long, but for me it involves first a retreat from language, the cultivation of a state of apparent stupidity.

... At this stage in the coming of a poem, I haven't any idea as to what the paraphrasable content of the poem is going to be when it comes—its prose meaning. I don't know what the poem is going to "say." At most I'll have some ideas as to the mood of the poem, its probable size, its probable scope, the extent to which it's going to ramify. The poem doesn't begin with a meaning, it works towards meaning—it finds out what it's about.

... The stage of creation called illumination seems to come at various points and in various ways.... For me, the poem is likely to start with the recognition of some resemblance between ideas or fields of experience.... You don't know where you're going, but you do know you're going somewhere. In other words, you have an overriding premonition that the poem is going to take shape. The writing of the poem is a matter of making moment-by-moment choices among possibilities proposed by the unconscious.

John Ferren also made a remark that may point up the essential differences between the approach to creativity of the artist and that of the scientist. He said, "Traditionally, scientists speak conservatively from a sense that truth must not be betrayed, and artists speak extravagantly from a sense that truth is a large affair anyhow, and it is all right to snipe at it from any unsuspected corner."

Many of the common characteristics of so-called "artistic creativeness" may be observed among scientists. The basic variations all seem to stem from differences in individual personalities or from differences in major interests. For example, a member of Princeton's Institute for Advanced Study, who was privileged to work with both Albert Einstein and his fellow mathematician, John Von Neumann, compared them this way: "Einstein's mind was slow and contemplative. He would think about something for years. Johnny's mind was just the opposite. It was lightning quick—stunningly fast. If you gave him a problem, he either solved it right away or not at all. If he had to think about it a long time and it bored him, his interest would begin to wander. And Johnny's mind would not shine unless whatever he was working on had his undivided attention." And yet both men made tremendous accomplishments in the field of mathematics.

Princeton's Institute is, of course, a wonderful place to observe the "scientific mind" at work. Its prime purpose is to give great minds a place, time, and the atmosphere in which to think.

In discussing differences between the ways scientists work, Dr. J. Robert Oppenheimer, Director of the Institute, said, "Physics is a more gossipy field. When a problem gets hot, everyone talks about it." This is so, reports another observer, because many of the great minds frequently get stuck, even as you and I. They work by fits and starts, by sweat, by torment, and by that beautiful phenomenon called inspiration. They may spend many long hours and days working at a problem and getting nowhere. Then, one day at dinner, or while mowing the lawn, "Suddenly something occurs to you and there it is—beautiful, simple, elegant."

Another of the Princeton scientists said, "You try to let your mind wander looking for correlations between elusive points. Suddenly, while you're walking, or chopping wood, something clicks. Things fall in place. Then you start scribbling, trying to put something down on paper in mathematical form, working out definitions and good statements of theorems and proofs. The thrill lies in the discovery of the unknown and how it fits in. It's almost as though you have discovered a new animal and how it grows and how it relates to its environment."

And through all the analyzing of scientific minds runs the intense striving for comprehension—the seeking for truth. So intense is this drive that it can probably be said that a scientist who would rather refute than comprehend has demonstrated that he has chosen the wrong calling.

There are many other examples of commonness in the mental patterns of creativity in different fields. Writers, for example, have been most generous in supplying directly, or indirectly, evidences of their creative processes. The only field in which we are shy of good examples is that of business. It is possible to trace out the patterns and actions of business executives and demonstrate that they do, indeed, follow the same patterns as those of people we are more apt to think of as "professional" idea men. But because executives themselves frequently do not have a full appreciation of the creative processes that they employ, they have not as yet analyzed themselves to the extent that creative workers in other fields have.

This is unfortunate, because it also means that they have not analyzed their weaknesses. And since even great leaders in business (or any other field) may also have great weaknesses, these tend to propagate along with the occasional strengths. In business, more than in almost any other field, the "followers" tend to ape their leader to a great degree—even to the point of blindly adopting his weaknesses and bad habits. Therefore, these weaknesses can have a multiplying effect in an organization. Let an executive be a poor communicator, and chances are his subordinates will also be poor in communication. On the other hand, let a manager show some dash and courage in his conduct of the business, and his subordinates will also "catch the spirit."

This is one of the basic reasons why an executive should familiarize himself as much as he can with what is known about creativeness in all fields. All through the ages, there have been individuals who have stood apart from the mob by virtue of being independent of spirit and independent of thought. If they were also bold, curious, discontented, and imaginative, they were usually able to inspire others to follow them in their efforts to improve the world and build a civilization. Today's business executive, sometimes by virtue of some demonstrated ability, sometimes by virtue of chance or circumstance, also stands apart from the crowd. Whether he can muster the imagination to be a creative leader is up to the man.

Now exactly what makes a creative person different? One important fact that emerges out of the welter of observations, analyses, and critical examinations is that he usually has the ability to relate two or more things that were not previously related. He has the ability to see relationships that the noncreative person misses.

As an example, a novelist may take a few traits of a personality he has met, put them with some character traits of a second person, put his composite personality into a set of circumstances he has also met or just read about in a news story, and, through imagination, weave a completely new integrated and interrelated story. Or a scientist learns of a new chemical, becomes familiar with its properties, sees its possibilities for affecting or modifying some other chemical he is also familiar with, and, by combining, creates still a third chemical or even a new material. The same process goes on for the business executive who is handed a sample of a new material developed by his laboratory for, say, a floor covering. On noting its properties, he begins to see possibilities in it for other uses: as a grip for tool handles; as a sound-deadening material; as a decorative wall-covering, and so on. By the time he is done relating it to other needs, the company may forget all about going into the floor-covering business in order to concentrate on these other areas.

In exercising this facility to combine and recombine elements into a new whole, there are several things that "go on" in the creative mind. Some of them are individual steps in the thinking process; others may be used in combination. Where they are in combination, it usually is in an alternating or "oscillating" form. There have been many attempts to assign specific words as names for these steps, but, because of their nature, there are still some questions about what, exactly, they should be called. In this examination, we shall describe the characteristics in these terms: *Use of the Familiar; Ability to Hypothesize; Ability to Suspend;*

Involvement; Withdrawal; Recognition of Autonomy; Permission to Develop.

1 · Use of the Familiar

The *familiar*, the *commonplace*, and the *mediocre* are all important tools for the creative mind. A hissing teakettle was the familiar that started the invention of a steam engine; a chunk of soft rubber, used for cleaning wallpaper, was the commonplace that led to the idea of attaching erasers to lead pencils; a barber's clippers suggested to McCormick the idea for his mechanical reaper. A baby's crying, a sound ignored for hundreds of years, started Walter Hunt on experiments for a new way to bend wire and produced the first "safety" pin. The sight of a wife accidentally spilling paint on the floor, while trying to pour it from one can into another, gave another inventor an idea for a clamp-on pouring spout for paint cans.

Every new idea *must* have its beginnings in something familiar —something old. The inventor or creator cannot start with nothing—he must borrow his beginning somewhere. This is usually something familiar, accepted, and often ignored by everyone else. But it is something more to the creative mind: something that bothers the individual so that he either wants to put an end to it or wants to get away from it through a leap to a better "something." The creative "urge" comes from realizing this—then realizing that the familiar must be changed.

For a business executive, this suggests that the more things he can make familiar to himself, the more opportunities he will have to materially improve both himself and his business. He should, therefore, know and understand such commonplace business problems as the unions with which he must deal; the government that regulates, taxes, or controls the business; the communities in which his plants are located; the economy in which the ups and downs of wages, prices, and interest rates are significant.

Good ideas come when a person is alert to conditions, has the imagination to see opportunities and the common sense to follow through. And it all begins with something so familiar that it is easier to ignore it than challenge it.

2 · The Ability to Hypothesize and Suspend

Hypothesizing is making a statement of what may possibly be true, and then using that statement to make assumptions and to reason upon, just as if it were true beyond a shadow of a doubt. The objective of hypothesizing is to enable you to reach some truth that is not known with certainty at the time you begin.

Suspension, in the sense we use it here, means to stop, or cause to stop temporarily, the act of hypothesizing. In this way, an assumption which has carried you to a certain point may be temporarily "frozen" for closer examination and analysis.

These are two mental processes that usually occur in combination. The creative mind will alternate or oscillate back and forth between the two. This is necessary, because in the creative process you must, to a large extent, speculate—you must assume that what has not yet happened, or what is not yet known, is still possible. However, the starting point, as we have seen, is the familiar. And the step from the familiar into the unknown is through speculation. Therefore, the creative thinker must use hypotheses of various kinds, because they are often the only bridge available from where he is at the moment to where he thinks he wants to go.

Often a speculative answer or theory will look good enough to test and experiment with in an attempt to prove it out. Or there may be a great temptation to capitalize on even a small step into the future. This is where suspension comes in.

Rather than quit with an immediate profit, the creative thinker will hold that first possibility in suspension—"put it on a mental shelf"—where he can always come back to it if nothing better turns up. He is then free to continue his speculation and try to improve still more on his "suspended" theory, or he may go off into a completely new direction to see if he can find something still better.

This process can readily be visualized by thinking of it as a mental progression up a staircase, as in Figure 2. The "familiar" used as a starting point is the "tread" marked No. 1. Now, through hypothesizing, the creative mind rises to a new level—No. 2. At this point, a new idea is in existence—possibly good, possibly bad.

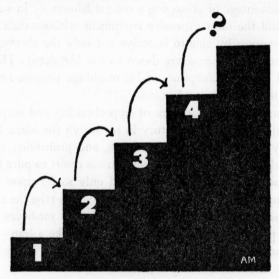

Fig. 2

The creator may stop here and try to utilize this new idea, or he may temporarily *suspend* his judgment and continue through new speculation on up to tread No. 3. Here, again, he arrives at a new hypothesis, now twice removed from the familiar down at No. 1 level. Now, at No. 3, he again has the choice of settling for his new idea or of suspending, and going on to No. 4. And, once at No. 4, the choice is again to go on or stop. If, at any of the steps, further speculation did not yield a new progression, he could then go into experimentation with any of the ideas that had been developed.

This may sound strange or involved in view of the more popular concept of an inventor or artist at work. Most people believe that the way an inventor gets his start is by going into the laboratory or workshop and beginning to "try things out." But actual experimentation is generally the *last* step—wherein ideas are *tested*—rather than the first. It was said that Nikola Tesla, mentioned earlier as the inventor of the alternating current generator, had the advantage of possessing a mental laboratory in which he could build the most expensive equipment without cash outlay. He was supposedly able to conceive not only the abstract ideas, but the machines themselves down to the last details. He never bothered to make blueprints of his machines, because he stored these brilliant images in his mind.

In exercising these faculties of hypothesizing and suspending, the creative worker is predatory in his search for ideas. He will use every tool, fact, reasoning process, and probability to build his hypothesis. If necessary, he will at times resort to pure fantasy. This is because the mind can proceed only so far upon what it knows and can prove. And this is not enough to raise the thinking above the already familiar, commonplace, or mediocre. There comes a point when the creative mind must take a leap—a jump to a higher plane of theory or knowledge—even if it cannot then prove or discover how it got there.

In this respect, of course, the creative process is a regenerating one. It never ends. No sooner has one "familiar" been left behind than the new speculation becomes a familiar. At this point, the creative mind is ready for a new leap. It wasn't so very long ago that we "knew" that the atom was the smallest unit of matter. This was the familiar—the commonplace—belief. Then, through speculation, our scientists theorized that the atom could be a whole universe in itself. Experiments confirmed this. Today this great new concept is a "familiar," taught even in high school physics courses. What new scientific insights and leaps into the future this new "familiar" will generate we can only guess. But one thing we do know: the speculations have started.

An important point to realize about this dual procedure is that it is a "fail-safe" method when you are looking for even just an improvement on a present situation: if your speculations carry you up to one promising possibility, and you suspend it at that point while you go out looking for something still better, you know you can always fall back on what you already have. Therefore, there is no reason to stop with the first "better" idea that comes along. You can always go back to it if further effort, or a deadline, leaves you without a higher-level idea.

3 · Involvement and Withdrawal

Involvement, in the creative sense, means to become completely absorbed in what is being done. *Withdrawal,* on the other hand, means a voluntary stepping back, or retirement, that is temporary in nature. These two mental processes are also alternating.

The creative mind must not only participate in the job of creating, but it must also reserve at least a part of its attention to being a spectator. Neither of these two acts can be allowed to suffer at the expense of the other. What actually happens is that the mind keeps shifting continually back and forth between the two. An analogy is the way an artist puts a daub of paint on his canvas, and then steps back to get a long-range view of the effect of the daub on the canvas as a whole.

The value of this procedure is to make your traveling over unknown paths easier: the "withdrawn" self steps out for a look at the road ahead that the "involved" self will soon be following. In this way, it tries to avoid bumps, ruts, blind alleys, and other traps that can dissipate both time and energy. During the time that your mind is actually involved in the problem, you will probably be much too busy smoothing out bumps and filling in ruts to pay much attention to the road ahead. Then, when you have made sufficient progress, or when you hit a really bad chuck-hole, you again withdraw from the problem, look to see what you have accomplished, and estimate what remains to be done. Therefore, the creative "flow" of mental effort is not usually continuous or in one direction. Rather, it is pulsating—moving forward in surges and pauses, but always in a forward direction.

4 · Recognition of Autonomy

Autonomy is reached when the problem solution becomes independent of its creator. There comes a time, in developing the solution to any kind of problem, when the object or situation being worked on begins to have an independent life of its own. It begins to make suggestions to the creator—it takes a hand in developing itself. Or just the opposite may occur: the object may tell you by its nature that what you are proposing won't work. Charles Kettering, in developing the high compression automobile engine, used to admonish his assistants to "Let the engine tell you what it needs!" This was perfect recognition of the autonomy of engines.

Such recognition is important to the speed of a creative solution. If the creator ignores the natural inclination of a problem solution to be good or bad, he is only causing himself needless effort and wasting resources. There is no point in developing a chair capable of holding a 130-pound person if the people who will be using it will average 180 pounds or more. At the same time, it is poor and wasteful design to build a chair capable of handling 180 pounds when the greatest load it will ever be subjected to will be a 40- or 50-pound child.

5 · Permission to Develop

The recognition of autonomy immediately brings into importance the creator's willingness to give his creation the freedom to develop itself. It means knowing when the creative process is complete. In the case of a machine, it may still be necessary to decide whether a bushing should be of brass or bronze, but you know a bushing of a certain size, shape, and general composition is called for. In the case of a management action, you may still have to decide whether Tom Jones or Ed Smith is the man to implement it, but at least you know what "it" is going to be.

The development may also be negative. When this happens, the creator will immediately drop it and start over again, usually in a new direction. But the creative thinker should realize when his creation is complete, when he can put it into use, or turn it over to someone else to use—even if it still needs some refinement.

Now in spite of all these steps, processes, methods, and procedures, the nature of a creative person is essentially simple. The first and most basic characteristic is the love of his work and his devotion to it. The second is that he takes a mature approach to problems. He is extraordinarily aware of people, of surroundings, of situations, of "things," and the problems they cause. He will usually approach all these with humor and trust and confidence. He is flexible in his thinking, and ready and willing to try new things. He is always looking, and has confidence in his own resources and knowledge to feel that what he finds, while it may be bad when he finds it, can always be set to rights and be made good.

And the creative mind believes that "the concept paves the way for the fact." What he can imagine should be so, can be made so.

6

The Nature of Problems

So far we have covered some of the basic fundamentals about creative *people*—what types of personality characteristics they exhibit; what mental factors can inhibit their problem-solving abilities; and the ways in which they approach, generally, the job of solving a problem. This chapter is concerned largely with what the shooting is all about—or at!—fundamentals of problems themselves.

It is a common occurrence in business, or in your personal living, to meet up with a major problem that only you can solve and immediately begin to experience a feeling of being very much alone in the world. It seems as though this is the very worst problem anyone has ever had to face; or that there has, at least, never been anything quite like it before. The next mental short circuit leads you to the frustrating feeling that, since you yourself have never faced this before and neither has anyone else, you are certainly not equipped to cope with it. It is an impossible situation, and why waste your time on it?

These "feelings" we experience probably inhibit our problem-solving abilities more than any other type of block. And they are completely false and misleading.

84

A man who suddenly finds himself in marital difficulties, with a divorce threatening, can easily go to pieces because of his inability to cope with this completely new emotional experience—new to him, that is. For when he finally gets around to seeing a divorce lawyer, he will find several very thick books detailing case after case just as bad as—or worse than—his.

The engineer frequently struggles in a mental aloneness with a peculiar design problem that may take months to solve. During this time he can become embittered, frustrated, and lose a great deal of his self-confidence. But finally, he produces his idea and it works. And a week later, a competitive design embodying many of the same problems and similar solutions is on the market. It is only then that the engineer realizes that he was not alone—that somewhere else another lonely man was also suffering the same emotional strain because of the same problem.

The industrial salesman may work over a particularly difficult prospect for months, or years, feeling all the while that this account is unique—nothing anyone else in the company has ever had any experience with is going to help him. He may even confirm this feeling by talking to other members of the sales force, actively seeking their help, and finding that they do not, indeed, have any suggestions to offer. But what the salesman is apt to forget is that *somebody* is now selling that account. And *somebody* is actively coping with the problems, whether they are personalities, price, quality, or supply. The problem is being solved so far as the customer is concerned, and so far as that customer is concerned, there is really no problem. This brings us to one of the first fundamentals you should know about problems: *Man makes his own problems.*

It has been said that if you give a monkey a peaceful stretch of jungle, and a lifetime supply of bananas, barring ill-health or physical accident, he will live quite happily for the rest of his natural life. But give a man a correspondingly ideal environment, as the Garden of Eden was said to be, and the man will get into trouble somehow! Our ability to get into trouble by creating problems for ourselves seems to be one of the great features which distinguishes man from other animals!

On this same theme, it has also been said that the only enemy man has is man. Man is a product of the universe. And the universe does not really care whether man unlocks its other secrets or not. A river, for example, has no interest in whether man uses its water to bathe, drink, or drown in. It doesn't care whether man wants to irrigate his lands, or create artificial barriers that will prove so inadequate the river is forced into washing away a town. When man succeeds in mastering the river's laws and using his knowledge of those laws to harness the water in the river, then the river will work for man. At the same time, if man does a faulty job of learning and causes the river to become a destructive force, then the man has succeeded in creating another problem for himself. But either way, the river does not care.

Another fundamental of problems that should be kept in mind: *No one has to solve a problem.* We always have a choice when confronted with a problem—we can try to solve it, which is the making of a problem; or we can put up with the present situation —in which case, there will be no problem. Frequently, we do put up with problem situations simply because solving them would cost more in time, energy, and expense than the solution could possibly be worth. This brings us to still another fundamental: *A situation should not be a problem unless its solution will have importance far greater than doing nothing.*

Many people fritter away their energies and mental resources on things that simply do not merit the expenditure of serious thinking. Like deciding what suit or dress they will wear for a particular occasion. Or which restaurant they will go to for lunch. Or whether they will see a movie on Tuesday night or Wednesday night this week. Or whether the car should be cleaned on Saturday or Sunday. These are not problems at all. Such situations call for routine decisions and they deserve no more mental attention than any other routine decision like brushing your teeth, or whether to take off your right or left shoe first!

What makes a real problem then? One good measurement is this: Will your decision on it be important to anyone *ten years from now?* If it will, then you've got a real problem—one that could call for real mental application and all the creative energy you can muster. And, chances are you have more problems than you realize that are just that important—they will affect someone else's life ten years from now.

Are you a parent? Every day you have problems—and the way you handle them can mean the difference between a responsible citizen or a juvenile delinquent in ten years.

Are you thinking about buying a house? In ten years the house you buy now will still be important to you and your family as a home.

How about your job? If you are an executive or a supervisor—or just someone that other people come to for advice—the way you advise other people may, in ten years, be responsible for the kind of people they are, or the attitude they have toward their job, or even whether your company will still be in business.

But in ten years it won't be important whether you wore your brown suit or your gray one today. And chances are you yourself won't remember what you had for lunch this noon even ten *days* from now.

There is a corollary that should be noted here, however: *Almost every big problem faced by anyone was at one time a little problem.* The reason it became big was that the responsible person missed the clues which indicated that it could or would grow.

A problem cannot be recognized as a problem until someone realizes there is something wrong: It may be something we don't know about a situation, and a mental "red light" goes on warning us that we should know this. It may be something that is out of place—or seems to be out of place. Or it may be something we have put into a situation which, upon later examination, does not seem to fit exactly. The Gestalt school of psychology refers to this type of "feeling" as the *principle of closure*—the efforts of the mind to "close" or complete an incompleted figure or pattern.

A simple manifestation of closure in action can be observed by watching the average "doodler": if he should, for example, doodle a series of parallel lines, then cross them with even one line at right angles, chances are he will go on to complete the pattern by crosshatching the entire design. Or if he should start a spiral drawing, almost inevitably he will complete the entire spiral before letting his pencil proceed to other patterns. If interrupted at his doodle, he will, at the first opportunity, go back to complete the pattern that has been set up in his mind. All this, of course, usually involves subconscious thinking, but it does demonstrate the operation of the mental mechanism.

In making deliberate use of this function, it is important only to remember that it is there and that it is operative. When you begin to get a "feeling" that something is wrong, your mind becomes sensitized to the "missing" element that will complete the pattern and make the situation "right." As long as you can avoid developing a fixation about some one missing element in particular—which would cause you to overlook others you may also be missing—your mind will be able to work with you in indicating the general direction you should go in pinning down the real problem.

There are, essentially, only two types of problems: *analytical problems*, which can be stated exactly and which can have only one correct answer; and *creative problems*, which can be stated many different ways and can have an unlimited number of correct answers. Here are two examples of how the same basic problems can be treated both analytically and creatively:

Suppose we were to give a design group the problem of *making a better toaster for bread*. This would be an analytical problem, calling, as it does, for an analysis of existing toasters to determine their shortcomings, and a routine substitution of parts, materials, shapes, etc. in order to come up with a more efficient and streamlined product. But it would probably still be quite similar to other mechanical toasters now on the market.

To turn this into a creative problem, we would ask the question in some such way as this: *What are some ways in which we can brown and dehydrate bread?* Now we have opened the possibilities to many different solutions. Our designers would be free to look at different types of heat treatments; to consider radiation or irradiation devices; to think about a special knife that might be coated with a material that would toast the bread in the act of cutting it. They might turn to chemistry and come up with a special butter that would "brown and dehydrate bread" when it was spread on it. The possibilities are almost endless. Not all of them would work or be practical. But only by taking the creative approach could we free our designers to break away from traditional concepts of toasting bread.

Or consider the problem of making a better oil filter. Stated this way, it is an analytical problem with a limited approach and a limited number of solutions. But look for *a better way of keeping oil clean,* and you have opened up creative possibilities that could even result in someone asking, "Do we need oil at all?"

Undoubtedly much more study has been made of analysis and analytical problems in the past than of creative problems. And most persons tend to handle the majority of their day-to-day problems in an analytical manner. Therefore, we will not dwell on this type of problem at any great length in this book, but will confine ourselves to the more creative problems and approaches to their solutions. It is, however, necessary to set up some guideposts to help you decide when you can take the creative approach and when you will find the analytical preferable. These are only guides and should not be taken as rules or formulas.

One such guide lies in the *needs of the situation.* For example, basic automobile styles change only every two or three years. The in-between changes that any particular auto maker brings out are just changes in trim, decoration, accessories, or minor lines. Because of the huge investment in tools, dies, and production changeovers, it is just not economical to make any major changes in body frames or basic body shells. (Where it is done oftener than every two or three years, it is usually an indication of trouble in the previous model. It probably did not sell.)

When the automobile designer is planning ahead for his major change model, he is free to assume a creative approach in every sense of the word. But in the in-between years, he has, at best, an analytical problem, because he is restricted by so many things he must retain and so many details that he can modify only slightly. In his work of solving the analytical problem here, he may not be able to stop himself from coming up with a completely new or creative approach; but it will be an idea of very little immediate value simply because it does not meet the needs of the immediate situation, which is to produce minor variations on a basic design.

Another important consideration, although creative minds may buck and fight it, is *the amount of time or money available* to accomplish a new problem solution. Generally, limited time or limited money may indicate that only an analytical approach is possible. Through analysis you confine your thinking to correcting an immediate wrong or making a minor change for improvement. With more time and more money you can begin to embark on a creative search for a completely new approach or concept to solving the problem. However, lack of either time or money should never keep you from being as imaginative as you can in making the changes you have opportunity to make. And frequently, a simple "change" idea can be a breakthrough to pave the way for a more creative approach at a later time.

Another fundamental of problems that should be understood is their *commonness*. Consider these:

An advertising layout artist is attempting to design an ad that will have one large photo and two smaller ones, all with explanatory captions; a separate block of text copy; the company logotype and trademark and a coupon. He must fit all these elements into a space 7 inches wide by 10 inches deep. His final arrangement must be dramatic and attention-getting, and all the elements must appear importantly ...

A textile production engineer is redesigning his production line for a new type of fabric made up of both synthetic and natural fibers. He has seven looms, of three different capacities, and, for greatest economy, wants to establish a continuous-production line that will be practically unlimited in the patterns and colors that can be handled ...

An office manager is moving into new space in his company's administration building. He has twenty-four desks and chairs, forty-two filing cabinets, and fourteen general storage units, as well as three duplicating machines, which have to be accommodated. He must arrange all these in the space so that they will be neat and attractive and, at the same time, enable the personnel to carry on their work with maximum efficiency ...

On the surface, these problems may not seem to have much in common. In fact, if you were to question any of the individuals involved, you would undoubtedly find that each of them considered his particular problem unique to his job and business. But basically, *they are all the same problem:* fitting a given number of units of specified sizes into a given amount of space. All three men are working with what is essentially the same problem, and all three will follow almost identical patterns of analysis in defining the problem. Whether they will all exercise the same degree of creativeness in their solutions is something else again. But they all have the same opportunity to do so.

Another example: there is basically no difference in the problem of a small town trying to attract customers from surrounding areas to its retail shopping center; the problem of getting more visitors to visit a company's booth at an industrial exhibition; the problem of boosting attendance at the games of the local baseball team; or the problem of filling a department store with customers the first day of a sale. All are really the problem of attracting people to a given location.

Being able to see such similarities lets us get to the "heart" of any problem much faster and helps us find the basic, underlying causes of troubles that may indicate the direction our search for solutions should take. For instance, when the United States was engaged in the 1958–1959 race to catch up with Russia on missiles and rockets, many theories were put forth to explain our lag. Everything from education to the congressional appropriations for basic research were being blamed. But when the famous German rocket specialist, Dr. Hermann Oberth, who had worked on the American rocket program, returned to Germany where he could take a closer look at what the Russians were actually doing, he was able to cut through the fog and point his finger at the American design problems. "The Russian rockets," he said, "remind me of simple alarm clocks—you can throw them at the wall and they'll keep on ticking. Compared with the Russian space vehicles, American rockets are ladies' wrist watches that look nice but tend to stop frequently."

What hampers us from seeing such basic relationships between apparently "different" types of problems are largely word blocks. Each of us tends to think in terms of word symbols for our particular job or industry or craft. We read about or hear about other people's problems, expressed in their own particular word symbols, and even though they may be absolute transfers of our own problems, we are blocked by the words from making the transfer.

In many cases, we have different words for the same thing, depending on where in the country we live or come from. For example, in some parts of the country, a certain type of cooked batter is called a "pancake." The same cooked batter, in other parts of the country, may be called hot cakes, flapjacks, slapjacks, fritters, flannel cakes, batter cakes, batty cakes, and griddle cakes. Is it any wonder that words often get in the way of understanding!

Then, too, different people tend to think in different ways. The mental associations we make with any particular word or phrase will depend, to a great extent on our education, experience,

temperament, or other background characteristics. Sex certainly af-
fects the way we "associate" on any particular word. Here are the
results of word-association tests that were given to groups of men
and women. Each person was asked to say the first word that
came to his mind when he or she heard a given word:

Word	Men	Women
Closet	Door	Clothes
Charm	Snake	Beauty
Garden	Weeds	Flowers
Blue	Spectrum	Dress
Flesh	Meat	Pink
Home	House	Happy
Powder	Bullet	Rouge
Fair	Weather	Blonde
Religion	God	Church
Stout	Strong	Fat
Gentle	Horse	Mother
Hunt	Shoot	Find

It is important to be conscious of these differences in word
interpretations. The fact that each job or industry or craft does
have its own word symbols or "jargon" means that words may
get in your way in trying to understand your own problems.
Once you become conscious of this, then you will find yourself
better able to look "beyond" the words and see more basic relationships in problems. And this will, in turn, enable you to make
more of almost any kind of experience you have ever had or heard
about for solving your problem of the moment.

It is possible, as one example, that the three men we considered
earlier, who were trying to fit given units into given space, may
have actually done that same job dozens of times in their lives—
in packing luggage for a trip, fitting the family's luggage into the
car trunk, or even fitting their home furnishings into a new house.
Persons trying to solve the problems of attracting other people
to a given location could draw on experience they had in high

school trying to make the annual "Harvest Moon Dance" a financial success; or the experience they have regularly on a church program committee in attracting members of the congregation to the various socials, dinners, and so forth. When you can get basic enough in your approaches to cut through the blocks that words, terms, and surface appearances set up, you will find that you have practically an inexhaustible storehouse of previous experiences in your mind which can greatly speed up your mental process of getting started on any problem.

And many times the best place to start on a problem is the most obvious, direct way of tackling it. Not only do we human beings make our own problems, we also have the faculty for overcomplicating them:

One of the greatest naval battles in history was the battle for Leyte Gulf between the United States and the Japanese in World War II. It turned out to be the victory that changed the course of the naval war in the Pacific. Between October, 1944, and December, 1958, more than two hundred books, including the official *History of United States Naval Operations,* were written referring to this particular battle. Each of these books left many unanswered questions and made many assumptions as to what had happened to enable the American force to defeat the powerful Japanese force so decisively.

Finally, after fourteen years, a sixteen-year-old California high school boy decided to try the direct approach. He wrote letters to several of the Japanese admirals and simply asked them. One of the replies, from Vice Admiral Kiyohide Shima, has become a prize document of naval history. He admitted several mistakes in judgment and explained several previously unknown circumstances about which the older, wiser, and more experienced naval historians had been making guesses and assumptions simply because it never occurred to them that they could get the truth by such a simple expedient as writing a letter asking for it!

We even tend to overlook the direct approach to a problem in much simpler affairs. One New Year's day a man had a real problem: he was notified that his father was seriously ill in a distant city. It was suggested that he fly there immediately. Being a businessman with many connections, he tried to think of someone who might be able to get him space on the crowded plane on New Year's day, and called a friend that he knew had some connection with the airline. This friend, in turn, called another man from his office who was directly concerned in doing business with the airline. This man began to call people at the airline to find out the possibilities of getting this one seat. But here he hit a stone wall. All of *his* connections were out of town or otherwise unreachable. Then it occurred to him to try the direct approach. He called the number listed under "Reservations" for this airline in the phone book and asked the young lady who answered if there was any possibility of getting a seat to the distant city for an emergency trip. The reply: there were *several* seats available on a flight leaving one hour later! If the first man had tried the same approach, instead of making the assumption that all seats were sold out because it was a big holiday travel time, he would have had about twenty-five minutes extra in which to pack his bag and make the flight!

Sometimes the people whose job it is to get facts are the last to think of the direct approach to getting them. A major department store was overhauling their entire advertising and public relations program. They had decided to make themselves seem a little less formidable and a little more friendly to the people of their city. Under consideration was a change in the official company name. They had been using the formal corporate title ever since the founding of the company, but there was some question whether this was what the public thought of as the store's name. A research consultant proposed a survey, with a price tag of several thousand dollars, to go out and sample the opinion in the city. A member of the store's advertising department thought of a more direct approach. He, and three other members of the department, went down to the sidewalk across the street from the store; each stopped twenty-five persons, pointed to the store, and asked, "What store is that?" Every single person answered with the shorter, abbreviated name of the store, and the whole survey took less than one hour.

Even people whose entire training and experience has been pointed toward finding the simplest, most direct approach to solving a problem sometimes forget the obvious. Here is a true story of how such an oversight may have changed the course of history:

When Germany started development of the V-2 rocket, one of the problems that stood out was the need for a high-pressure pump to get fuel into the combustion chamber. A top engineer was assigned to the project, with the job of investigating various designs to see if something could be found that would serve. The specifications were rigid: the pump had to maintain constant pressure within + or — 0.4 per cent; it had to be capable of being stored for long periods of time, and yet be immediately available for use; and, after being out of service for some length of time, it had to come to full- and constant-pressure delivery within three seconds.

The engineer worked on this project for *six months*, during which time he succeeded only in refining the specifications. After that time, he recommended that all the pump manufacturers in Germany be called together and have the problem presented to them. His prime hope was that once these seemingly impossible specifications were presented, the manufacturers might be able to suggest some other new ideas that could be worked on to eventually develop the pump.

The audience of manufacturers listened quietly as the specifications were read off. When they were finally asked, "Does anyone have any comments or any ideas?" one manufacturer rose and said, "Sir, it looks to me like what you need is the standard firefighter's pump. A standard fire pump has to deliver large volumes of water in order to put out a fire; it has to deliver the water at a high pressure in order that the firemen can be at a safe distance from the fire; the pressure must remain very constant, because otherwise the stream cannot be directed. A fire-fighter's pump has to be stored for long periods, because fires may not occur for six months or a year, and yet, when they do occur, the pump has to work and it has to come to full-pressure delivery in a very short time."

In his *History of the Second World War*, Sir Winston Churchill said that if the V-2 rocket had become operational six months sooner, the favorable outcome to the Allies would have been seriously in question. Perhaps this is one case where the Allies can thank fortune that it took a German engineer six months to think of the direct approach of asking specialists how to solve the kind of problem they specalized in!

There is another advantage in starting with the obvious direct approach to a problem: *it at least gets you started.* Frequently, the most difficult part of solving a problem is deciding where to begin. But once you do begin, it is like deciding to jump into a cold lake: once you are in the air and falling, the problem no longer exists—you are on your way. So if no better place exists to start on a problem, try the direct approach—do the obvious thing first.

Of course, the direct approach to a problem will not always be successful. But if you are down to a basic problem, you can then see other approaches quite readily. For example:

If the direct approach just will not work, what about the indirect approach?—how about doing just the opposite?

If your problem seems to have almost an unlimited number of subproblems (for instance, in management we often think of our working force as one mass or one unit, when, in reality, it is a large number of distinct individual people), group the subproblems for group treatment (which you do when you treat with one department or section at a time).

If something is unnecessary in a problem situation, do the opposite of grouping, try removing it entirely and see what the results will be. (Many types of machines have been greatly improved as the result of taking things away from them instead of adding more!)

Frequently, if all your possibilities turn out unfavorable and your problem remains unsolved, you may be able to change the problem itself. This proved to be the solution to the problem of eliminating printing ink from newsprint and other paper in reclaiming operations. No solvent could be found that would get the ink out of the paper once it had been printed. So they changed the ink formulas.

One of the key factors in how well and how quickly an individual can point up, simplify, and solve any problem will be his own attitude toward problems. If, through our attitudes, we approach every minor problem as a major crisis inflicted upon us by nature, other people, and the misfortunes of circumstance, we will not be nearly so effective in solving problems as will someone who is more realistic and realizes that problems are a part of living. We make them ourselves, and if we don't like a particular set of problems, we can always get away from them. (No company *owns* a man—no one can force you to keep a particular job you dislike!) And when we can take the more detached view of problems, solving them becomes more fun—it can actually become a game of skill or wits to see just how fast you can lick any particular problem. Then any minor setbacks or complications you meet—not enough time or not enough money—become just factors of the problem, more cards in the decks, or the particular position of your problem-opponent's checkers on the boards.

It may help you to remember that, as Napoleon Hill said, "A man is only as big as the circumstances he allows to worry him." Your whole approach to life, to living, and your job will depend on how positively you can face up to the problems you have selected to make your own. And if you feel that you shouldn't have problems, that you shouldn't have to face them, then the chances are you should trade in your present job for a South Sea Island beach where you can pick food off the trees and sit in the sun. It is still possible to find such spots, where no one has to work, and no one has any particular problems. But if you elect to stay in civilization and continue with your present job, the choice is yours. It is not being forced upon you. The problems you meet go with the choice. They are not being forced upon you either. Therefore, why fight problems? It makes much more sense to conserve your energy for the game and chase of finding solutions!

7

Steps in Deliberate
Problem Solving

One of the most interesting, vital, and promising arts to be placed at the disposal of business executives in several hundred years is the concept of *deliberate* creative problem solving.

The idea that you can "force feed" your mind into finding ideas and problem solutions is a relatively new one. Like all new ideas, it has far to go in winning complete acceptance from everyone who meets up with it. There are many people who still feel that you have to depend upon inspiration to incite creative activity. And there are others who dislike the idea of working as hard as you sometimes do to force an elusive idea out into the openness of your mind. These people want "bright" ideas to come without any expenditure of effort. The truth is that both these methods do occasionally produce ideas, some of which might be called brilliant. But, in the long run, they are certain to be erratic and, therefore, unreliable producers of innovations.

As was mentioned earlier in this book, the man most responsible for focusing attention on the ability to be deliberately creative is probably Alex F. Osborn. Although he had famous forerunners in the theoretical applications of disciplined creativity, such as Aristotle and John Dewey, as well as contemporaries, notably James Webb Young, author of *A Technique for Producing Ideas*, and Robert Crawford, author of *The Techniques of Creative Thinking*, Osborn's series of books, culminating in *Applied Imagination*, were the ones to win widespread readership and popularity. Much of his success was probably due to the almost overnight popularity of the "Brainstorming" procedure, which was described in his last two books, and which literally took the country's brains by storm. It may prove, in the long run, that the greatest contribution Brainstorming *per se* made to creativity was to get many more people interested in studying up on the subject than would ever have done so without the technique. If so, Brainstorming has rightly earned its place as a creative contribution to mankind!

In the wake of Mr. Osborn's writings and stimulation, came the interest of business executives and less dogmatic types of educators. Among the latter may be counted Dr. John Arnold, whose Creative Engineering courses, conducted while he was on the staff of the Massachusetts Institute of Technology, gained national fame. Dr. Arnold has since moved to Stanford University, in California, where he continues to innovate and to challenge more conventional educators with his teaching methods.

Probably the greatest impetus to the movement toward more creativity in business, science, education, and government came with the establishment of the annual Creative Problem Solving Institute at the University of Buffalo, New York, jointly sponsored by Mr. Osborn's Creative Education Foundation and the University. There, leaders and thought-leaders from all fields of endeavor gather every June to study, assimilate, and examine every aspect of deliberate creativity. Leaders for the Institute are selected on the basis of contributions they can make in specific fields, and the objective of each Institute is to present the latest news to interested people who can, in turn, use the information they gain as a base for adding to our knowledge of the elusive creative process.

The methods advocated for deliberate problem solving are not, in any way, magic formulas or mystic rites that will produce imaginative thinking. Nor are the principles underlying the use of the techniques to be considered as absolute dogma that must be accepted at face value. Rather, both principles and methods are the result of closely observing the great creative minds of history and the present; and, through cross-comparisons, arriving at some basic characteristics these minds seem to have in common. The working methods are those that creative persons seem either to prefer or to use in common.

The steps, or principles, observed in attacking a problem are basically five:

Orienting, or defining, the problem
Getting the facts needed to work on the problem
Getting ideas as tentative solutions
Incubating the problem
Evaluating the tentative solutions produced

By comparing these steps with the observed and reported methods used by known creative people covered in Chapter 5, it will be seen that the translation from creative theory to recommended creative practice has been almost a literal one. These steps are really simplified statements of the normal, often unconscious, operations of creative minds when confronted with problems.

It should be pointed out that you would seldom follow these steps in just this order in the normal course of working over a problem. In fact, it is frequently difficult to see where one step leaves off and another starts; and sometimes it is difficult to see any clear-cut order whatever. A person may begin to get ideas while he is still consciously in the fact-gathering stage. After finishing incubation, he may decide that he wants still more facts —the facts that, when he first plunged into the problem, he did not know he would need. But in deliberately trying to court ideas, it could pay you to deliberately follow the sequence—at least to the point of making sure that you have covered all the steps.

Step 1 · Orienting the Problem

Perhaps the most important step in solving any problem is to make sure that you understand it before you try to do anything else. Frequently, eagerness to "get on with it" and "get it over with" can lead to attempts to press for solution before the problem itself is clearly understood. Problem definition, essentially, boils down to *finding out where you are going with all your subsequent work so that you will know when you get there!*

Business or administrative problems seldom come to us in clear-cut, easily recognized and defined forms. Often, personal opinion or interpretations get in the way. For example, how many times have you heard someone say, "Gosh, the boss is in a bad humor today—everything I do is wrong!" Now let's just turn this statement around: "Everything I do is wrong—the boss is certainly in a bad humor!"

You'll notice that we've said almost the same things in the same words, but the nature of that problem is certainly changed!

Other business problems are often obscure because of lack of facts. For example, a national consumer product sells well everywhere but in the New England states. As an academic problem, it would be easy to brush off—to say that it was due to the vagaries of consumer behavior in the New England states. But the sales manager for that company cannot brush it off—he has to start by digging out the facts to pin those vagaries down and then produce the ideas to solve them.

Some business and community problems are difficult to define because they get into the chicken-or-the-egg question. For instance, nearly a hundred small cities throughout the country are fighting to keep what may be a key to industrial and commercial growth for them: scheduled airline service. The Civil Aeronautics Board has set a 150-airline-passenger-a-month minimum for any community that wants to keep scheduled service. And the service is important if the community is trying to attract new industry. In fact, if a town has the service, it is almost a safe bet that growth will follow. But on the other hand, before they can get the service on a permanent basis, they have to produce the business for the airlines.

Other problems become complicated by the human element which must be accommodated. A good example is what happens when, for economic or other reasons, a manufacturing company must close down a particular operation or plant, or move a plant to a new community. Younger workers may have the flexibility to accept transfers to other cities or to learn new skills on reassigned jobs, but workers in their fifties and sixties may be reluctant to give up the town they have called home for many years, or they may not have the ambition to learn a new skill or even to learn to work under a new supervisor. The problem then becomes a highly complex one of effecting the changeover with a minimum of emotional or economic disruption, and of fulfilling whatever moral obligations the company feels it has.

Frequently, as in medicine, the symptoms of the problem can obscure the disease. When this happens, the executive is apt to find himself putting out a continual series of small fires that seem to crop up in all directions, but around one central source. Until he gets to the base of the trouble and thoroughly quenches any latent sparks, he will never be able to put his fireman's hat away. As an example, a plant manager is concerned about his production —it is running behind schedule. Upon investigating, he finds that absenteeism is running at an abnormally high rate. Thereupon, he puts into effect various punitive and regulatory measures to deal with the absenteeism. But somehow, production does not respond. When his top management finally sends in a personnel specialist, the finding is that the plant morale is extremely low, and while the measures to curb absenteeism had indeed curbed it, the basic cause of the production lag was, if anything, aggravated.

Therefore, the key to effective problem orientation is a complete and thorough break-out of all the angles that may possibly affect the problem solution. It is important that you deliberately search for parts of the problem which may be hidden or obscure. One good way is to start out by writing down your first impression of what a problem is. Then try to list every factor you can think of that could be a part of the problem. Don't worry too much about the sequence of your parts or their relationships to each other at this stage. The important thing is to get just as many subproblems out of the main problem as you can. Once this is done, then you can begin to rearrange these factors into logical relationships and sequences. Then look for the *key* factor. Frequently, when you run through such a list of problem parts, one will stand out—a person, a material, a design, or a need—which will so obviously be the key that, if you can solve that, everything else becomes a detail.

Another good device to try, in attempting to define a problem, is that of writing it out in several different ways. Try to write it out in ten words or less. Try to turn it around—see what happens when you transpose the cause and effect—as we did in the example of the worker complaining about his boss's bad humor. Try to explain the problem to someone who is completely unfamiliar with it—and have him restate it in his own words—not just repeat what you have said. Such devices as these can often help you clarify your own thinking on a problem.

Another way to limit or break down a problem is to concentrate on the elements of it that you yourself have some control over. In other words, start where you are. This may, of course, include the necessity of "selling" someone else—your boss or your secretary or someone in another department—on the idea of cooperating with you. But this saves you from wasting mental energy on things that you could not possibly do anything about anyway. (But be sure before you say something is not under your control that you aren't just taking an easy way out for yourself!)

The creative problem solver should select his target for initial attack only after he has studied the problem as much as time, money, or the relative importance of the problem itself allows. One of the greatest aids in defining problems—and isolating the real heart of a problem, free of fiction, fantasy, opinion, or misconception—is the use of the creative, well-aimed question. This also includes the development of opportunities.

In his Creative Engineering course, conducted at M.I.T., Professor John Arnold advocated the use of questions like these to uncover new possibilities for improving a company's product:

> Can we increase the *function?* Can we make the product do more things?
>
> Can we get a *higher performance level?* Make the product longer lived? More reliable? More accurate? Safer? More convenient to use? Easier to repair and maintain?
>
> Can we lower the *cost?* Eliminate excess parts? Substitute cheaper materials? Design to reduce hand labor or for complete automation?
>
> Can we increase the *salability?* Improve the appearance of the product? Improve the package? Improve its point of sale?

Notice that each of these major questions approaches the problem of redesigning the product from a different angle. This is the key to creative questioning—to make sure that you question *around* a problem, so that you continually uncover new directions as well as new possibilities for exploration.

Once you are aware of what your real problem is, of course, you must then be able to state it clearly, concisely, and exactly so that you can communicate it to others with the same degree of understanding that you yourself have. But be sure, in presenting your problem statement, that you do not limit the possible types of solutions. Don't ask a man to think up a new toaster if what you want is a new way to brown and dehydrate bread; or don't ask for an improved oil filter if you want to eliminate filtering entirely.

As you can see, just defining the problem calls for imagination, as well as analytical judgment. It takes imagination to search out and find the hidden aspects of a problem. It takes imagination to think of the kinds of questions that are going to produce useful answers. It takes imagination to recognize a specific aspect of a problem as the key or vital aspect. Generally, it will take an alternating of imagination and judgment to define and refine the usual problem "mess" down into a workable problem statement that everyone can understand. What it nets down to is this: never try to tackle a *big* problem—instead, break it down into little problems and tackle them one at a time, starting with the one that is going to gain you the most ground right away!

Step 2 · Get the Facts

There is a saying that "The devil you know is a lot friendlier than the devil you don't." This is especially true in problem solving. If you can gather enough facts about a problem, the facts themselves may point out what the solution to the problem will be or must be.

The human thought processes are complex. But there is one basic that cannot be ignored: they are all dependent upon a body of reliable information. The mind—even the speculative, leaping, projective creative mind—must have facts to feed upon. In the absence of some facts, you can use hypothesis. But until you can prove out the hypothesis, you must remember that it is just theory—it is not fact, and you must be prepared to relinquish your theory, no matter how beautiful, when fact comes along that is contrary.

Furthermore, any individual's thinking, on any subject, will necessarily be limited by the boundaries of his information on that subject. Thus, Leonardo da Vinci, certainly one of the great creative minds of all time, could not have built a television set. He may have thought of the idea of transmitting pictures through the air, but without the preliminary factual background of electricity, ether-wave transmission, and electronics, even this brilliant mind could not have invented television.

In gathering your facts about a particular problem, you want to look for information that can make up a part or parcel of the problem solution. You want to study the conditions of the needed solutions, and the relationships of the facts to those conditions. You want to learn to recognize truth in facts. And all "facts" that you meet up with are not true. Charles Kettering, shortly before he died, made the statement that "Forty years ago everything about fuel engines was in a row of books 18 inches long. Today not one word of that is true, because it was not true then."

There was a time when scientists believed that when the water vapor in a cloud was cooled to 32°F, the vapor would freeze, as any water would, and there would be snowflakes. But when they tried to duplicate this in the laboratory, the reality did not always work out that way. Sometimes the temperature would get down as much as 60° colder than the "freezing" temperature, and still the stubborn vapor would refuse to turn to snow. Then someone found that just a handful of dry ice would turn a whole skyful of cloud into a raging snowstorm!

The humorist Mark Twain pointed out that even the seeming bulwark of truth, the statistic, can be faulty. His example: "In 176 years, the Lower Mississippi has shortened itself 242 miles. This is an average of a trifle over one mile and a third per year. Therefore, anyone can see that 742 years from now the Lower Mississippi will be only a mile and three-quarters long, and Cairo and New Orleans will have joined streets together."

One of the important points to remember in going after facts is that other people's opinions are not always reliable. It is a characteristic of a human being that he is seldom bothered by insufficient data, and often the less he has, the more willing he is to give a firm opinion. And, unfortunately, some people prefer even a wrong answer to the necessity of digging further for verification or amplification in their factual quest. Consequently, it is easy to fall into a "blind-leading-the-blind" pattern in compiling information, so that you end up with inaccurate information, a confused mind, and a still unsolved problem.

One sure symptom of possible trouble with the "facts" you

have is that you find yourself in an argument when discussing them with someone else. No matter how you look at it, argument is an indication of lack of facts. When all the facts are known and verified, there cannot be argument.

Once you are reasonably certain your facts are facts, then you should classify or categorize them. Separate the usable facts from the nonusable; separate the important facts from the nonimportant ones. Just as you can separate out the key subproblem in a given situation—one that, if resolved, will make all the others details—so you can also separate out the "mountain-moving" facts: those so important that if you act on them, they will serve to cancel out many unimportant, even though completely opposed, ones.

Where do you get facts? Many are probably readily available in your office or in your home library. You can talk to other people to find out what *firsthand* experiences they have had (beware of the "I know a fellow who had a friend" type of fact!). Visit the library and read up on the problem. If you know what you are looking for in advance (and you should, if you have suitably oriented your problem before you start), you can make your fact-hunting time much more productive. John Gunther, the author of the "Inside . . ." books, is noted for his ability to make lightning visits to various cities and countries and come away with all the pertinent facts that other authors spend weeks or even months gathering. His secret? As one who worked with him reports, "He is a master of the art of brain-picking—and of choosing the right brain to pick. From careful homework, he knows precisely what information his story needs, and can extract it with the efficiency of an automatic orange squeezer!"

And that brings up one of the most efficient methods of digging out facts: tough questioning. "Tough," not with people, but with the information people give you. One of the country's most successful new product companies uses a highly detailed checklist to make sure it has all the facts before committing itself too deeply on a new idea. Although you may never need such an exhaustive list of questions on your problems, this will give you an idea of just how far it is possible to carry question-asking when you want to be sure you have all the facts:

Can we sell it? Is there a market now?—if not, can one be developed? Is it compatible with present products? Selling price all right for the expected market? Consumer education needed?

Can we make it? Sources of required materials? Do we have personnel in the company to manufacture it now? Need for technical staff to develop?—to manufacture? Do we have machines to make it?

What investment is required?—to develop?—to market? Distribution costs? How soon will it pay its own way?

What will the product be like? Size? Weight? Handling properties? Perishable? How will we transport the finished product? Can related products be developed?

How will we sell it? Present sales force?—new sales organization? What kind of sales promotion necessary? Manner of merchandising?

If the answers to any of these questions are unfavorable, the standard follow-up question is then, "Can we change this situation?"

Of course you have to be sure that in this quest for facts you don't let any of your own preconceived ideas of what the facts should be deter you from getting the real facts. Frequently, "facts" will contradict your own notions of what something should be. To try to distort them, in this case, will only result in your weakening your ability to solve the problem. So, in searching for the truth in a situation, make sure you are not like the coed on her way to a political rally, who stated: "I'm going with an open mind, a complete lack of prejudice, and a cool rational approach to listen to what I'm convinced is pure rubbish!"

When do you stop your fact searching? This will call for exercise of judgment: it may be you will stop when the facts you get seem to be duplicating each other—when you are no longer getting usable new information. Or perhaps it will have to be when the cost of gaining any additional information will be higher than the possible value of the information. It is probably true that no one ever has *all* the facts pertaining to a problem, and there will come a time when you will have to work with what you have. But before abandoning your search, it might always be well to remember the remark made by one of the staff physicians at the famous Mayo Diagnostic Clinic. When asked why it was that this clinic could successfully isolate a disease that had baffled even the best doctors in a patient's home town, or why they were able to accurately diagnose a new disease that other doctors had given up on, he replied, *"We just probe a little deeper, and keep at it a little longer!"*

Step 3 · Get Ideas

Once you have suitably oriented your problem, and after you have collected a sufficient body of facts so that you have something to work with, then you are ready to begin your systematic search for ideas—but *lots* of ideas—all you or anyone you can get to help you can think up.

Remember, it is a basic characteristic of any problem that can be solved with imagination that there are *many* feasible solutions. The only guarantee you have that you will eventually pick the best solution to a problem is to be sure you have thought of every possible solution. (One prominent and successful design engineer claims that there are at least eight ways of doing anything, including diapering a baby!)

Somerset Maugham, the novelist, once wrote, "To conceive ideas is exhilarating, but it is safe only when you conceive so many that you ascribe no undue consequence to them and can take them for what they are worth. People who conceive few find it very difficult not to regard them with inordinate respect!"

A biographer of the famous artist, Toulouse-Lautrec, records that "always he was sketching—everything, everywhere, with any kind of pencil. When his drawing pad ran out, he used a menu, the back of an envelope, any scrap at hand.... He tore up thousands of these drawings, but thousands still exist."

Even in higher mathematics, where there can be only one possible exact answer to a problem, there is always more than one way to arrive at that answer. Furthermore, even though you may be searching for only one idea at the moment, one idea is hardly enough to be self-sustaining. You will need supplementary ideas to bolster up the weaknesses you are bound to find in your original "big" idea. And if you make an intensive enough search at the beginning, you will probably find that many of your "secondary" ideas will serve to supplement your prime idea.

To draw an analogy on this all-out search for ideas, we might consider the techniques used by a pearl diver in his search for pearls: the pearl diver puts on his swimming gear, dives down to the oyster bed, cleans the bed of every oyster that is there, and brings them all up to the surface with him. Only after he has completely cleaned the bed does he remove his swimming gear, put on his street clothes, and begin to open oysters to see if he has a pearl. He does not stop to change into street clothes after each individual oyster, open it to see if there is a pearl inside, then get back into water gear, go down and bring up another single oyster, and repeat the whole time-consuming process. And yet that is the way some people try to work with ideas:

They get one idea; expend time and effort and money to prove or disprove it; go through the whole process of "warming up" their minds all over again; get another single idea; again expend time and effort to prove or disprove it, and on and on. It is wasteful of time, effort, and the company's money. When you are after ideas, stick to getting ideas.

And this brings up a key point—one that is vital if you want to improve your production of ideas: *don't* let your judgment interfere when you are on the hunt for ideas. It is like trying to drive a car with the brakes on!

Imagination and judgment are diametrically opposed mental functions. Either can cancel the other out; either has the power to weaken the other. Yet both functions are present, or at least available, in any individual's mind. It is possible to separate them in use. This is not, as some people suspect, a new concept being promoted by the new group of "deliberate problem-solvers." The distinct character of these two functions was recognized and stated quite clearly by the eighteenth-century German poet-philosopher Johann von Schiller. In a letter to a friend, who had complained of a lack of creative power, he wrote:

> The reason for your complaint lies, it seems to me, in the constraint which your intellect imposes upon your imagination.... Apparently, it is not good—and, indeed, it hinders the creative work of the mind —if the intellect examines too closely the ideas already pouring in, as it were, at the gates. Regarded in isolation, an idea may be quite insignificant, and venturesome in the extreme, but it may acquire importance from an idea which follows it; perhaps, in a certain collocation with other ideas, which may seem equally absurd, it may be capable of furnishing a very serviceable link. The intellect cannot judge all those ideas unless it can retain them until it has considered them in connection with these other ideas. In the case of the creative mind, it seems to me, the intellect has withdrawn its watchers from the gates, and the ideas rush in pell-mell, and only then does it review and inspect the multitude. You worthy critics, or whatever you may call yourselves, are ashamed or afraid of the momentary and passing madness which is found in all real creators, the longer or shorter duration of which distinguishes the thinking artist from the dreamer. Hence your complaints of unfruitfulness, for you reject too soon, and discriminate too severely.

In the next chapter, we shall examine some of the devices that can aid you in developing quantities of ideas. One final word about what makes an idea for now, however: Don't kid yourself with vague suggestions that you think might be ideas. Discipline your mind to think in terms of specific propositions—make your ideas as concrete, as "real," and as solid as the problems you are going to be hurling them against.

Step 4 · Incubate!

If you have labored over a problem and haven't found a satisfactory solution, you run the risk of frustration. Creative people of all sorts—writers, artists, composers, and scientists—often get the feeling of being "blocked up" on a problem—their minds just refuse to function on it any more. The best thing to do when this happens to you is to *get away from the problem*—let up on your mind.

Your conscious mind is only a small part of the mental powers at your disposal. Back in the memory cells of your mind may be dozens of facts and associations that you have completely forgotten about and so haven't brought into use on your particular problem. But they are still there, in the subconscious. If you can just open up the communications channels, they may come out to help you find the solution to your present problem. In fact, you may find that a subconsciously produced idea is better than any that you were consciously able to develop, simply because it will have the benefit of all the experience and knowledge you have accumulated in your lifetime. The human brain actually has ten thousand times as much "memory capacity" as the best present-day electronic computer, and it can store and retain and recall this data for sixty to ninety years or longer.

There are other advantages to incubating, also: For one, it can give your mind a change of pace—a chance to inject new light into your search for a solution. For example, one business book author reported that while he was working on a rather "meaty" volume, he was incubating a sexy novel! And, he claimed, in mentally developing the characters and situations of his novel, he found that he would occasionally gain a new insight into the psychological aspects of his heavier subject and was able to improve the contents immeasurably. "Besides," he said, "It was nice to be able to get away from business once in a while!"

This touches on another prime advantage to incubation periods:

they give ideas time to "grow." Psychologist Allan B. Chalfont put it this way: "Perhaps in the course of several days or weeks this thing that started with just the germ of an idea has developed into a full-fledged idea, complete with trimmings. And, in its full-fledged state, it is many times as exciting as before."

Still another advantage of learning to deliberately harness your subconscious, which is what incubation amounts to, is that it greatly increases the mental energy you have at your disposal. Some authorities consider this a significant "secret" of powerful minds: they have established a high degree of compatible co-operation between their conscious and their subconscious think-ing processes. After all, a man's conscious mental effort is some-thing that is subject to fatigue and exhaustion. Experiments have demonstrated, however, that the real thinking part of the brain, the cerebral cortex, is never completely at rest unless it is under the influence of powerful drugs—and even then, we are not sure that it can be put completely to "sleep." This means, of course, that your so-called "subconscious" can be kept working for you even when you are asleep.

Among the people who believed in the power to incubate deliberately were such minds as Josef Hofmann, Paderewski, and Fritz Kreisler, all great musical composers who made it a practice to spend hours in "idle" thinking. Charles Tellier, the French engineer, claimed that his greatest discoveries were made in the course of quiet strolls while his mind was busy enjoying the peaceful scenery. One observer reported that John Jacob Astor's most striking characteristic was the patience with which he would wait for one of his ideas to come "into full flower." Sir Isaac Newton was another scientist who believed in thinking continually by harnessing his subconscious, as was John Von Neumann. Von Neumann is reported to have believed that pure concentration alone was never enough to solve difficult mathe-matical problems and that these were solved in the subconscious. He would, therefore, frequently go to bed at night with a problem in the unsolved state and wake up in the morning and scribble the answer on the pad he kept on the bedside table. And therein probably lies the key that these minds used to unlock their subconscious mental powers: ,

To make your subconscious work for you intentionally, you have to give it specific assignments. You must turn your problems over to your subconscious mind in the form of definite jobs to be done after giving it all the essential facts, figures, and arguments to work with. This may seem to be a contradiction of the statement that incubation consists of forgetting the problem, or putting it out of your mind, but it is not, really. The trick is that just before you deliberately put the problem out of your mind, you just as deliberately review everything you have done on it. And then change your pace.

The great mind of Leonardo da Vinci was kept at work full time in this manner. Leonardo described his method this way: "I have found in my experience that it is of no small benefit when you lie in bed in the dark to recall in imagination, one after the other, the outline of the forms you have been studying." And, he reported, he would frequently awake in the morning with a solution to such a problem.

Many creative people have, of course, benefited from nondeliberate incubations. They would work on a problem until they had just plain "fagged out" on it; then, through fatigue or other necessity, would have the current of their thinking changed. And then would come the "bolt from the blue." Those creators, like Leonardo, who have studied themselves generally agree on what happened, and from them we have learned what we know about this subconscious "tool."

There is, of course, something else that must go along with this deliberate charge to the subconscious: an open, receptive mind, sensitized to the possibility of a new idea ready to be born. When the first hint of a solution creeps into your conscious thinking, you must then be ready to grasp it firmly and pull it bodily out into the light of conscious examination. You should, at the very least, make a written note of it. If it can be visualized, make a sketch of it. And make sure that either the note or the sketch can be deciphered later. The idea that comes in a flash can go in a flash!

The process of incubation has often been referred to as "sleeping on a problem." In actual practice, particularly in business, where problems can come thick and fast, the time you will have to incubate any particular problem may only be time that you can readily "make" in the course of the day. It may be just a matter of breaking away from your desk for a walk to the water cooler or for a "coffee break." Or it may be timing your activity on a problem so that you can mentally lay it aside while you go out to lunch.

It is nice when you do have overnight or a two- or three-day spell in which to let your subconscious take over the problem, and if you can allow yourself the time, then take it. But, at the same time, don't let incubation become an excuse for procrastination. You can polish and refine and improve on an idea to the point where the original spark of the idea is smothered and lost. So give yourself enough time to incubate—but don't make it forever. After all, you are after accomplishment—not mere mental gymnastics!

Step 5 · Evaluate Your Ideas

All the steps in our method so far have had as their aim the eventual production of a quantity of worthwhile ideas. But the gathering of ideas is not an "end" in itself. The creative process is never completed until the ideas are evaluated, some idea selected as a possible solution, the possibility worked on and developed, and some need filled.

All ideas are not worthwhile. Some of your first, second, or third ideas will probably prove on final analysis to be "old hat." Some ideas you produce will not have substance—they will be hazy, nebulous, or too general in scope. Some will prove to be completely impractical.

In sorting out and evaluating your ideas, it is well to keep in mind the fact that many of them are going to be duds. Not only will this keep you from becoming disappointed when every scheme of yours does not pay off, but it will also aid you in keeping your perspective through the whole evaluation process. And, in spite of the experience all of us get every day in making decisions and in the constant and sometimes instant evaluation and selection of alternatives, most people don't have enough appreciation for the potentials of ideas to be able to evaluate them creatively.

Just watching most businessmen in the process of making decisions, you get the feeling that the deciding is still done on the basis of intuition, hunch, emotion, personal bias, or not enough facts to decide otherwise. Often these methods are satisfactory. (You can flip a coin and stand a good chance of being right 50 per cent of the time!) But if you are trying to build disciplined creative habits into your mental workings, it will pay you to build discipline into your decision-making also. And decisions are not easy to make—especially in the selection of ideas.

In making a decision, it is important to be objective, unbiased, and unemotional. And yet your decision may have to take into account other people's emotional reactions to what you decide.

Decisions can become precedents for future decisions. But any decision you make will probably be based, at least in part, on some past decision. Your problem then is to make a decision that will allow for the past, provide for the future, and yet not limit the present!

And, of course, any decision involves risk. You could decide wrong. However, no decision also involves a risk. Your procrastination may allow the problem to grow.

When you are trying to decide on the relative merits of an idea, or group of ideas, you need your judgment "full strength."

But there is also plenty of room for imagination in evaluating ideas. Often a seemingly impossible idea may be susceptible to a switch which would make it usable. Therefore, you must not let your judgment take over so completely that it excludes all imagination. Again, it is a case of alternating, or oscillating, to make sure that you will be able to see any hidden, partially hidden, or otherwise obscure possibilities in an idea.

So how do you begin the job of judging ideas? How can you be sure that you will consider, seriously, the best, won't overlook the possibles, and won't waste time or effort on the impossibles? The first step is to turn on your objectivity. In the creative stages, we suspended our judgment temporarily to let the ideas come through the gates. But when you get to weighing alternatives, it is often a big temptation to hop on the idea you favored all along because "It's obviously the best of the lot!" So rather than switch from hot ideation to cold judgment, it is better if you make the changeover gradually.

If you have a quantity of ideas to select from, and you should, then do your evaluating in two steps: First, give them a "loose" evaluation—screen them roughly for such categories as "immediate possibilities," "possible possibilities," "research project," and, of course, "no goods." Then, tighten up your evaluation first on the "immediate" and the "possible" categories. The best way to do this seems to be to measure all the ideas against some common yardstick. This yardstick will probably be whatever standards or criteria you can set up (or that may already be established) which will satisfy the needs of the problem.

It would literally be impossible for any book such as this to provide comprehensive criteria for any problem that might be met by any executive in any kind of business. Furthermore, the best criteria will usually be specifically made for any specific problem. However, problems do have "commonness," and here are some examples of criteria listings that have been used successfully to "measure" ideas of various types:

First, a rather general type, that may have its chief value in helping you sort out the "possibles" and the "maybe's": Ask—and answer—these questions *about each individual idea:*

Is the Idea Simple?

Does it seem obvious?—or is it too clever?—too ingenious?—too complicated?

Is It Compatible with Human Nature?

Could your mother, or the man next door, or your cousin, or the service-station attendant all accept it? Is it direct and unsophisticated?

Can You Write out a Simple, Clear, and Concise Statement of It?

Can you do this in two or three short sentences so that it makes sense? Can it be understood and worked on by people of the average intelligence level found in the field?

Does Your Idea "Explode" in People's Minds?

Does someone else react to it with "Now why didn't I think of that?" Can people accept it without lengthy explanation? If it does not explode, are you sure you have really simplified it?

Is It Timely?

Would it have been better six months or a year ago? (If so, is there any point in pursuing it now?) Will it be better six months from now? (If so, can you afford to wait?)

The U.S. Air Force has a "Key Criteria" list that is adaptable to many business and management decisions on ideas. They suggest that in using this list you rank the criteria in order of importance for any particular job. In other words, rank them so that any standards that an idea *must* pass will get more weight in the final decision, and those which it would merely be nice if the idea did meet will have a secondary scoring. Here are the three points:

Is It Suitable?

Will this solution do the job? Will it remedy the problem situation completely or only partially? Is it a permanent or stop-gap solution?

Is It Feasible?

Will it work in actual practice? Can we afford this approach? How much will it cost?

Is It Acceptable?

Will the company president (or the board, or the union, or the customers) go along with the changes required by this plan? Are we trying to drive a tack with a sledge hammer?

One suggestion in the Air Force list—How much will it cost?—has been expanded out into still another method of evaluating ideas that has much to offer business executives. Rather than ask, "How much will it cost?" however, you ask of each and every idea on your list, "How much will it be *worth* if it can be made to work?"

This system, used by the General Electric Company, among others, accomplishes many things by making sure that potentially good ideas get the attention they deserve. You will often find, in evaluating any list of ideas, that some of them *could* be put into effect immediately. But when you evaluate them on the basis of their *worth*, you may find that they would cost you more to implement than they could possibly be worth. On the other hand, an idea that seems to offer only a vague possibility of being useful, if it has enough potential worth, might justify even years of engineering-development time to bring to fruition. The only other suggestion for using this system is that you try to assign your dollar-values *before* you let any other form of judgment get in to cloud or prejudice your thinking!

One of the most difficult types of problems to establish criteria on are social problems—those dealing with solutions which are going to affect human lives and living. But even here it is possible. Witness this "Four Way Test" which has been widely distributed by Rotary Clubs throughout the United States:

Is it the *truth?*
Is it *fair* to all concerned?
Will it build *goodwill* and *better friendships?*
Will it be *beneficial* to all concerned?

If you can answer "yes" to each of those four questions, chances are your idea will at least be "socially acceptable."

One final example of a criteria listing, also from the military: Some departments of the U.S. Navy use this listing, which will also be applicable to many types of ideas for business problems:

> Will it increase production—improve quality?
> Is it a more efficient utilization of manpower?
> Does it improve methods of operation, maintenance, or construction?
> Is it an improvement over the present tools and machinery?
> Does it improve safety?
> Does it prevent waste, or conserve materials?
> Does it eliminate unnecessary work?
> Does it reduce costs?
> Does it improve present office methods?
> Will it improve working conditions?

If the answer to any of these is "yes," then, says the Navy, you've got a constructive idea.

As mentioned, the best criteria listing you can develop will be one tailor-made to your problem. You might want to start out by adapting or adopting one or more of the example listings that seem to be close to your own type of problems and ideas. However, the actual questions that you ask about the ideas you are trying to evaluate are not nearly so important as is your attitude in asking. If what you are trying to do is to "knock down" someone else's ideas, or discourage a particular line of endeavor, then you are defeating yourself. The creative thinker looks for possibilities to solve problems—he looks for the 90 per cent that is "right" in any idea, rather than the 10 per cent that may be wrong. And the creative mind realizes that the 10 per cent may be so obviously wrong that it can almost obscure perception of the 90 per cent "right."

Furthermore, a creative evaluation of an idea will include looking for possibilities to improve or develop the basic idea, even if it is pretty good to start with. And, not surprisingly, the way to go about this search for possibilities is again to ask questions and get answers. When you have an idea that looks possible, or even just hopeful, ask yourself questions like these:

What is the simplest possible way of doing it? If a seven-year-old boy were tackling this, how would he approach it?

List on a sheet of paper every part or factor in your idea, then ask of each part: "Is this absolutely necessary?"

Are you sure you were starting fresh?—or were you being inhibited by customs, traditions, and "the way we've always done it?"

Suppose the whole solution were completely reversed? What new possibilities does this open up? What restrictions does it remove?

Can public (or management, or worker) acceptance be measured? Can you check the feasibility of your idea out where life is going on? Can you learn anything you ought to know by *asking* the public?

What opportunities are being overlooked either in the problem or in the idea, because no one has bothered to develop them? Have you overlooked "the invisibility of the obvious?" What is the commonplace in the new idea?—can this be still improved upon?

What are the special needs of the situation? Does this dictate any idea specifications? Are there any situation needs that haven't as yet been expressed?

If your idea won't satisfy the needs of the problem, how could it be modified to strengthen it?

Asking questions like these can frequently lead you to ways to strengthen and improve your ideas.

It is important to remember, when you are evaluating ideas, that instant acceptance of an idea is as self-defeating as instant rejection. Establishing and using criteria or other measurement devices may seem to be a great deal of work to someone used to making quick or "snap" decisions. But it is the only way to discipline your thinking; it is the only way to be absolutely "fair" to all ideas; it is the only way to make sure that you "squeeze every drop" of value out of any potentially good idea. Too often, a person with a problem will go through all the motions of being organized and methodical in orienting his problem, gathering his facts, collecting literally dozens of ideas as possibilities, and then will throw all the previous work out the window because he cannot maintain his objectivity and discipline to the end.

A final word on evaluating your ideas is to pass on what may probably be the best single criterion ever developed. It was Charles Kettering's advice, and he believed in it so strongly that he had it painted on a large sign and hung in the laboratory where he worked. The sign read:

"This problem, when solved, will be simple."

8

Help Yourself to More Ideas

Of all the traits that are helpful to a creative person, one of the most valuable is undoubtedly *idea fluency*—the ability to generate sheer *quantities* of ideas against a given problem. If enough ideas can be thought of, the law of averages says that some of them are apt to have potential. And if a person will persist long enough, chances are he will try to approach his problem from different directions in the attempt to build up a quantity of possible solutions, and benefits will also accrue from this self-driven flexibility.

In attempting to build your fluency of ideas, there are artificial "spurs" you can use. These are not magic formulas or sorcerer's secrets that will automatically make you a "big idea man." They are, rather, an organization and codification of techniques and methods found to be common among people known to be creative—"tricks of the trade," if you want to call them that, but with enough general usage and acceptance in enough different fields to make them seem worth learning.

Furthermore, experiments have demonstrated that people who

learn these methods and practice them to the point that they become habitual, do show an increase in their idea production.

The basic aim of the different methods is to stimulate your mind in one way or another. Some help encourage your memory-recall; others build or activate your powers of association. And some, like checklists and questions, merely stimulate your mind into a more exhaustive analysis of either the problem or the possible ways to solve it that you might normally make without some "formal" type of discipline. As you get into these, don't be surprised if you find one or two which you already use, possibly without ever realizing that you do. Most executives unconsciously do use such techniques from time to time. The value of having them "formalized" lies in the confidence it gives you to know that these tools exist; that they have a purpose; and that you can use them whenever you feel the need of them.

1 · Make Notes

Note-making can be a big help in idea producing if the right kinds of notes are made and the right uses are made of them. The use of notebooks, "Think Books," or "Idea Traps," as they are sometimes called, is almost universal. Nearly every businessman carries at least one pocket notebook or some substitute such as 3 x 5 index cards, pads of scratchpaper, etc. Unfortunately, carrying it is often as far as he gets. Or, if used at all, it is merely a recording device for statistics like names, addresses, or what to remember to tell the serviceman about the car the next time it goes in.

But the habit of making notes is a good one, and it can work for you in several ways. One of the most obvious is that it can keep you from forgetting something. But more actively, it can help you out on your actual thinking.

For example, often a "first-impression" idea seems to block any further thinking on a problem. But by giving it the token embodiment of a written note, you may be able to help your mind move on past the obstacle and into the search for new possibilities.

Another way that writing things down can help you is by encouraging your powers of association. This is the mental function first pointed out by Aristotle over 2,300 years ago. He laid down the three laws still considered basic today: *Similarity*, *Contiguity*, and *Contrast*.

Similarity is when your mind asks, "What is this *like?*"—or when it jumps right to the answer, "This is like the time Brown Brothers had that overstock on shovels..."

Contiguity is when your mind asks, "What is this *related to?*" —or suggests the answer, "Well, this operation is much closer to a design than a production function, therefore the responsibility should probably be assigned to engineering."

Contrast is the opposite of similarity in that your mind will ask, "Now how is this *different?*"—or answer, "Brown certainly acts a lot like Smith, but he doesn't have the sense of responsibility and the broad knowledge of the business."

It's obvious that once you can start your mind asking such basic questions, you can then move ahead on your problem merely by thinking through answers. The way to "trigger" such associations as you take off on a problem is to sit down with a pencil and paper and begin to put your thoughts down just as they come to you. Try to list the thoughts separately—on separate lines or separate sheets of paper. Then, when your ideas have finally stopped, start reading back over what you have done. Ask the three associative questions about each of your notes— *What is it like?—What is it related to?—How is it different?* Continue writing down your answers or ideas. Chances are that, if you can get five or six ideas on paper in this manner, just by reading them over you will get numbers seven and eight. One thought will spark another. One idea will lead to another. The important step is to get your mind rolling in the direction you want it to go. Making notes—writing things down—is a good "primer" for the mental pump.

In the more permanent class of notes, the most useful type is certainly the note that will capture a stray idea. You have probably had the experience of "going to sleep on a problem" and waking in the middle of the night with a good idea. It was so obviously good that you knew you would remember it in the morning. But came the dawn—and disappointment. The problem was still there, but the idea was gone! "Idea men" who really mean it keep pencils and pads all over the house and capture those stray ideas immediately before they can get away.

In your permanent notes you can record your observations of circumstances: plant operations, personnel conflicts, office procedures, production problems. Later, when you find yourself with even a few minutes' time, you can use such at-the-moment notes as a base for giving the circumstance some thinking time.

Learn to record your conclusions or opinions on problems you have been thinking about. Frequently a person spends hours, or even days, working on a problem. After reaching some good conclusion (an idea or a decision) and taking action, he firmly puts the problem out of his mind to work on the next one. Later, the first problem may recur in the same or a different form. The man may recall that he thought that problem through once; but without a record of *why* he did *what* he did, chances are he will have to do all that thinking again (when there are other problems he hasn't gotten around to yet) or else take the risk that all conditions are still the same and the same action is still appropriate. Or, if the action was not successful the first time, he will find himself without a base to use in analyzing the cause of failure.

The statistical note does, of course, have a place. You should certainly form the habit of noting anything down that may have possibilities for future use to you, however remote those possibilities seem at the moment. Psychological (*Gestalt*) tests have established that on information of "average" interest (i.e., neither slight nor vital) the *rate of forgetting* is 25 per cent within the first twenty-four hours and 85 per cent within a week. In the face of this, pure memory-substitute notes do make sense. In this class of notes, you should also include clippings from newspapers and magazines, letters, book references, etc.

Along with your note-*making* system, however, you will also have to develop a note-*using* system to which you transfer your spur-of-the-moment notations at the earliest opportunity. This can be as simple or as elaborate as the problems you are making notes on. Actual systems used by successful and creative executives range from a simple cigar box (which never fills up because the owner constantly pulls out and uses his ideas) to an elaborately indexed and cross-indexed library of loose-leaf notebooks, a system used by a leading physicist. (He does the filing and indexing himself—claims he gets the same pleasure and relaxation out of it that other men get out of arranging stamp catalogues!)

One highly creative plant manager is the bane of his secretary because his personal "file" consists of a shelf behind his desk on which is heaped several years' accumulation of records, notes, papers, clippings, and pertinent letters. "Best filing system there is," he states; "nothing ever gets lost!"

Whatever system you devise, remember that the objective is to enable you to quickly gather everything you have seen, read, heard, or experienced on a problem or problem area when you need it. Then, when you have the problem, be sure to use the notes! Frequently, the hardest part of solving a problem is just getting started on it. Your notes can provide a "take off" or starting point to get you off dead-center in your search for ideas.

2 · Pick Your Time

Every individual runs on a daily cycle. Each of us has a time during the day or night when we are most capable of creative or imaginative thinking. Conversely, we probably also have a time when we are most capable of cold-blooded analytical thinking.

Your personal cycle is something you will have to find out for yourself. Try analyzing your normal "quiet" times—when you are taking a bath, or driving to or from work, or walking about the neighborhood. These are apt to be times when your mind is more sensitive to new ideas. And once you find your most creative time, set it aside and guard it zealously for ideation —use it for thinking about problems with a view to getting ideas.

The practice of spending a definite time just in searching for new ideas can be one of the most productive techniques you can adopt. When you really concentrate your mental energy on a problem, it tends to spark your mind into reaching further back into your memory cells and exposing a greater fund of experience and knowledge to bring to bear on your problem.

It is a common complaint of business executives that they "don't have time to think." They are so loaded with detail and routine problems, which need on-the-spot or immediate solutions, that they cannot seem to clear any time whatever for long-range thinking and planning. And when these men meet someone who seems able to handle and balance a great deal more activity, and still seems relaxed and cognizant of the need for thought, the first question is usually, "But how do you find time to do all those things?"

Actually, no one "finds" time to do anything. You *make* time to do the things that you consider important. The same people who complain that they can't find time to think, or work on extra problems, or do extra research into the problems they have, usually waste more time in a week than they would ever need to double their productivity. Next time you hear someone complain of not having enough time, try this: Keep the conversation going. Get it around to the subject of TV programs. Or baseball. Or nearby golf courses. Somewhere along the line, you will ring a bell. Some of the loudest complainers about the shortage of time are practically walking guidebooks to every television comedian, Western hero, and detective on the air. When you actually analyze all the programs they are fully familiar with, you find that they must spend a minimum of twenty hours a week just watching TV.

This is not to say that a person shouldn't have some mental relaxation or a chance to "recharge his batteries." Both of these are musts. But you can carry them to extremes. If what you *really* want is to get more time to think, take a long hard look at some of your extracurricular activities and make sure you are not dissipating your time in nonproductive and passive mental activity.

Your work-habits should also be looked at in a cold analytical way. There is a saying that "You can tell the condition of a man's mind by the top of his desk." From observation of many executives and would-be executives at work, this would appear to be true. In most cases, the cluttered desks belong to people who haven't learned to appreciate the true value of systems.

Systems can be extremely valuable in gaining thinking time because, if you work them out yourself, they can take over much routine administrative detail for you. Such details as record keeping, budgets, allocations, and other purely statistical work can be put into forms of various types that can be completed and checked with a minimum of time.

Letting yourself get bogged down in petty details is another time-waster. Somebody has to take care of details, it is true, but if you are in an executive or supervisory capacity, the chances are that "somebody" should *not* be you. Perhaps it is your secretary (one of the biggest wastes of executive time is failure to make the most effective use of secretarial time!); or it may be a subordinate or even someone in another department. With details that you just cannot pass off, the best approach is to group and organize them. For example, get your dictation out of the way at one time during the day. Group your telephone calls so you can make several at one sitting. Plan to have any interviews or conferences at the most convenient time for all concerned, and make appointments in advance—this will cut your waiting time. Insist on punctuality for meetings—for yourself as well as others. You can easily lose an hour a day waiting for tardy people. When a meeting starts, get it started—if six men sit for ten minutes telling stories as a preliminary to a meeting, that is one hour of manpower wasted. And learn to plan and schedule your work. If you can do it daily, then do it daily and stick to your schedule. If you can make it weekly—even to the point of starting off on Monday morning with a meeting to coordinate your activities and the activities of others for the week —then schedule your time for the week and stick to the schedule.

If you analyze your activities closely and honestly, you will undoubtedly find that you can gain at least some time every day and every week just by cutting out the time-wasting habits that you have fallen into through indifference and lack of planning. If you want to gain time to think, this is the way to do it.

And if you want to make the most of that time when you get it, then learn how you work best and work that way: steer clear of mind-weakeners like fatigue, noise, and other distractions. They divert your attention and interfere with concentration. And don't be misled by stories you hear of great ideas coming out of all-night coffee-drinking or liquor-drinking sessions. For every "great" idea produced this way, there are a thousand that have come out of clear, rested, incisive minds owned by men who knew that the "only job of the body is to carry the brain around," and who, therefore, kept their bodies in good condition and their minds free of dulling fatigue. A good night's sleep and moderation in diet, exercise, and pleasures will do more for your thinking than any artificially induced stimulants.

3 · Give Yourself a Deadline

It is human nature to procrastinate. Yet prolific idea men find that they are at their most creative in spurts, and they get their best ideas when they go "all out" to get them. Sometimes, of course, there is a real and practical deadline to supply the urge to push yourself mentally: the customer wants to see the new design *tomorrow;* the planning committee is meeting *next Wednesday* to decide whether your department or Ed Brown's is going to get the extra money for expansion; you have only *ten days'* supply of material "X" on hand and the only supplier has a strike still going on. In any of these cases, you would find yourself really mentally involved in finding a solution. But you can also simulate such pressure by giving yourself a deadline —just make one up. To get yourself equally involved emotionally in meeting that deadline, just tell someone else—your boss, or his boss, or the planning committee—that you are going to have ten or twenty new ideas at such and such a time.

The idea of personally stimulating yourself to be creative through the practice of setting personal deadlines should not be interpreted as a recommendation for continual "crash programs." To be sure, there are times when crash programs are necessary (even mindful of the Pentagon wag who defined a crash program as "getting nine girls pregnant in order to make a baby in one month"!). In research or product development, crash programs may have value if the paths to be followed are clearly defined and there are no major unsolved problems in the way. Then an all-out "drive" to finish a project may be justified. But by and large, you cannot keep any machines, especially mental machines, running at top speed all the time. They need "rest periods" and time for maintenance and refueling. But so far as your personal thinking is concerned, the occasional made-up deadline may be just what you need to spur your mind to a new and better problem solution.

4 · Set a Quota for Yourself

The aim of building up idea fluency is to enable you to generate quantities of ideas against any problem you may have. So start shooting for quantity right away any time you have a problem. Give yourself an actual number quota of ideas to get down on paper before you try to evaluate or organize them. Don't set an impossible task for yourself, but if you can usually think up two or three ways something might be done, try setting a quota of at least five ways. When you can make five, up your quota to ten. When you get to ten, try fifteen or twenty. You shouldn't have to keep this up too long before you will find that quantities of ideas begin to come easier, and you will be able to produce any given number of ideas in much less time than it took you when you first started the practice. You will also notice that when an on-the-spot problem presents itself, instead of making a "blind stab" for a solution, your mind will automatically start running through many different ways of handling it.

You will also find that the *quality* of your ideas is improving with the quantity. This gets back to the basic advantage of idea fluency: If you have a problem, and you have only one idea how it might be solved, then good, bad, or indifferent, one idea is all you have. If it fails, then you are right back with *no* ideas. If you have two ideas, chances are one will be somewhat better than the other. If you have twenty or fifty or a hundred ideas, your biggest problem may then be to decide which is best.

5 · Use Checklists

You have already met examples of checklists in the previous chapter: the "Question Listings" to help you explore problems, dig out facts, and evaluate ideas. And, of course, you probably use other types of checklists every day in your normal business routines. The most common business checklist is aimed at reminding a person not to make mistakes in an accepted procedure. But another type, such as those we have already considered, is aimed at reminding us not to forget to be original.

Such checklists usually consist of operational-type questions that challenge the obvious aspects of a problem. Using them can often stimulate your mind into exploring areas you might otherwise miss through mere acceptance of routine. We have already mentioned the General Electric Value Analysis service as an example of applied systematic creativity in business. Here is the checklist used by a value analyst when he first meets up with any particular part or component:

1. Does its use contribute to value?
2. Is its cost proportionate to its usefulness?
3. Does it need all its features?
4. Is there anything better for the intended use?
5. Can a standard or a vendor's standard be found which will be usable?
6. Can a usable part be made by a lower cost method?
7. Is it made on the proper tooling, considering volume?
8. Do material, reasonable labor, reasonable overhead, and reasonable profit total its costs?
9. Will another dependable supplier provide it for less?
10. Can anyone buy it for less?

You will note that a lazy thinker *could* answer most of those questions with a simple "yes" or "no" because many of the answers lie purely in the realm of *fact*—they are either yes or no. But a man with a creative mind, rather than take this obvious way out, uses such questions to aid him in "thinking around" the problem at hand. For example, consider question No. 2: "Is its cost proportionate to its usefulness?" The answer to this may be a simple "yes" or "no," but it may also be "maybe." It could be that a "yes" would still leave some room for doubt whether the part was being utilized to its fullest potential, even though the cost was fair. On the other hand, a "no" could open up a whole stream of questions aimed at narrowing down the causes of the excessive cost and suggesting ways to reduce the cost. In this manner, a creative thinker can develop his whole problem solution from knowing which questions to ask and what kind of answers to hunt for.

One of the most basic of all question checklists was formalized by Alex Osborn and presented in his textbook, *Applied Imagination*. He lists more than seventy types of questions to ask yourself when you are searching for new ideas. It is interesting to note that most of these questions require the "commonplace" as a starting point. In going through this sampling, it will be helpful if you pick some common object, such as a pencil, ash tray, paper clip, or other familiar item, and try to answer each of these questions in terms of that object:

Can It Be Put to Other Uses?
Is there a new way to use it as is? Other uses if modified?

Can It Be Adapted?
What else is like this? What other ideas does this suggest? What could I copy? Whom could I emulate?

Can It Be Modified?
Give it a new twist? Change the meaning, color, motion, sound, odor, form, shape? Any other changes possible?

Can It Be Magnified?
What to add? More time? Greater frequency? Stronger? Higher? Longer? Thicker? Multiply? Exaggerate?

Can It Be Minified?
What to subtract? Smaller? Condense? Lower? Shorter? Lighter? Omit something? Streamline? Split up?

What Can We Substitute?
Who else instead? What else instead? Other ingredients? Other process? Other power?

Rearrange It?
Interchange components? Other patterns? Other layout? Transpose cause and effect? Change the pace? Change the schedule?

Reverse It?
Transpose positive and negative? Turn it backward? Upside down? Reverse roles?

Combine It?
How about a blend? An alloy? An assortment? An ensemble? Combine units? Purposes?

You will note that not all of these questions are directly applicable to any specific product or situation. But if you made a conscientious effort to answer each of them, you will also note that they do stimulate your mind into thinking channels it might not normally follow.

The best type of checklist is, certainly, one you make up yourself to fit your own recurring problems. Using such checklists takes a certain amount of initiative, however. It takes initiative and application to analyze your problems thoroughly and compile the question-list that will make you think around the problem. It takes effort to really ask the questions and find the answers; and it certainly takes initiative to review your checklist from time to time to make sure it hasn't become outdated. Using an outdated checklist can be a major pitfall: we get lulled into a sense of false security through feeling that everything is under control just because we religiously ask questions about what we are doing as we go along doing it. But situations change, and we may end up predicating our thinking on outmoded or no longer pertinent questions.

What's more, just a mechanical use of a checklist does not produce originality. The purpose of such questions is to provide challenges to obvious ways of doing things. Therefore, the answers to these questions must be well thought out—even if the answer results in a "No—this is the best we can do right now."

Checklists can often be improvised, also. An open-minded sales manager looking for new customers might get real benefit out of just leafing through the yellow pages of a telephone directory. An office manager, trying to develop a more efficient utilization of space, might get some ideas by paging through a trade publication devoted to hotel or kitchen planning. Since you are simply trying to find new or different ways of solving a particular problem, you can never tell when or where you will find an idea to borrow. The originality may consist of the fact that this has never been used in your particular field before—and if that will solve your problem, settle for that!

6 · Use Creative Questioning

Checklists are one technique which will aid you in asking questions. But questioning should be almost a continuous process throughout a problem-solving effort. The questions and the answers provide the bricks and mortar with which you build toward your solution of a problem. A strong sense of curiosity, coupled with a well-developed capacity for questioning, is vital to creative thought of any kind.

Questioning is an art. Like any other art, learning it is best accomplished by acquiring some understanding of the aims and methods and adding a large amount of practice in the technique.

Much of this needed learning could, for an adult, be better classified as "relearning" because it involves methods and techniques that you probably used quite instinctively and intensively as a child. After all, the time of your life when you were learning at the highest rate possible was probably between the ages of four and six. And you were undoubtedly asking more questions per unit of time during those years than in any years since.

For an adult to recapture this questioning attitude and ability (which was lost largely through the indifference of parents, school teachers, classmates, and the "big kids" of the neighborhood and their unwillingness to put up with "silly kid" questions) calls, first, for getting over the feeling that he is parading his ignorance in asking. An adult, through constant exposure to the school of success that says, "Never show what you don't know," is usually afraid to ask questions. Some of this fear is undoubtedly the old fear of sounding foolish when asking a question. Some of it may be due to not knowing how to ask meaningful and worthwhile questions. Actually, it is only through questions that a person can learn. Only by questioning other people's thoughts and asking questions of your own mind, can you hope to uncover theories, new ideas, and new combinations of thoughts that will lead the way to new and better ways of doing things. And it is always good policy to start by questioning yourself first. Your own experience and knowledge, if they have been properly acquired, are probably as good as anyone else's. You start questioning others when you run out of answers yourself.

There is, needless to say, a difference, and an important one, between questions of idle curiosity ("What's the weather like outside?" or "Read any good books lately?") and what Einstein called the "driving spirit of inquiry" of the truly creative person. The questions asked by a person driven by this creative spirit are not usually asked, nor can they be answered, lightly. So in trying to build your own questioning ability, keep in mind that it is somewhat like taking setting-up exercises. If you take them halfheartedly—just now and then—very little good will result. However, everyone realizes that such exercises taken for a purpose—and taken purposively—can do wonders. In the same way, purposeful use of questions can work wonders for your imagination and your general thinking abilities—and can do so in a short while.

(Before going any further on this subject, the executive must never forget that his questioning should be done in a *positive* frame of mind. Too many people use questions as a way of establishing their presence in an organization. They never go after the answers—they just raise questions. The object of creative questioning is to uncover new possibilities for better ways of doing things. The person who asks a *creative* question does so with the intention of finding the answer himself!)

Here are some general types of questions that may suggest productive avenues of inquiry that you can follow in pursuing your problems:

Ask about What Is Around You. These questions will largely concern the "which," the "what," and the "how" of things. Such questions help you uncover problems—or opportunities. As examples: Questioning your present methods may lead to the elimination of unnecessary operations or to simplications of your procedures. Asking about working conditions can lead to improved safety measures or to the elimination of accident hazards. Such a simple question as "How can we reduce the waste on this particular manufacturing operation?" may lead the way to more profitable production throughout the plant.

Maintain a Healthy Skepticism. Ask questions about the "why" of things to keep yourself (and others!) from getting into ruts. This kind of question can, of course, make you highly unpopular with certain types of people because it forces them to think. And, frequently, a "why" challenge to an accepted procedure can uncover the fact that the only reason for doing something a certain way is that "We've always done it this way." If that "always" covers a period of more than six months, a whole salvo of questions may then be in order to establish whether or not this is still the best way to handle that particular problem. It may well be that it is—but if you question it, then you *know!*

Ask When and Where. In business, good timing can often be the crucial factor in the success or failure of a venture. Marketing, sales, and advertising efforts are especially vulnerable to mistakes in timing—and just as susceptible to help through good timing. ("Timing," of course, includes termination of an effort as well as initiation.) Asking "where" is logical in the case of a new plant location, new markets to be opened up, new sources of raw materials, and even the location of a new water fountain in the shop (Where are the largest number of workers located? Where does the traffic flow? Where are the present water pipes? Where are the drainpipes? Considering these, just where is the best place for the water fountain?)

Learn about Personalities. The acceptance or rejection of any new idea or new method of doing things is largely dependent upon the people involved. So is the degree of probable success in getting an order carried out. So ask about the "who" of things —Who will have to approve this? What are his likes, dislikes, strengths, weaknesses? What are the qualities we need in a man to handle this operation? Who comes closest to filling those qualities now? Who could be trained? Probably every executive believes in Harriman Hill's advice, "Never do anything yourself you can get someone else to do for you," but if you hold the responsibility for the success or failure of a venture, you should be very concerned with questioning the "who" of things!

And don't be afraid to go "off-beat" with your questions. The story is told about what happened in the metal-fabrications department of a major manufacturer when they were trying to weld a tricky new aluminum assembly. The aluminum had been anodized, for reasons peculiar to the application, and the development people had about given up the whole project because it seemed impossible to get satisfactory welds on the material. At the meeting, where the vote was to abandon the project, one engineer dissented. He said, "Let's not quit. Why don't we try doing it the way an Indian would?"

"What do you mean, do it the way an Indian would?" asked the engineering manager. "What do you have in mind?"

"I don't have anything in mind except that I know an Indian wouldn't weld it," replied the engineer.

To make a long story short, the engineer was given the assignment of seeing "what you and the Indians can do." He began working with people who knew how to fabricate from wire—by crimping, bending, forming, and so forth. Three months later the problem was solved, and the company began enjoying savings of $2.5-million a year!

Of course, eventually you have to stop asking questions and start doing. Knowing when that exact point is reached calls for tough judgment. Often it is easier to convince yourself that you still haven't all the answers you need, and therefore should keep on looking, than it is to get down to the job of solving the problem. So you should know how to tell when your questioning is efficient and when to stop.

The first principle is *know what it is you want to find out.* This may sound obvious, but it is deceptively so. To do a really efficient job of questioning, you have to "back off" from your problem initially. Then you begin to ask questions that will first establish the "big picture" of the problem—its boundaries, limitations, history, and general characteristics. Once this is established, you can again step back and look for the area that seems to offer most immediate possibilities for attack.

Gradually, and with your big picture constantly in the back of your mind, you reduce it into a series of smaller detail pictures about which you ask detailed and specific questions. It is probably a good idea not to try to zero in on details too soon. If you do, you may miss something important in the over-all picture. Furthermore, if you begin asking questions to pin down details before policy is clear, you may end up wasting a great deal of time. A shift from an assumed policy could make all your detail decisions obsolete or even wrong.

As to when you stop, it is again a case of getting a worthwhile return on your investment. You stop when what you "get back" in information and ideas is no longer worth what you "put out" in time and effort.

But always conclude with one final question: "Have I overlooked any sources of new answers?"

7 · Other Aids

The individual spurs to ideas covered so far are the most popular with the greatest number of people largely because they can be used any time, any place, under any circumstances, and they are general enough to be adapted or adopted for almost any type of problem, whether personal, business, social, or environmental. There are several more specialized techniques that may also be of interest. These are usually favored by persons with highly specialized types of design, engineering, or other problems dealing largely with tangible items.

They may be classified generally as *analytical* techniques, in that, like checklists, they force you into an analysis of all the various factors involved in changing or improving your commonplace beginning.

Attribute Listing. This technique was developed and formalized by Professor Robert Platt Crawford of the University of Nebraska (and is explained in detail in his book, *Techniques of Creative Thinking*). Basically, it consists of listing all the attributes or qualities of an object, product, or situation; then systematically considering each attribute or group of attributes in turn, to try to change each of them in as many ways as possible. The object of each change should be to do a better job of satisfying your new need. For example:

If the problem were to develop a different kind of picture frame, you would start by listing the attributes of an ordinary frame and looking for possible ways to change them:

Ordinary Frame Has ...	*Could Be Changed to ...*
Rectangular shape	Round, oval, triangular, etc.
Glass covering	Lucite, plastic film, ornamental tracery, louvers, etc.
Wooden construction	Aluminum, plastic, rubber, no frame, built-in, etc.
Wire hanger	Magnetic, double-faced tape, suction cups, hook-and-eye, etc.

If you carry this far enough, you can soon get into such questions as "What other objects are like picture frames?" (window frames, wall-panel mountings, mosaic panels) and "What can I borrow from them?" "What other materials used in decorating anything might lend themselves to decorating a frame?"

The "X" Method. This is a method formalized by Professor George B. Dubois of Cornell. Professor Dubois suggests that if you have broken your problem down completely and still can't seem to get started, you substitute "X" for any unknown and go on to the next step. It's a little like the way General MacArthur "island-hopped" in the Pacific during World War II: His strategy was to by-pass enemy strong points and capture less well defended islands beyond and around them. The "X" method lets you attempt the same thing on design or development problems: when you hit an impasse, go on to the next phase that you can tackle. You may find the solution to your "passed" problem while working on another aspect of the total problem.

Input-Output System. This method serves first to define the problem, and then to provide a framework for its solution. You start by determining what it is you want to accomplish—the final objective. Let's say this will be a new lamp base. This would be the *output*. Then, you determine your *input*, or what you have to work with—tools, materials, skills. In between these two, you list any limitations—cost, structural requirements, aesthetic considerations. Now you begin to work from one side of the problem to the other and back again—from the input of one particular detail, such as tools available, over to the desired output to see what you can accomplish in view of the limitations you have established. If your analysis is exhaustive enough and you are creative enough in looking for possibilities, the input-output system can frequently produce a multitude of ideas for incorporation into your final design.

It is well to note that in using any such analytical techniques as attribute listing and the input-output system, the value and quality of the results will be largely determined by the care and accuracy of the original problem analysis. If vital angles of the problem are not included in the initial framework, or if facts are inaccurate, you will not be able to make accurate or useful transformations to final ideas. Therefore, if you must make some unverifiable assumptions in order to go ahead on the problem, be sure you put mental "flags" on them to indicate possible danger spots. In many cases, of course, your final result will prove or disprove the validity of your assumption; but if, in the course of working your way through an analysis, you get the opportunity to check out a key assumption for accuracy, you may save yourself much time and trouble by stopping to pin it down right then and there.

All the self-prodding techniques covered in this chapter can be useful in helping you to produce more ideas; they will enable you

to take an orderly approach to a problem and to avoid ordinary
blank spots which might be caused by faulty perception, haste,
or emotional or cultural blocks. But, to be effective, they must all
be used with intelligence and imagination. Before you consider
any particular technique, you should consider its suitability for
what you want to accomplish. In many cases, it may be useful
to mix or combine the devices you will employ. At every stage
you will have to use your imagination in deciding just which tool
is the best for your needs at that particular stage in the problem-
solving sequence. It is, in a way, like playing golf or trying to
catch fish. There are no hard and fast rules to tell you just what
to do next—you have to use judgment in deciding how you will
play the ball or lure the fish or solve the problem.

Finally, always remember the basic aim of all idea-spurring techniques: to help you keep an open and receptive mind. You never
know where or when the solution to any particular problem is
going to come to you. So don't get all wrapped up in the techniques, methods, procedures, devices, or what have you. They
are only means to an end—not the end itself. Be receptive—be
ready to "receive" when your mind starts "sending" a promising
idea or ideas.

And don't let yourself be blocked out of a good idea by what
anyone else says about it, or even by what you see in front of you.

9

When to Use Creative Groups

So far everything in this book has concerned itself with improving individual creativity. This, and the following two chapters, will be concerned with uses for a type of creative operation that is becoming almost indispensable in certain areas of business— creative teams and groups.

When our first Explorer satellite was put into orbit, American technology moved irreversibly, if somewhat belatedly, into the realm of 18,000 mph-and-up speeds. In spite of the wishes of many people, we can never go back to the relative horse-and-buggy days of even 1955 when the fastest man-made machine moved at the "leisurely" pace of 500 to 600 mph. The age of space-travel speeds is here, and we have to learn to live with them.

This means we also have to gear ourselves to new speeds in thinking and problem solving. Even pre-Explorer scientific problems were so complex that it was a rare individual who knew all there was to know about just one of the subspecialties within a scientific specialty—let alone the complete science.

And, of course, complex sciences make problems just as complex. Nearly, if not entirely, gone are the days when a lone scien-

146

tist can suggest a simple "formula change" that will immediately solve a major chemical or processing problem. We just don't *use* chemicals that way anymore! And in other fields, too, we seldom hear of a great individual inventor today. Most of our advances seem to come from groups, out of laboratories or engineering sections. No single individual can claim invention of atomic energy; there is no name tag on the automatic transmission of your car; legal departments of large corporations will tell you that one of their biggest problems in planning patent protection for products is settling on just which three or four names out of a dozen or more should be put on the patent application as "primary inventor"!

This situation exists chiefly because research, development, and production people frequently find that today no one man has the knowledge or experience to solve the new "superproblems" they are meeting. Individualists will tell you that the solution lies in educating our scientists better—or more. Or in teaching them to use more than the 15 to 20 per cent of their mental powers that the average person uses now. Both of these goals are worth striving for and should certainly be explored and encouraged. Unfortunately many of the problems of 18,000 mph-and-up science and business can't wait for the human element to catch up. Not if a company (or the nation!) wants to stay in business. And with technologies increasing at an estimated rate of 22 per cent a year, it seems somewhat doubtful whether we *can* catch up if we depend solely upon the improvement of the individual.

Not only have problems become increasingly complex, but we have, in recent years, tended to make our individual problem-solvers more specialized. This pertains to business executives as well as scientists. There are strong indications in business that, in breeding new specialist executives, we may have shortchanged ourselves on the "generalist" types so necessary to cope with broad, over-all business problems. As any individual becomes more specialized, his sphere of knowledge and capabilities drops off in the broader areas, and he finds himself in need of other specialists in order to survive. The more we specialize, the more dependent we become on one another—and the more we must cooperate with others. For a business or scientific specialist of any kind to declare himself independent of his fellow men today is literally to commit professional suicide.

The scientific or management "team" of two or three men has provided a partial answer to this. But even teams find their joint imaginative efforts inadequate at times. So more and more we are being forced to turn to group efforts to come up with ideas and answers, particularly when those ideas and answers are needed in a hurry.

It is unfortunate that the necessity of using groups has pushed many people into the practice before they have taken the time to seriously explore the use of groups or teams as problem-solving tools. In some fields, group use has become almost a fad: a meeting will be called on almost any pretext, and the group is turned loose on the problem without adequate preparation, direction, or leadership—and without achieving any close feeling of responsibility for solving the problem. In such cases, it is probably true, as critics charge, that the group will seek, or settle for, a compromise rather than the best answer, or that it will settle for the most daring idea that the least daring member can accept.

Consequently, many of the more responsible types of creative persons have become somewhat suspicious of group creative activities. As a result of one or two bad experiences with improperly used groups, they have developed a resistance to the idea that groups can be valuable adjuncts to a problem-solving effort, and even to the thought that groups can be creative at all. This is unfortunate because, if used properly, a creative group can be a powerful tool for helping the individual move along toward a problem solution.

One of the important points to remember in using a creative group is that the objective is to help you get ideas that will help solve problems. Not ideas just for the sake of having a list of ideas, but ideas to solve the problems you or your company consider worth solving.

Secondly, anything we can do to get those needed ideas is "fair play." In this sense, a creative group in no way competes with or replaces the individual. In fact, a creative individual becomes even more important. He becomes the "problem planner" or "coordinator" who uses his imagination and knowledge of the various problem-solving tools, both individual and group, to quickly and efficiently plot and execute the approach to the problem solution. This type of individual will regard the group as a tool to be used where that particular tool will do the best job.

When you consider a creative group of any type as a tool, it then becomes apparent that you will have to learn a few things about it and develop some skill in using it before you can expect maximum results. And you have to learn enough about each type of creative group to know when it is the best tool for the job in hand. An analogy could be made with a hammer. If you were going to build a house by yourself, and someone said to you, "Well, then, you'll want a good hammer," you wouldn't interpret that to mean that a hammer is the only tool you would need, or that a hammer should be used on every job in constructing the house. But you would realize that a hammer would be a very useful tool to have in your kit when you started construction on your house. The same holds true for any of the creative group techniques: none of them is the "universal" tool which will solve any or all problems or even aid you on every problem. But it is well worthwhile to have them in your mental tool kit for the times when they can do a job more efficiently than an "individual" tool. The really creative person in business today is one who is willing to use any tool he can to obtain solutions to problems. To this kind of individual, other minds are tools. And the way to begin a study of creative groups is by studying groups in general.

Let's say that a business organization, or a department of an organization, is made up of 100 individual people. These people all have different temperaments and different racial, religious, and family backgrounds. Each of them is a product of his particular heredity, early home environment, and parental training. Each can, therefore, be expected to react somewhat differently to other people, to business situations, and to any experiences with which he is confronted. Their emotional reactions to any stimulus will be quite individual and completely automatic. Their mental reactions, in the form of associations and thought processes, will also be automatic and individual. There will exist differences of opinion on almost any problem and differences in reactions to almost any type of challenge. All these individual differences in backgrounds, education, experience, and emotional responses, then, constitute an available "pool" of mental resources to draw on in a search for a problem solution.

(This, incidentally, is where the *understanding* group user differs from those critics who complain of "group-think" tactics: the usual sense of "group think" implies that all members of an organization think alike—will have the *same* responses in the same situation. To a creative group user, such people are useless—what he needs, and, in fact, must have, are the *differences* in thinking!)

In selecting people from this pool, the creative group user will draw them on the basis of the contributions he expects them to make from their own individual backgrounds, and he will work to focus these varied characteristics on a solution to the problem. He is after a cross-fertilization, rather than an inbreeding, of ideas. There are times when the group organizer will want a flint-like mind on his problem. He may also, in order to ensure some sparks, include a more "steellike" mind. There will be times when the heavy, ponderous, serious thinker is the person needed for a particular problem. But it may be, in order to keep the group from being overwhelmed by such a mind, that one or two frivolous, lighthearted types will be needed for balance. It may be that the nature of the problem will be such that you will want to cross organizational or functional lines in making up the group. Research scientists and the sales department, for instance, are usually pretty well isolated from each other in a company. But if your problem involved the planning of a new product, you might get some very interesting results from mixing representatives of the two interests.

Such planned, intentional, and intelligent mixing and intermixing of personalities and interests is a key to successful group usage on creative-type problems. Each member of the group should be individually selected on the basis of a specific contribution you expect him to make. If you are so fortunate as to be able to select specific contributors who are also highly creative individuals, then you will find yourself handling what can be an extremely "hot" tool, and how well or how poorly you handle it will determine the degree of success that the group can achieve. Now let's see what happens, in a general sense, when you organize a business group to attack a problem creatively.

The Individual in a Group

No two people in any group ever "join" it for exactly the same reasons. In a business conference, each person present will have a different degree of motivation and interest. Some will be staunch proponents of either the pro or the con of the subject—if there are pros and cons; others will be present as "resource people," who were invited to contribute their experience or specialized knowledge, but otherwise will not be concerned with any action taken or decided upon; still others will be there purely and simply because they were ordered to attend. Initially, these may be completely indifferent to the purposes or causes of the meeting. And finally, in any group, at least half the members will be composites to varying degrees of any or all of these characterized members.

(Although we are concerned here primarily with business groups of "conference" size it should be noted that most of these principles and methods are equally applicable to social groups as well. For example, the main concern of a religious group may be to probe and explore the values of the human soul and spirit. However, there will undoubtedly be individual members of any such group who will be in it purely for the social opportunities which the group provides. This can, at times, lead to a conflict of interests which may threaten the primary purpose of the group.)

Most groups of six or more persons will include one or more individuals who may be almost fanatics for "group thinking"—they consider the group the only efficient and impersonal arrangement for objectively disposing of a problem. They may or may not enjoy participating in the group action, but they do believe in it.

Then there are other individuals who consider group participation an emotionally satisfying experience to be prolonged and savored to its fullest. (In this respect, it is important to remember that one of the biggest things you can "give" any person is recognition. Group methods do give people a sense of being recognized through participation and experience. This is a mixed blessing: on the one hand, participation in a group can be used as a motivational tool or as a reward to an individual; on the other, there exists the danger that such participation will "go to the head" of a member and he will devote much time to scheming how he can be included in more of it!)

The most satisfactory group member, however, will be the one who finds the group personally satisfying to the extent that he is motivated by participation to contribute, but who, at the same time, realizes the true purpose of the group as a problem-solving mechanism and will work efficiently toward that end.

Specific types of individuals who can be anticipated in any group meeting will include representative samplings of these:

The Power Jockey. This type has a hidden agenda in any meeting; he is seeking to build his own personal power or prestige, either as an individual or as the leader of a clique. He gives himself away by frequent stubborn and usually uncalled-for attacks on other members or on ideas or suggested lines of action for reasons which have nothing to do with the main issue.

The Deflator. This individual may be an incipient power jockey, or he may be supporting a jockey. His troublemaking usually takes the form of an attack on a personal level which is intended to deflate and reduce the prestige of another member.

The Loyal Outsider. Here is an individual with a real problem. He is usually a willing and helpful member of the group—at least, he tries to be. Nevertheless, as a loyal representative of an outside organization or department—and only incidentally a member of the meeting group—he suffers from divided loyalty. He wants to help the group do its job effectively, yet he feels he must resist any attempt to blame, examine, or involve his parent group in any way. He can usually be spotted by the appearance of confusion, irritation, or stubbornness when the subject being covered gets close to his primary-group interests. Other times, he will be a most cooperative and useful member of the larger group.

The All-wise. This is the member who comes to a meeting with a problem-solution all thought out and decided—at least in his own mind. Instead of being present to share knowledge and consider other opinions, he has his answer in his hip-pocket. (A minor subtype is the *snap-judger*—he gets his answer in the opening minutes of any meeting, then tucks it away for the proper time to present it.) The all-wise is usually intelligent enough to realize that a premature revelation of his solution will not sit well with other members of the group (such a revelation might imply that he as an individual is smarter than the group), so he waits until he judges the time to be ripe for a solution suggestion. In the process of this judging, his mind is pretty well closed to any other solution or suggestion, and he will probably not be either objective or even active in contributing to the major group effort.

The Withholder. Either lack of confidence or mental laziness can be the root trouble with this member. He may hold back an honest opinion or answer because of a fear that someone will disapprove, and he will lose stature. Or he may come to the meeting in the first place with a determination that this is not his problem, that someone else can do the thinking and the work. He is satisfied to be "a good listener." To switch this member's participation from the passive to the active is one of the toughest jobs a group leader can face. Occasionally, you may be so unfortunate as to meet up with an entire group of withholders. Then it will take every trick in your leader's bag to get the meeting moving. (Some such "tricks" will be covered in Chapter 11.)

These individuals are seldom met in a "pure" state in any creative group. (In any event, it need not be disastrous for the meeting, if the leader can spot the type he has to deal with early enough!) Any individual may move from one category to another as the meeting or conference progresses and as the subject being covered moves nearer or farther from the individual's particular interests or field of knowledge. Furthermore, in a fast-moving group situation, the leader cannot always attend to each person as an individual. He must deal with a composite of all of them. Fortunately, a kind of law-of-averages comes into play to help the leader.

The Group Personality

Whenever people are mixed together in a group, a different personality takes over: that of the group. This personality is real and positive to the point that a skilled observer can analyze it for any given group much the same as an individual's personality can be analyzed. This group personality consists of all the factors that make up all the individual personalities present in the group, intensified or modified in direct relationship to how many times each of those individual factors appears in the group. In other words, a group made up of predominant extroverts would tend to have a sharply extrovertic personality; one made up of predominantly hostile or suspicious individuals would be most disagreeably hostile or suspicious in its group behavior.

The executive who is attempting to use a group for problem-solving must be sharply conscious of the effects of this group personality. Just as the group personality is affected by the individual factors involved, so too will continued exposure to any group affect the individuals. Many people, over a period of several adult years, acquire their attitudes, beliefs, and feelings from their experience with groups. Therefore, one of the tools of prediction for group behavior is to know in advance the outside interests the individual may have in other groups.

By balancing out the individual personalities you select for a group you are putting together, you can make reasonably sure of a group personality that will have the best opportunity to solve the problem.

This is demonstrated clearly by the composition of many research and development task groups: depending on the nature of the problem, R&D group members may include a balanced ratio of chemists, physicists, metallurgists, electronics specialists, and engineers. Each would be selected because of a specific knowledge contribution he was expected to make. And the group can be directed or steered toward a specific type of group action by including more of one type of personality than another, or by carefully selecting individuals of one type who are known to be more aggressive in their personalities than the others. The predominant or aggressive specialists then tend to take over the leadership of the thinking, with the secondary members dropping back into the roles of resource people—specialists who will be called upon by the group as their specialized training and experience are needed.

An effective use of groups depends, however, on how well the various personalities and interests can be pulled together by the leader into an integrated and smooth-working whole. Therefore, the prospective group leader would do well to familiarize himself with some of the resistance factors that can be encountered once the group personality has come into being.

Pressures within a Group

The ills that bother a group action, once it begins to function as a group, can be oversimplified by considering some of the characteristics of a family:

Though it may appear unified and close-knit to the outside

world, there are, at the same time, minor and almost continuous conflicts going on within the family group. Husbands attempt to influence—or even pressure!—their wives into certain lines of thinking or action; wives attempt the same with their husbands. In trying to guide their children, parents, with the best of intentions, frequently run head-on into conflicts of interests among the children. In attempting to accept parental guidance, the children, in turn, often find themselves in a state of conflict with their own emotions and instincts, which tends to set off a chain-reaction of confusions and even frustrations. These family conflicts, of course, seldom break out in open warfare between the participants because the bonds of the family are strong enough to override them. Nevertheless, they are present. And such conflicts are also present in adult groups gathered to solve a business, community, or social problem. They are usually described by social analysts as "group ills." Here are some of the more common:

Confusion of Purpose. Members of the group become dissatisfied or openly hostile in the process of group operation. There may be flights into endless discussion of petty or completely unrelated details. There may be long arguments over points that could more easily be resolved by a single individual at a later time. Such symptoms may indicate that the group lacks a clear understanding of its purpose. This is usually the fault of the leader— either he failed to give them suitable orientation as to *why* the group was called together in the first place, or he failed to impress upon the group the importance of their activity to the extent that they are motivated to undertake it to the exclusion of personal and more selfish interests.

Incompatible Personalities. These conflicts can arise between individuals or subgroups who may, ordinarily, work in perfect accord. For example, a normal boss and subordinate relationship may be a smooth, well-coordinated team activity. But put them together in a larger work group where, ostensibly, everyone is on an equal footing, and a defensive conflict arises: the boss feels he must maintain his position of authority by demonstrating it, and the subordinate is really afraid to challenge that authority by publicly refuting the boss. Symptoms of this frequently show themselves in the domination of the discussion by a boss or sub-group of bosses; or in the passivity of a subordinate or subordinates; or in too enthusiastic support by subordinates of essentially mediocre ideas or opinions ventured by the bosses. The two most satisfactory cures for this are both preventive. The first, logically, is to avoid any opportunity for conflict by careful selection of the group members in the beginning. As an example, for a group that is intended to be a creative group and to produce creative results, it is better to avoid putting a boss and a subordinate together. Keep your group make-up on the same level—either all bosses or all subordinates. The alternative is to plan your program in such a way that opportunities for conflict simply do not happen—neither the boss nor the subordinate is put in a position of having to define or challenge a normal relationship. On the other hand, of course, if the issue is one that needs to be faced squarely, the principal antagonists, whoever they may be, should certainly be brought in, and the leader can brace himself for the battle and attempt to ensure that any wounds inflicted will not be fatal or long-lasting!

Leader Hostility. In every case of a leader-directed group, there will be a certain mixed-emotion feeling. The group member wants to be independent and free-thinking. At the same time, he wants to be told what to do and be given guidance for the doing. This means that if the leader attempts too much to dominate the group, the result may be either passive resistance or outright revolt. On the other hand, if he avoids leading, the group may react with apathy and disintegrate or—possibly worse—accept real leadership from a more positive member whose aims and objectives may in no way resemble those of the leader. Suggestions for coping with this will be found in Chapter 11. For now, we will just say that the leader must keep firmly in his own mind the fact that the easiest and fastest way to lose control of a group is to first lose his own temper!

10

Creative Group Techniques

Creative groups are a relatively new concept in business operation. It is true there have been committees, conferences, and various types of small group organizations working on problems ever since there have been problems (the tribal "elders' meeting" for instance). But the idea that you can deliberately put a group of people together and, through planned use of a formal technique, encourage these people to be creative is relatively new—so new, in fact, that we are only beginning to learn how such groups function, and how they can be made to function better. The techniques themselves are still in rather "crude" stages, and we have much to learn about improving them. The important thing to remember is that they do work now—and that an executive who will take the time to learn and understand them can give himself and his company potent tools to use in searching for ideas and problem solutions.

You will recognize from our study of creative individuals that it is not always easy to find one person with all the attributes of a highly creative thinker. However, you will also recognize that at least some of these attributes will be found in varying degrees in most people. Creative group techniques focus the creative characteristics, as well as the educations, experiences, and backgrounds, of a group of people against some problem on which they share, or can acquire, some common knowledge. What you are doing is putting a mental "team" to work on a problem—you give them a set of rules, which all understand and agree upon, in order to coordinate them into a single "master mind." The objective is to accomplish more than an individual mind could alone, or, at least, to accomplish it in less time.

Another reason for the more or less "formal" organization of creative groups is the same as that for putting a definite discipline into your own personal attack on problems: it is a much more efficient way *to think*. Nearly everyone in business has at some time attended a meeting or conference which was a complete waste of time. This, however, is no reason to condemn the idea of using groups. It is, rather, a condemnation of the *individual* who allowed a wasteful use of the group tool. There are many reasons why groups fail at their intended tasks. But they are all caused by individuals failing. The group itself is a tool—and it can be used wisely, audaciously, poorly, or disastrously. It depends entirely on the skill of the individual who is using the tool.

When you think of groups in terms of tools, then many of the nuts-and-bolts questions about using them become somewhat easier to answer. To repeat an analogy, consider what you go through when you use more tangible types of tools:

When you pick up a hammer, you don't just start hitting things to see what will happen. You wouldn't even take a handsaw off the rack unless you had a specific need for a saw—and then you would pick a specific saw for the particular type of cutting you had to do. By extension, you don't call a creative group together unless you know what it is you expect the group to produce or create. If it happens to be a group aimed at getting ideas, the answers to the questions of how the ideas should be evaluated, and who should do it, should be practically predetermined. And the worst possible way to use a creative group—one that can kill off all interest and any spark among your most creative people—is to turn to it simply because you don't know what else to do.

Knowing when and where to use any kind of tool demands an understanding of both the characteristics and the functions of the tool. You can't acquire skill in using a tool just by looking at it, so proper understanding will also require some practice. It will require making mistakes and wasting materials—"materials" such as the time consumed and the disruptions of other activities every time a group is organized. Therefore, please do not consider that the descriptions of group methods and techniques which follow are going to give you everything you need to make productive use of groups right away. (They may, but it will be pure luck!) The rules and methods come first; the understanding and skill will come with experience and analysis of mistakes.

1 · The Creative Team

Strictly speaking, two or three persons probably cannot be called a "group." The creative team is, however, such a commonly used working unit today that it deserves some consideration to set it off from its opposite, the individual.

Teams have probably won their widest acceptance in scientific and technical fields. They are, however, coming increasingly into use in management and administration. Where they are used wisely, they can produce effectively. Where they are used carelessly and casually, they can end up as prime villains, breaking morale and destroying initiative. In far too many cases, unsuccessful team operations have resulted from a lack of understanding of the objective of a team: to put two complementary minds into proximity so that each will help and strengthen the thinking of the other. It was Emerson who said that "Idea and execution are seldom found in the same head." By a proper combining of the "heads," therefore, a team can be built that will combine both ideas and executions. The trouble starts when the selection of teammates becomes a haphazard thing, done on the basis of expediency and without regard to the compatibility, or lack of it, of the two or three individuals involved. A good team operation will utilize strengths to offset weaknesses. If both members are weak on the same characteristics, or if both are strong in the same directions, there will undoubtedly be failure or outright conflict rather than a self-complementing cooperation. At the same time, an outright conflict of completely opposite personalities will probably never produce an effective team. The focus of team efforts must be against a common problem—*not* against the teammate!

Another reason for giving special consideration to the team operation is that it is the normal work pattern for almost every person in business: the executive-subordinate relationship; the executive-secretary team; department head *A* and department head *B*, who have to coordinate the work of their respective interests. And even a key administrator, with several secondary management men reporting to him, will usually find himself dealing with them one at a time, on a strictly two-man team basis. For this reason, an understanding of the principles of good team operation, together with a knowledge of what makes good team technique, can make almost anyone more creative and productive when working with another person—even if the other person just happens to be the man's wife.

To start with principles, there are two that can make a team collaboration more productive: the separation of creative and critical (or judicial) thinking; and the alternating of team and individual effort.

Separating your creative from your critical thinking is, as we have seen, basic to imaginative thinking under any circumstances. By alternating the team thinking with individual thinking, you combine the advantages of introspection and mind-searching, which can best be done by the individual alone, with the benefits of cross-fertilization and sparked associations which come from one mind stimulating another. For purposes of clarity, the various steps the team goes through to combine these principles will be broken down as separate activities. It will readily be recognized that, in actual practice, many of these individual steps can be, and are, compressed into single sessions or single phases of processing the problem:

1. The first step is a *creative* act done by the individuals alone. This is to try to define the general problem area. It is better to start with at least two conceptions of this.

2. Next is an *evaluative* step taken by the team together. They compare their initial understandings of the problem, and either reach a final agreement on what the general problem really is or submit their disagreements to an arbiter for clarification. At the conclusion of this phase, both members of the team should have exactly the same problem in mind, and both should be certain that this is the right problem.

3. This, again, is an *imaginative* step to be taken by the individuals alone. It consists of each of the team members breaking down the general problem into its component subproblems. It is best done by the individuals, because no two minds will ever work in exactly the same way, and you can be sure that, working alone, both members will come up with at least slightly different lists of minor problems to be solved in the over-all general problem.

4. The next step is a two-part activity for the team that will call mostly for evaluative thinking: consolidating the individual lists of subproblems and searching for the *key* subproblem. This is the most important of the minor factors, the one that seems to offer the greatest danger of holding up solution of other parts of the big over-all problem. Once this "key" is agreed upon, the team can then go to work on it as their problem (and for the rest of this outline, the word "problem" will refer to this key subproblem which has been selected for the initial creative attack).

5. Next the individuals go back to being individuals in a separate search for the facts needed to solve the agreed upon key problem. This again takes advantage of the diverse characteristics of two minds, since the two minds will each approach the job of collecting information in a different way. It multiplies effort where effort can stand multiplication. (This is distinctly different from a *duplication* of ef-

fort. Duplication would result if the team were to search out factual background as a team.)

6. The team do get together, however, to consolidate their information. In this step, which will be largely evaluative, they compare and discuss, combine and discard. For almost any problem, such a comparing of "facts" will disclose at least some discrepancies and, possibly, outright conflicts caused by an acceptance of faulty information by one or the other of the team members. Depending upon their relative importance, such inconsistencies should be resolved or the questioned information should be dropped from consideration.

7. Once all information has been pooled, the next stage is for the individuals to go into individual creative sessions to think up ideas as possible solutions to the problem. It would make sense if, at this stage, they were working on some agreed upon quota. ("Let's see if we can each think up at least five different things we could do.")

8. The next step is to pool ideas and try to add more possibilities as a team. All ideas should be listed for later consideration by both team members as individuals. During this stage, no evaluation whatever should be attempted. It is a purely creative step.

9. Now, individually, working from duplicate lists of all the ideas produced, each spends time evaluating and judging the ideas. As a refinement of the method of each person selecting one single idea, it is better if they each try to select what they consider the best two or three possibilities out of the combined total listing.

10. The next step is, again, an evaluative one, but this time as a team. Here is where the team finally turn into a "supreme court" on everything they've been doing so far, and attempt to reach agreement on which of their ideas is the best, or seems to offer the best opportunities for future development. The team should come out of this with one idea rated "number one"—even if it means that they rank two or three others as first- and second-choice "alternates."

11. Another "creative" step follows in which the individuals, as individuals, pit their imaginations against the problem of determining what the next step should be—some course of action, either investigating or activating, which will result in action on the idea or ideas they have developed. This is followed by—

12. The team, again evaluating, agreeing on the course of action to be taken and then initiating the action.

Any "seasoned" business executive reading through such a detailed breakdown can be excused for scoffing somewhat at the thought that he has to go through any such rigmarole in order to get something done with another person. However, we are not, in this book, concerned with the way people have always done things. The team method outlined has been tested and refined in actual use and has been found to increase productivity. And, if you will find yourself an open-minded teammate and try it a few times, you will be pleasantly surprised at the increase in quality of your problem solutions.

As already mentioned, however, you will seldom, in actual practice, work in such clear-cut steps as these. But again, if you are deliberately trying to solve an important problem, it could pay you to deliberately follow these steps. Or, if you find that you and a co-worker are having trouble resolving a problem, it might be beneficial to check back through this method to see if you have missed any steps that might have been vital to the progress on your problem.

2 · Buzz Sessions

The "Buzz" technique was originally developed as a device, for large groups, to encourage full-audience participation in discussions. Its originator was Dr. J. Donald Phillips, of Hillsdale College in Michigan. His concept of the technique was that groups of six persons would discuss a problem or assigned topic for six minutes. Hence it has been tagged with such names as "Discussion 66," "Phillips 66 Sessions," and "66 Buzzing." But the most popular term is the simple "Buzz Group."

The basic goal of the technique is to gain democratic participation in a meeting or conference. Instead of a discussion controlled by a minority who may simply be more vocal than the other members, without having more to contribute, the Buzz session is intended to allow everyone to participate. It starts with a discussion target in the form of a carefully prepared question on a specific point, and has both a stated objective (the answer to the question; or suggestions for action; or a recommendation) and a limited time in which to reach that objective. It is an extremely flexible technique and can be used in many ways. In its original form, for large audiences, it has been used during the traditional question-and-answer period following a speech; it has been used as the basis for an entire meeting; and it has been used in conjunction with other more standard discussion and participation devices. Here is the way it can be applied to an audience of even hundreds of persons:

Start by dividing the audience into groups of six, using any convenient method of doing so. A very simple method is just to tell the audience to "Look around you and find five other people." Another is to have them "count off" by sixes. Ask each group to appoint a chairman and a secretary. (The chairman's job is to see that all members of the group have an opportunity to participate in the discussion and idea production, and that the group keeps moving toward its objective so that it will reach a definite conclusion at the end of the given time period. The secretary records such notes as seem pertinent to the subject at hand, or, if the purpose is straight idea production, he records the list of ideas produced.)

The chairman should be instructed to see that every member of his group is acquainted with every other member. The organized groups are then given six minutes to discuss a specific problem, or decide on specific questions, or arrive at specific recommendations. When the discussion time has elapsed, the group is then given an additional few minutes, if necessary, to screen their ideas or synthesize the thinking. Each secretary then reports the conclusions or ideas of his group to the entire membership of the audience as the summarized thinking of the six people.

Although the original purpose of the Buzz technique was for large-audience use, it has quickly found acceptance, in modified forms, as a business-conference technique. The two key principles of a stated objective and a limited time to reach that objective can give regular business meetings discipline and objectiveness that most do not ordinarily have. When used this way, the official leadership of the group generally evolves upon the man who called for the meeting in the first place. It then becomes his responsibility to enforce both the principle of democratic participation and the principle that the group will progress toward a stated goal without digressions or distraction. In most such adaptations of the Buzz technique, the six-minute time limit is changed to a longer interval in order to obtain a full discussion in depth of the problem or situation.

One of the best methods the chairman of such a group can use to obtain full participation, without interference, is the so-called "circular response." The members of the group, seated in a circle or around a conference table, are asked to comment in strict turn upon the problem presented. Members are allowed to disagree with other members' views and to express contrary opinions, but always in turn. The chairman should encourage all members to present such divergencies of view as positive counterarguments rather than the nebulous "Well, I don't agree with that." This method is based on the simple assumption that persons who share knowledge and background adequate to discuss a problem or situation should also be capable of engaging in a cooperative evaluation of that knowledge.

Buzz methods will be found to be most productive on problems where it is necessary:

> To present information about a program, a problem, or an area of interest, and, through discussion, to make certain the information is understood.
>
> To pool the knowledge or share the experiences of workers or executives from different departments or divisions on a problem of interdepartmental interest.
>
> To inspire people by unifying them around an objective or a program. This will work best if the members of the group actually par-

ticipate in building or outlining the program or stating the objective.

To gain backing or support for an idea or a policy. Through participating in a democratic airing of pros and cons behind a new proposal, a group will often "sell themselves" on its merits.

To explain a new program or policy, with the circular Buzz being utilized to give everyone an opportunity to ask questions and clarify their thinking.

To plan a long-range program. In this case, members are asked to contribute their forecasts or opinions on any factors that will affect the success or failure of the long-range forecast. In fact, they might start by outlining which factors should be considered in making any forecast.

The executive attempting to use the Buzz discipline for the first time in an organization can expect to be greeted with a certain amount of resistance and skepticism. Too many people look upon a business conference as a "social" break in the day's occupation, rather than an instrument for getting things done. They are, therefore, somewhat inclined to favor long, rambling, and disorganized meetings in order to prolong the sociability. However, business-minded participants will quickly take to the Buzz principles, once they have the opportunity to learn that meetings can be both productive and efficient.

3 · Brainstorming

Probably no group technique has ever been so widely publicized, acclaimed, used, and, at the same time, so misunderstood, damned, and abused as Brainstorming. In some fields, it has been hailed as the first really "great" development in democratic participation. In others, it has been looked down on as a product of commercial hucksterism, fit only for extrovertic advertising and sales promotional types.

Part of this latter attitude is undoubtedly due to the name "Brainstorming," which does, in a way, suggest a flash-in-the-pan approach to problem solving. Part of it is undoubtedly due to the

origins of the technique. Developed by advertising man, Alex
Osborn, and introduced into his advertising agency, Batten, Barton, Durstine & Osborn, in 1939, Brainstorming more or less cut
its teeth on promotional problems. And it was the advertising and
promotional departments of BBDO's clients who were the first
"outsiders" to be exposed to the results of the technique, and who
began to spread its use. Therefore, Brainstorming's history is
replete with new product names, supermarket promotional ideas,
and wing-ding, razzle-dazzle whoopdeedo's which, though they
did solve the problems for the people who needed just such ideas,
did not contribute anything to gaining a respect for the technique
among more conservative minds.

It is not really important to a business executive that Brainstorming is called "Brainstorming," or that it was originated by an
advertising man, or that its chief advocates are still "promotional
types." The only thing that is important is whether or not the
technique has any value in the kinds of problems your company
faces.

Basically, a Brainstorm session is a conference aimed at producing ideas. It has no other objective. It differs from conventional
conferences in that all criticism is ruled out during the Brainstorming, and evaluation of ideas is strictly reserved until a later
time. Thus participants are free to express any and all ideas they
can think of, without fear of censure, ridicule, or disagreement.
It works because of the interstimulation of the group—each member of the group stimulates every other member. The power of
association becomes a two-way stimulus: when a panel member
spouts an idea, he immediately spurs his own mind toward another
idea. At the same time, his ideas stimulate the associative power of
all the other members of the group.

Much of the misunderstanding about Brainstorming stems from
a lack of understanding of both the aims and the use of the technique. Brainstorming is used as a supplement to individual thinking. In fact, in the sense that it is a tool of the individual, it should
not be used if the individual responsible for solving the problem

feels that he can do it entirely alone. It should never be used until and unless an individual has had opportunity to attack, orient, and define the specific problem he wants Brainstorming assistance on.

Brainstorming should always be thought of as a three-step procedure: the preparation to brainstorm, which includes orienting the problem and careful selection of panel members; the Brainstorm itself; and the follow-up to the session wherein the ideas are screened and evaluated and the best possibilities selected for further development or action.

One of the chief causes of failure to obtain usable ideas from Brainstorming is undoubtedly failure to select the "right" kind of problem. The basic aim of Brainstorming is to pile up a quantity of alternative ideas. Therefore, the problem must be one that lends itself to many "possible" answers. As an example of a wrong and a right type of problem, an experienced Brainstorm leader was once called in by a metal-working firm and asked to conduct a session to help them find distribution outlets for a new line of metal office furniture they had developed. On a hunch, he requested a copy of the telephone book and, flipping to the yellow pages, found "Office Furniture." He showed the manufacturer the fifteen firms in town who handled such furniture, and showed, further, how these were actually grouped in only three basic types of retail outlets. To have attempted to brainstorm the problem as presented would have ended in failure. But, at the expert's suggestion, the problem was changed to "Ways to gain distribution for a new line of office furniture against existing competition." This turned out to be highly Brainstormable, and the company was able to plan a successful and profitable marketing program utilizing the ideas produced during the session.

You should not try to brainstorm problems that require value judgments—or judgments of any kind. This includes questions like "What's the best time to start our new campaign?" Brainstorming, being a nonevaluating technique, cannot make a decision for you.

Your problem should be specific, rather than general. Do not try to brainstorm something as broad as "How can we improve our packages?" Instead, point it more specifically toward "How can we improve this particular package?"

If a problem is large and complex, break it down. Instead of "How can we promote our new flashlight?" brainstorm three separate problems: "How can we promote our new flashlight to (1) drivers of automobiles? (2) homeowners? (3) law-enforcement agencies?"

Once you have suitably defined your problem and stated it in a way that will invite group participation, the next step is to select your panel and brief them, by means of a letter or memo, on the problem they will be brainstorming. This is to allow a period of individual thinking on the problem before the time of the Brainstorm. Generally, the memo should be sent about forty-eight hours before the time of the session.

In selecting your panel members, remember to balance them out on the basis of their expected specific contributions. Don't limit your panel to "experts." Occasionally the best ideas come from people who "don't know any better"! The panel should have between eight and fifteen members—eight being the minimum that experience indicates can get a session self-generating; fifteen being the maximum that even an experienced moderator can control with ease.

It is a good idea to include a few "self-starters" on your panel— the kind of people who can produce ideas on anything and everything at the drop of a question. Such persons can help you get your session off and rolling. (But be sure you don't let them dominate once it gets under way—one of the prime purposes of Brainstorming is to get the benefits of full participation in the idea production.) And keep top brass away from the session. No matter how democratic and impartial they try to be, the mere fact that they are in the room will tend to put a damper on the panel. This goes for "visitors" also. If there is some reason why you can't avoid a visitor, make him a participant.

The actual session itself should be conducted according to the four basic "ground rules" of Brainstorming:

1. *Criticism Is Ruled Out.* Adverse judgment of ideas must be withheld until later. (To first-time Brainstormers, you can explain that allowing yourself to be critical at the same time you are being creative is like trying to get hot and cold water from one faucet at the same time. Ideas aren't hot enough; judgment isn't cold enough— all you get is lukewarm thinking. Criticism, therefore, will be reserved for a later screening session.)

2. *"Free Wheeling" Is Welcomed.* The wilder the ideas the better; it is easier to "tame down" than to think up. (Explain that off-beat "blue-sky" suggestions may trigger practical ideas from other panel members which they might not think of otherwise.)

3. *Quantity Is Wanted.* The greater the number of ideas, the more the likelihood of good ones. (This, after all, is the basic aim and prime legitimate use of Brainstorming: to generate such a quantity of ideas on a problem that you have almost a mathematical certainty of finding one or more usable ideas.)

4. *Combination and Improvement Are Sought.* Suggestions by others on an idea give better ideas. Combinations of ideas lead to more and better alternatives. (This is basic to any creative activity. Synthesis, combinations, mutations, and other idea-mixing forms are the basic methods for producing any "new" ideas.)

The chairman of the Brainstorm session is the key person at the conference table. It is his responsibility to get ideas from the panel members and to see that each person has an opportunity to take part. A good chairman will carefully "pre-Brainstorm" any problem he is asked to moderate. He will look for categories of possible ideas and develop ideas of his own as well as leading questions which he can use to stimulate the panel to think "around" the problem in the course of the session. Usually, the chairman of the session will do a better job if he is *not* the man with the problem.

In running the Brainstorm itself, the chairman should have some kind of signal, usually a small bell, which he can use to warn anyone who forgets himself and criticizes an idea. The bell is also handy for enforcing orderly conduct of the session. Although some Brainstorm advocates feel that the conduct of sessions should be informal, others are inclined to "ring the bell" also on comedians, "wise guys," and those who try persistently to "sell" their ideas. These leaders feel that since the purpose of a Brainstorming group is to solve a business problem, and since there is apt to be a sizable amount of company time and talent tied up in the session, the Brainstorm itself should be run as a business meeting.

The leader also has the job of keeping all the minds working together—he has to be alert to any tendency of his panel members to break up into smaller groups. And, although the four rules and the activities of the moderator should serve to keep the session disciplined, the chairman should also strive to keep the mood as relaxed as possible. He may do this with some preplanned, completely "wild" ideas himself; he may accomplish it with his own relaxed method of conducting the session. And, by all means, the chairman should keep shooting for quantity of ideas.

All ideas produced during a session—mild, wild, mediocre, or magnificent—should be recorded by a secretary. She can take the ideas down reportorially, rather than verbatim, because when she later types up her list, she will have the opportunity to put back missing words and make complete sentences out of her key phrases. If you expect your session to be a fast-moving one, you can use two secretaries, having them alternate the ideas recorded.

Although there is no hard and fast rule on how long a Brainstorm session should run, it is recommended that you set your "extremes" at forty-five minutes and an hour and a half. The minimum of forty-five minutes (which should be announced to the panel right at the start) will ensure that after "surface," "tried and true," and "what someone else tried" ideas are out of the way, the individual panel members will not sit back and feel they are finished. It is frequently noticeable in a session that about ten to twenty minutes after it has started, there is a definite lull in the idea production. This is when the "easy" suggestions stop coming, and the panel members have to "dig in" and really start thinking. This is also a critical point for the moderator to watch for, because he will have to "move in" fast to get the session going again, or risk having it die out completely on him. The hour-and-a-half maximum time represents what is generally a "fatigue point," beyond which panelists will decrease in productivity.

Brainstorming is a relatively simple procedure. In reality, all it amounts to is a group of people tossing out ideas, without self- or outside evaluation, as fast as they can be thought up and recorded. There is no "discussion," "elaboration," or "selling" of any particular ideas. And when the flow of spontaneous ideas begins to slow, the moderator or chairman moves in to get the flow going again. Members of the panel listen to each other and try to improve, modify, or combine their ideas to increase the number of alternatives. When the time limit is up, or some arbitrary quota of ideas has been reached, the chairman closes the session by thanking the panelists for their efforts, and requests that any "after-session" ideas be written down and sent immediately to the secretary for inclusion in the typed list. And the whole session is kept relaxed, informal, and friendly.

That is all there really is to Brainstorming, but simple as it is, there are some real pitfalls to be avoided in introducing the technique into a company.

One of the first is to avoid overselling the technique before it has produced anything worthwhile. It takes time and experience to learn to lead a Brainstorm session effectively. It takes a certain amount of indoctrination and practice before people can participate to the full extent of their capabilities as members of a panel. Therefore, a good way to initiate it, or any group method, in a company is to suggest trying it as an "experiment" to explore the possibilities. As long as you keep your Brainstorming on an experimental basis, and everybody understands and is sympathetic with this objective, you have both time and freedom to make mistakes, analyze them, correct them, and gain the experience you and your Brainstormers will need.

Another major difficulty of Brainstorming is attempting to use it as a substitute for individual thinking. This can quickly earn you hostility from your panelists. Brainstorming should not be used on a problem simply because an individual is too lazy to work out solutions himself. It *may* be used to supplement the work of the individual by *adding to* what he has already produced. But it is not a substitute for individual thinking.

A prime pitfall is failing to orient your problem correctly. A problem that is too broad will cause the panel to flounder and go off in far too many directions for them to really explore or exhaust the possibilities in any one approach. On the other hand, a problem that is too narrowly confined does not take advantage of Brainstorming's ability to uncover many different approaches. And in between is the problem that is just plain misdirected: trying to design a better mouse trap when what you really want is a new way to get rid of mice.

As mentioned before, it takes a certain amount of indoctrination before panelists are ready to brainstorm. So another major pitfall is to fail to give this indoctrination. Brainstorming, for all its simplicity, *is* different from any other kind of meeting, conference, or group activity. This means that, initially, the average person will lack an understanding of just what he is expected to do, and how he is supposed to do it, and, most importantly, *why* he is doing it. All these questions should be covered in an indoctrination meeting with panelists before they are expected to participate in a Brainstorm session. It is also a good idea to put new Brainstormers through a simple practice session at the time of this indoctrination so they can get the "feel" of participation without, at the same time, feeling that they are on the spot to produce. A simple, nonobjective problem like "How many uses, other than writing, can you think of for a common pencil" makes a good practice problem.

Two major pitfalls of Brainstorming lie in the area of follow-up: failure to take action on ideas produced; and failure to report back to the panel members with any "successes." Either of these failures can result in discouragement and apathy toward the Brainstorming process and make future participation and cooperation difficult to obtain.

Here are general types of situations where you might consider the use of Brainstorming, with some observations on the results you could reasonably expect:

Exploring the Possibilities in a Product or Situation. Example: "What changes could we consider to make this product more salable?" (or to increase the performance or the function or to cut the costs). In this type of problem, you can expect that your ideas will be largely broad, general leads—but only leads or approaches —which will have to be developed. In this case, you should know in advance that the next step will be for an individual (or, perhaps, a team) to evaluate those leads for possibilities. Chances are you will also know who that man is, because he should be the one who requested the Brainstorm in the first place.

Creating a List of New Needs. Example: "What new food products, not now on the market, would you like to be able to buy?" This was actually brainstormed for a food-products manufacturer who wanted to diversify his line. There was no question about how he was going to screen and evaluate his ideas—he knew in advance what he wanted them for and had set up criteria covering his production abilities, research budget, and general plant and financial considerations. These effectively limited how far afield from his present lines he was willing to go. (These criteria were not, however, given to the panel members for fear of restricting their thinking.) And this manufacturer got what he was looking for: a *few* ideas for promising products that merited further attention and development.

Uncovering Potential Uses for New Products or Raw Materials. A chemical company use Brainstorming in this way. When a new chemical or seemingly promising material comes out, they brainstorm for possible new products they could make with it or possible replacement uses in their present products. These ideas are considered only as *starters*—the list is then turned over to a development group to evaluate and research. Sometimes this group reports complete blanks. But this is not considered a failure. It simply means "no potential for this material at this time." This is what the company wanted to know in the first place.

As a "Crash Program" Knowledge-pooling Device. Brainstorming is primarily an orderly method for concentrating the knowledge, experience, and education of a group of people on a problem. By mixing a variety of specialists, who, as individuals, know *something* about the problem, you may be able to save time in gathering information. Notice, the word was "information" not ideas. This use of Brainstorming utilizes the rules and framework of the tool for the sake of discipline and expediency, but the objective is different. If you do happen to get a few promising ideas, they are side benefits.

As a Group Test. This can be an effective and productive use of Brainstorming, particularly on technical problems. When an individual, or a team, has what looks like a feasible solution to a problem, the problem and the solution are given to the Brainstorm panel with the challenge: "What improvements can we suggest on this solution?" To evaluate the resulting ideas, you simply measure them against the test idea on standard criteria of cost, function, dependability, efficiency, etc. Again, you may not get anything worthwhile. On the other hand, you may get some new approaches or good modifications or simplifications. Either way, you know your final solution is probably the best you can come up with at the moment—even if it is not completely satisfactory.

4 · The Operational Creativity Technique

The "Operational Creativity" technique is sometimes called the "Gordon Technique" after its inventor, William J. J. Gordon, of the Arthur D. Little Company, a research and consulting firm in Cambridge, Massachusetts. This technique is the basic group method used by that company's Design Synthesis Group. It is the job of this group to invent products to order for their clients. They claim that, so far, they have never failed to produce a requested invention, using the Operational technique as a basic creative step. Among the products they claim for this technique are a revolutionary new kind of gasoline pump; a new type of can opener; and a new method of building construction.

The basic objective of Mr. Gordon's technique differs from that of a Brainstorming session in that, with this method, only *one* radically new idea is wanted.

The principal characteristic of the Gordon session is that only one man—the group leader—knows the exact nature of the problem to be solved. There are two main reasons why Gordon feels that the other panel members should *not* know what the problem is:

First, he feels that Brainstorming produces superficial ideas because solutions are arrived at too soon. He avoids this by not revealing the problem initially.

Secondly, he seeks to avoid "egocentric involvement." He feels that a participant in a Brainstorming session, or in some of the other group techniques, can become infatuated with one of his own ideas—perhaps, he will even go so far as to consider it the only logical solution to the problem ("the all-wise"). Such involvement or infatuation does, of course, seriously hamper the participant's effectiveness in the group search for solutions.

Because group members involved in the Gordon session do not know the exact problem being considered, it is extremely important in choosing the *subject* for discussion to choose one that is suitable—one that is actually related to the real problem, but does not reveal its specific nature. Here are a few examples of the subjects Mr. Gordon has used: for a new toy, *play or enjoyment;* for a fishing lure, *persuasion;* for a new can opener, *opening.*

Utilizing some such subject, the group begins to discuss it with only enough guidance from the leader (who does know the final objective problem) to keep them from going completely astray. When the leader feels that the group has either exhausted all the possible aspects of thought surrounding his problem area, or when he feels that the group has uncovered a particularly good idea worth following up, he then reveals the exact nature of the problem. At this time, the group begin to channel all their efforts into synthesizing all the previous exploratory and speculative thinking toward solving the real problem. After a promising initial idea is obtained, and as much spontaneous development of it as is possible has taken place, the project is then turned over to a development group and the finished product is worked out by more conventional engineering means.

In attempting to apply this Operational Creativity technique, Mr. Gordon makes several suggestions:

He feels that the session length must run a minimum of two to three hours. In practice, this usually results in about 75 per cent of the time being devoted to "deconditioning" the group through the broad, general field discussion, and in the remaining 25 per cent of the time being given over to spontaneous development of ideas. These figures should not be taken literally, however: the exact moment of revelation of the problem is entirely up to the discretion of the panel leader.

The group leader should be exceptionally gifted in group dynamics and thoroughly trained in the use of the Gordon technique. The leader is unquestionably the key man in the group, and his judgment and running analysis of the group progress is vital to the success or failure of the effort.

In selecting personnel, try to obtain a group with diverse backgrounds. Try to get a balance of highly active and quiet members. You may want to mix groups of men and women, especially on consumer problems. Mr. Gordon feels that his groups are most effective in sizes of from four to nine members.

For this type of group, a secretary *and* a tape-recording machine are almost musts. Ideas and thoughts are produced in rapid-fire cross-discussion, and must all be recorded. Frequently, once the problem has been revealed, the group will want to refer back to a previous theoretical discussion. This can be done easily with the tape. It is a good idea to have blackboards available for members to sketch out or visualize any ideas they may have.

There are some obvious drawbacks to the Gordon system, but also some obvious advantages. Mr. Gordon himself feels, and probably rightly, that the only way any company can determine the value of the system to their particular problems is to "plunge in" and experience and experiment with the technique. For this reason, he is somewhat loath to give too many suggestions or to reveal his own specific experiences.

One of the prime drawbacks, obviously, is the requirement for a skilled and gifted leader. Any personnel man who has attempted to find or develop a good leader for even ordinary business conferences will immediately recognize that "skilled and gifted" leaders are hard to come by. Furthermore, there are certain other difficulties to be overcome for a good Operational session:

Group members will frequently try to "guess" the real problem in their attempts to get down to more concrete thinking or in their attempts to take over leadership from a leader who must necessarily remain "withdrawn" to a certain extent.

Some group members suffer major inhibitions in this type of meeting, because they feel that purely theoretical discussions are too impractical. This will limit the types of thinking they contribute.

Operational sessions can be extremely fatiguing. The two or three hours mentioned was a minimum—some sessions actually go on for days before the group begins to come near to a solution. This also interjects the question of the time investment —will the group really produce an idea good enough to merit the cost of the continuing session?

And, of course, the statement of the problem, in the form of a key word or phrase is vitally important. It is possible to mislead a panel through selection of the wrong word or key, and thus to completely waste the entire effort.

At the same time, Operational Creativity does offer some highly interesting possibilities for group-technique development: The avoidance of preconceived ideas and ego involvement holds distinct possibilities for improving creative exploration of a problem area. The very broadness of the initial problem statement is a spur to complete flexibility in searching out approaches.

For a company willing to invest the time and cost of experimenting with this technique, it would probably be a good one to have "on tap." So far, it has been limited largely to problems of design and of a technical nature. But it would also seem to offer distinct possibilities in many other fields, including management (to develop a new form of organization structure based on fundamental organizational principles, rather than tradition); sales management (to develop a marketing concept completely free of such inhibiting factors as past experience and competitive threats which are often imaginary); and even in the field somewhat preempted by Brainstorming, advertising (for the development of new campaigns to appeal to specific segments of the market). Probably the greatest contribution of the Operational technique is its possibility for synthesis with other group techniques to help them overcome some of their major drawbacks.

Just as one example, if it is true that Brainstorming tends to produce superficial results by revealing the problem too soon, it might be possible to strengthen this technique by borrowing from Mr. Gordon and starting out the Brainstorm on a more general subject. Let's take the problem of improving a specific package:

The first problem given to the panel, in the form of their regular briefing memo, might simply be to think about packaging anything. The Brainstorm could then start off by developing a list of "Positive characteristics of good packages." These would be listed on a blackboard. After a few minutes—say ten or fifteen—of this, the actual package under consideration could be revealed, and the problem would become "Specific improvements we could make on *this* package."

5 · Practical Combinations

Probably the greatest potential for the various group techniques lies in making intelligent adaptations and combinations of the different methods. It is important that the group participants be indoctrinated into the "formal" methods first; but once they know and understand what is expected in each type of group, they can then utilize various principles and operating techniques "on the spot" at the discretion of the meeting or conference leader. As examples:

In opening a standard conference on a production problem, the person running the meeting might want to call for a ten-minute "Buzz" on the present state and condition of the production line, or on special equipment or workers on the line, without making any particular attempt to relate this to the basic problem that is to be discussed. This would serve the purpose of encouraging broader thinking on the problem and put the entire problem, when it is finally presented, into a relationship with the over-all line. In other words, it would be a "deconditioning" process to open minds up to new possibilities.

Later, in the same meeting, and when the specific problem was beginning to be more defined, the meeting leader might call for ten minutes of Brainstorming, with the ideas being recorded on a blackboard or large pad, so that everyone could see them later. This would give the group an immediate "stock" of possibilities which they could then evaluate and discuss. And the Buzz rule of an over-all time limit is a valuable one for even a conventional conference.

The Hotpoint Company has developed a modification of Brainstorming which they call "Reverse Brainstorming." This has as its objective "creative destruction." In operation, a specific product or problem or system is put before a group. One person has pre-Brainstormed an accepted or proposed method to find everything he can that is wrong with it. In the group meeting, he then takes each of the flaws he has uncovered and presents at least one suggestion for improving it. The rest of the group brainstorms improvements on his and all other suggestions on an exhaustive basis. This is a form of group test. The final result is usually a list of highly refined ideas. In one instance, such a group was able to take a planned $200,000 conveyor system, cut the proposal to pieces, suggest improvements and consolidate them, and come up with a new design that was installed and worked successfully for a cost of $4,000.

Another modification of basic Brainstorming that is meeting with some success, particularly in technical fields where it was originally developed, is one which, for lack of any better name, is called "Stop-and-Go Brainstorming." It was devised in an attempt to overcome one of the major deficiencies of regular Brainstorming: the difficulties in quickly brainstorming a complex technical problem from an original broad problem statement through to a usable idea, approach, or lead. It also overcomes one of the major weaknesses of the Operational Creativity technique: the absolute dependence upon a strong leader to direct the group. This is accomplished through having a more or less "set" procedure, comparable to the agenda of a conventional meeting. It does require a leader with the ability to maintain an orderly discussion at times, however.

In practice, the Stop-and-Go method utilizes both Buzzing and Brainstorming alternately. The sequence is usually some adaptation of this plan:

1. The broad general problem, without definition or other limiting restriction, is presented to the group of ten to twelve members.

2. Two Buzz groups or teams are formed. Each group then buzzes to break out all specific subproblems important to the solution of the general problem.

3. The chairman of each group then reports on the subproblem his group considers most important and why. Through conventional give-and-take discussion, under the strict control of the over-all

group leader, agreement is reached on which subproblem the group will take as their initial target.

4. In a full-group Brainstorm, ideas are then developed as possibilities for solving this particular problem. The ideas should be recorded on a blackboard or large pad so all members will be able to see and refer to them at later stages of the processing.

5. In two Buzz groups, members then evaluate the ideas to judge which seem to come close to meeting the requirements of the original problem.

6. Following the Buzz group reports, the whole work group should seek agreement on two or three of the best possibilities and then brainstorm each of these, one at a time, for any needed refinements or changes that seem required to put it really "on target" as a solution to the particular subproblem being worked on. Again, the ideas should be recorded on a board or pad for full-group visibility.

7. At this time, the two Buzz groups run independent over-all evaluations aimed at answering such questions as these: Are we making any progress? Can we now zero in on some specific direction? If not, where are we weak? These evaluations are then pooled, compared, and synthesized to indicate the next step the group should take. This may be to begin the Stop-and-Go process all over again with another subproblem or specific phase, or it may be to continue with further refinement of the progress that has been made.

8. Subsequent questions that the leader may want to inject for either Buzz or Brainstorming, whichever seems most appropriate at the time, include these: Do we have any specific real possibilities now? If none, what have we overlooked? Which direction seems to offer the best possibility for further exploration at this time? And, when a good possibility has been uncovered, In what ways can we economically test this possibility?

It will be apparent from studying just the few examples of combinations and variations given that Brainstorming is one of the basic creative group tools. And this has been proved in all other attempts to develop similar combinations. The basic separation of creative and critical thinking in the Brainstorming process seems to be one of the most efficient group operational techniques that can be used. As a matter of fact, instructors who have taught creative-thinking courses, including uses of all the various types of creative groups, generally agree that Brainstorming is so basic, and the principles so valuable, that they get their best results if they make Brainstorming the first introduction to group methods. Persons who have been indoctrinated into Brainstorming first—which is an easy method to teach—take much more readily even to Buzz groups and team operations. Therefore, it is suggested that any attempt by an executive to introduce group creative methods in his company start with at least enough Brainstorming to give members practice and skill in the technique.

It will readily be seen that the group leader is the key to any creative group's success. This, in a way, is further reinforcement of the theory that the group, at best, is a tool of the individual. This, in turn, puts a tremendous responsibility upon the leader to know and understand not only the basics of group dynamics, but also the various methods that make up the specific tools he is calling upon. And, throughout any creative group effort, from the time the leader first begins to plan and organize for it until he has submitted his final report, he must constantly keep in mind that a creative group is largely a medium of communication—it is a means to an end and not the end itself.

Too many people who meet up with the techniques and methods of creative groups become so intrigued with the things which can be done that the opportunity to "be different" becomes their goal for every conference or meeting. They play with the formats and formulas to the point where they completely forget that the aim of these devices is to produce some kind of result: a change of attitude, a supply of ideas, a redefinition of a problem, a broadening of possibilities, etc. They, in short, get "gimmick happy."

In practical business reality, overuse of methods may cause just the opposite reaction to what is desired. No meeting should ever be planned to be so out-of-this-world as to be unrealistic in terms of the participants' normal thinking, actions, and reactions. To go contrary to human nature will throw all members of your group into a role-playing situation where they will simply be acting out their parts, rather than giving you honest effort and true "thinking" based on their normal, previous experience and knowledge.

11

How to Lead Creative Groups

When the American Management Association surveyed top executives on reasons for inefficient meetings, it found the largest share of the blame laid to poor leadership. This included such factors as lack of a clear-cut objective; meeting called at the wrong time; wrong person or persons included; failure to prepare necessary information in advance; digressions; failure to summarize; unchecked repetitious argument; toleration of interruptions.

If these are faults in conventional business meetings and conferences, they could easily be fatal to the success of a creative group, wherein the full resources of the group are being called upon for active and imaginative response. In a creative group, the leader must remain in complete control of the group's activities, and he must do this without in any way inhibiting the group or restricting individuals from participating in a positive manner. And this is where so many creative group meetings fail: the leader has not sufficiently planned his own participation.

It is the leader's responsibility to think through such basic questions as these: What are we trying to accomplish anyway?

Are we in line with the company policy on this project? How are we tying in with the long-range plan? What objective will be reasonable and relevant to the problem for this group? What resources will we need in the group to help us accomplish the objective? This planning may take two minutes or two hours or two weeks, but until you have the needed answers, you are not ready to call a creative group meeting!

Furthermore, a basic planning step is to orient your problem thoroughly. This is important for individual creative work, and doubly so for group work. Frequently, a person thinking through a problem for presentation to a group will, in the course of his own orientation, hit upon a satisfactory solution. Or he may even find, after defining a problem, that no problem exists. In either case, of course, there is no reason to go on with the group meeting.

Once the leader has thought through the answers to the basic questions about the problem, he is then ready to plan his own part in the meeting.

He should keep in mind that the secret of success in leading a creative group is to manage the actions of the group and to manage to do it unobtrusively. A good leader accomplishes this by thinking through the problem in advance, and then matching up various work methods and continuity devices to the thinking steps he believes will be required. Then, in action, he suggests, rather than forces, the use of the procedures and techniques which might be of help.

The leader will try to guide the group in such a way that they will balance the narrow line between strict rigidity of methods and disorganized confusion. He will resist any inclination on his own part to "mastermind" the problem, knowing that this can backfire in the form of group reaction. (In fact, if the leader is in any position to "mastermind" a problem, he should probably go ahead and do so on his own, without tying up the expensive investment in time and disrupted work schedules that use of any group involves!)

And the leader must somehow manage to stimulate, encourage,

assist, and recognize group contributions on the problem, all the while keeping them on the track and moving toward a goal. In a truly creative group, calling upon the full resources of its members, it may be that the leader will make his greatest contribution by creating an atmosphere that permits free expression of opinion, along with giving directional guidance.

Finally, the group leader must maintain complete objectivity. He must learn to work, at least during the time that he is in a leadership position, impersonally. He must himself learn, and enforce on the group, if necessary, the art of give and take. He must realize that a group member who expresses intense dislike for a plan or an idea isn't necessarily disliking either the person who proposed it or the fact that it was proposed.

So far as the leader's own ideas or proposals are concerned, in a productive group the leader's own ideas are bound to be challenged. Moreover, his plans for the group and his own ideas of the way the group should go are apt to receive some jolts and may even be disrupted completely once the group begins to function as a group. Therefore, the leader will try to keep his eye on the basic objectives, rather than on any individual and isolated expressions of thought or opinion.

The leader's attitude is usually the determining factor in whether or not a creative group will succeed in reaching its objective. Skill in techniques he needs—but unobtrusive skill. Group members will usually respond to the leader who does not try to change their natures or force their thinking, but who uses both to the fullest extent.

The leader who seems to understand his members instinctively and to respect them sincerely will quickly command their respect in turn. But if the leader does not have a genuine regard for the people with whom he is working, he will never "get through" to them. There are no tricks, techniques, methods, or gimmicks to replace genuine understanding and respect in the communication and leadership process.

Much of the leadership of any creative group consists in

applying techniques and methods which are known as "group dynamics." Briefly defined, "group dynamics" is the art of giving an active "life" to a group. And because leadership is so largely a matter of communication, much of the art of group dynamics is based on ways to break down any social, organizational, or other inhibiting barriers to communication that may exist within a group.

Nearly everyone has seen or participated in a meeting or conference that was handicapped and inhibited by the carrying over of some "big shot–little shot" (such as boss and subordinate) relationship from the world outside the conference. What happens is that the big shots tend to monopolize the time of the group whether their ideas merit the time or not. The little shots always hesitate to challenge the big ones, even though they, the little shots, may actually have insights, ideas, and experience more relevant to the problem. As a further example, in many businesses, the same types of relationships exist in mixed groups of men and women: although the company, and any individual men in it, may profess to consider their co-working women as "equals," in reality such is not the case. Any female member of a conference or meeting can go only so far in challenging a male opinion or thought before she is in danger.

Nevertheless, in business it is frequently necessary to use different combinations of people and temperaments in seeking solutions to problems. The hidden or unmentioned conflicts do exist and will not disappear merely because you'd like them to. Therefore it is up to a meeting leader to see that these do not interfere with reaching the objectives of the group. It is the leader's job to create a climate of safety, so that group members know that they are free to express themselves and that their expressions will receive consideration. (Even in the Brainstorm process, for example, where head-on criticism of another's ideas is ruled out, a member can always interject a positive objection simply by proposing an alternative way something might be done. This alternative may be the exact opposite of a suggestion already given—but he knows it will be recorded and evaluated on the same basis as the idea he took issue with.)

In its bare essentials, a creative group is a group of people interacting to seek the solution to a problem. Good leadership of such a group calls first for the ability to plan such an opportunity to interact. Just as a wife will plan a party, so a business executive should try, where possible, to put together a creative group that will wear well and get things done with a minimum amount of friction when it comes to solving a problem or contributing to the solution of a problem. And just as a party-planner will try initially to "break the ice" and make guests feel "at home," so the meeting leader will plan his program to make his group members feel "involved" in finding a problem solution.

Some of the qualities desirable in a good group leader are these: a sense of humor (and the sense of "timing" that tells him when to be humorous); the ability to listen to people and to make them feel he *wants* to listen; a genuine liking for people; and the ability to accept the other person's point of view, even though he may not totally agree with it. In addition, it is desirable if the leader can remain calm and poised in the midst of a fast-moving group situation; if he can generate an aura of security when conflicts arise; and if, whatever happens, he can remain and act both optimistic and positive in his approach to the problem. He will use all these characteristics, or as many as he has, in setting the tone and atmosphere of the meeting in the hope that his own attitudes and attributes will prove contagious and spread to the other members. His chief aim throughout the group session will be to keep the channels of communication very wide, and very open, and make it very clear that they are that way.

There are certain physical helps that you can employ both for "breaking the ice" and for suitably communicating your problem to the group members. These are demonstration devices such as charts, slide presentations, movies, blackboard demonstrations, props, models, and even magic tricks. It is helpful to a group that is working on the improvement of some actual object, such as a product, package, or material, to have a sample or samples of that object to look at, poke at, examine, feel, or in other ways make themselves familiar with. The purpose of using any such physical or visual aids is largely educational: to help members of the group understand the problem or some obscure phase of the problem; or simply to broaden their backgrounds to make sure they have enough information to cope adequately with the problem being presented to them. Well-planned, such devices can stimulate early participation by getting the individual members' thinking "warmed up" ahead of time. In any case, the use of such informative or educational aids will contribute to the self-confidence the members have in their ability to make suggestions on a problem.

Once a creative group is under way, the actual things the leader does will generally reflect the kind of things that are done in any other type of dynamic group: the occasional summary; the probing question with a purpose; the trick of making a statement every member of the group can agree with to gain their support and friendship; or the reverse, to make a controversial or antagonistic statement to excite interest. The leader who is aiming for total group participation, however, will keep in mind that he is trying to motivate people to work with him, and not against him. He must also be extremely careful to impress upon his group that he really wants their contributions.

Any group will need a summary of where they stand from time to time: what they have accomplished; how far they have to go; exactly what route they are expected to take in arriving there. You may give them this yourself, or you may ask your secretary or recorder to summarize briefly, and ask the members to correct or supplement that summary.

It is also up to the leader to remind the group at intervals that they are working within a time limit. This should be done in such a way as to encourage them to stay on the track, but not to get anxious or feel pressure.

Probably the most flexible and all-round useful tool to keep a group moving is the probing question. It is, of course, necessary that the leader's questions should be asked in such a way as to place a maximum responsibility on the group to reply. If possible, they should be phrased to show that the leader is not only accepting members of the group as individuals but is also confident of their ability to come up with good answers. Some examples of good questions are these:

To Get Discussion Started:

What do you think about this problem as stated? What has your experience been on this type of problem? Can anyone suggest the kind of facts we ought to have or know at this stage?

To Get More Participation:

How does what we have been saying so far sound to those of you who have been thinking about it? We've heard from a number of our members now; does anyone who hasn't spoken want to give us his thinking? What other phases of the problem have we missed covering?

To Limit the Overactive Participant:

We appreciate the help you are giving us. However, it might be well to get some other thinking. Would some of you who have not spoken care to add your ideas? Or: You have made several interesting statements, and I wonder if someone else wants to add to them or modify them? Or, as a last resort: Since all our members haven't yet had an opportunity to speak, I wonder if you will hold off for a while?

To Orient the Discussion:

Where do we stand now in relation to our goal? For comparisons and a check, why don't I review my understanding of what we have said and the progress we've made so far? Your comment is interesting. But I wonder if it contributes to the chief problem?

To Keep Discussion Moving:

Do you think we have spent enough time on this phase of the problem? Can we move on to another part of it? Have we covered this section of the problem enough that we can shift our attention to another area? We do have a time limit to meet; should we perhaps look at the next question we have to face?

To Press for a Decision:

Am I right in thinking that we agree on these points? (Follow with a brief summary.) What have we accomplished up to this point? We seem to be zeroing in toward a decision now, so should we consider what it will mean if we decide this way?

The questions the leader must *avoid* at all costs are those which will complicate an issue or mislead the group members, or which will limit the group's thinking by taking away some of their latitude on the problem. This latter is a consideration that the leader must be especially conscious of throughout any creative effort. The leader, if he is really searching for new ideas, cannot, in any way, restrict the group effort to go off in new and different directions. This is what the group is there for. But, at the same time, the leader must be ready to bring the group back in case they wander too far. This can be done with a leading question or a contribution of an idea by the leader which is more "on target" so far as the basic problem is concerned.

On the other hand, if a group member should unconsciously launch into a brief speech or grow slightly fuzzy in expressing an idea, the leader should exercise restraint, overlook it, and carry on. Don't try to short-circuit or clarify someone's thinking by interrupting him—that is a dampener. Everything about a creative meeting should be aimed at developing free and easy thinking.

And this brings up the pitfalls the leader of any creative group has to watch out for. On the deep, and usually unconscious level, the leader may have a hidden purpose of his own: that of maintaining his leadership at any cost. The position of influence and power, even a temporary one, is pleasing, and most people resist letting it go. One of the most difficult jobs the leader of a creative group session faces is that of allowing the group to "grow up" and be less dependent upon him. He must, as parents frequently do, maintain his control in little ways that will not interfere with the development and expression of the group personality. Furthermore, groups can readily develop hidden agendas concerning the leader. If he is too dominant, the hidden reaction will take the form of passive resistance. If he takes sides on crucial issues or leaves the group with a feeling of insecurity about his fairness or objectivity, active revolt may take place. Frequently a group in revolt will obviously follow the leadership of one of its members, while it permits the nominal leader to go through the empty forms of leadership.

There are other troubles that can beset a leader also. For example, he may find himself fighting to maintain leadership against an individual member of the group with a hidden purpose. In many cases, this individual may not realize he has a purpose himself—he may be the type who is generally hostile to leadership in any form. If accused of trying to take over the group, he would strongly deny it, and be righteously indignant at the accusation. The leader himself may frequently have to make a quick analysis to decide whether his leadership is indeed being challenged for the purpose of taking it away, or whether the member is making a legitimate challenge of a mistake by the leader. It is not always easy to distinguish between the two in a fast-moving group action.

Another source of trouble has already been touched on: the apathy that keeps the meeting from developing into a productive session. Here again, the leader needs to make a quick analysis of what is going on. Apathy can be caused by many factors: the group may feel that they don't really have the procedural tools to move ahead on the problem (this is frequently caused by a lack of indoctrination and orientation into the principles, techniques, and purposes of the tool being used). The group may have the impression that their decisions or recommendations will not have any real stature in the final analysis of the problem or policy. One subgroup within a larger group may have a too zealous or personal feeling about the problem under discussion, and so may intimidate other members to the point where they actually block or shut off the outside thinking. Whatever the cause, when apathy sets in, a "What's the use?" attitude takes over.

Most such group ills, however, have their beginnings in the initial minutes of the meeting, at the time of the actual presentation of the problem and the suggestions for handling the problem. Many group members, for instance, will be slow to take a leader up on his invitation to "express yourselves freely." This is because from childhood they have been used to having the person in authority tell them what to do or to think. It is difficult to change a lifetime habit simply by being told to do so. The leader, recognizing this, will accept it and plan his meeting in such a way as to create a climate favorable to free expression and participation.

It is certainly helpful to the leader of a creative group if he knows its members. You can guide and direct people only on the basis of how much you know about them and their interests and feelings about a subject. If you don't really know the members of a group, you must at least make a quick surmise about them in order to establish your own behavior "base line." The old theory that a group leader has to be an inspirational evangelist to be effective is being severely challenged by today's crop of dynamic exponents of group techniques. Instead of using pep talks, which are, at best, transient in value, the true leader uses empathy to get at the real roots of his group's personality, interest, and capabilities.

In preparing to handle a meeting, then, the leader will think about the people who will be involved. He should study their natures and characteristics closely, and then use his own ingenuity, imagination, and resourcefulness to figure out how to produce the reactions that will be needed.

Leaders, of course, vary in personalities and temperaments just as members of the group do. Therefore, it would be a mistake to lay down any hard and fast rules for exactly how the leader should approach or operate with his group. Since you are trying to be sincere and friendly, it is usually good to be somewhat informal in your approach to the group. Some leaders can comfortably sit on top of a desk or a table in the front of the room. Others simply do not feel at ease unless they are on their feet (but a leader on his feet tends to be a "formal" figure to the members of the group). Still other leaders get a sense of comfort out of having a lectern to lean on. But the important thing is that anything you do to reduce the degree of formality in your meeting must be in harmony with what you can comfortably bring yourself to do. An ill-at-ease leader will only succeed in communicating his uneasiness to the group.

In dealing with a group that has never been exposed to creative group concepts before, probably the one most important introductory step is to let the members know how they are going to be expected to act—just what part they will be playing in the problem-solving effort.

Once you are sure you have suitably broken the ice, you can then get on with the business at hand. A good way of taking this step is to present the problem in objective discussion, but without divulging your own viewpoint on it. Or you may give several tentative solutions to help the group start their thinking. If you do this, you should be sure to mix and vary the suggestions in as many ways as possible to avoid giving the impression that you are in favor of any one particular approach or that you are trying to "steer" the group in their thinking.

Initially, the most difficult part of running a creative group meeting, particularly a Brainstorming session, may be just to get started. Therefore, the leader must be 100 per cent alive to any tendency by the group to begin to participate, and he must be sure that he does not, in any way, discourage participation when it begins. On the contrary, he should be working to encourage the group to "take over" as soon as possible.

Once the group makes its initial break into activity, the leader's job then switches over to maintaining the activity. He may have to suggest, cajole, challenge, tease, and otherwise motivate each individual to contribute in his own way and, at the same time, guide the individuals into working within the framework of shared commitments in both the job at hand and the methods being used.

He must, at the same time, be alert to any indications of confusion or hostility and exercise his guidance to reduce or eliminate the trouble before it can cause a breakdown in the group process. For example, if one member launches into a speech about some pet idea or proposal, it could quickly set up an apathetic reaction among other members. It is important for the leader to move in quickly at this point and get the group functioning again.

If you, as a creative group leader, are really sincere about getting the group to take over, you can only plan a creative session up to a point. Once the group reaches that point, the leader will find himself trying to adhere to the framework of his planned-out methods, but very definitely "playing it by ear." In a really productive group, the leader's original plans and ideas are bound to be challenged and strained. Moreover, you may find that some of your own favorite thoughts or pet predictions will receive some unexpected jolts and you may have to disrupt your whole plan in order to accommodate the new changes suggested by the group. It is a real challenge to maintain both your leadership and the cooperation and good will of the group when you suddenly find yourself thrust into strange territory by the group.

Perhaps we can sum up the leader's responsibilities in a general way:

He should, first, create a friendly atmosphere for discussion.

He should make sure the group members know and understand the "rules of the game" for whatever discussion or participation device he is using.

He must be ready to help individuals, or subgroups of individuals, or the group itself move ahead with continuity and focus.

He should see that all members have ample opportunity to

participate and that they realize and take advantage of a climate of safety.

He must, in the end, be the catalyst that will help varied interests, opinions, and convictions in the group come together to arrive at definite conclusions, suggestions, ideas, or decisions.

Many people, in surveying all these responsibilities, possible difficulties, and unfamiliar duties for the first time, get a feeling that this is not for them. It sounds too tough. They are even discouraged from trying such group activities by the feeling that they, themselves, could never lead such an activity. Actually, this is a mistaken attitude to take. Many of the things a creative group leader must do are just as important to the successful conduct of any other type of meeting or conference. Many of the difficulties never arise—at least, they never all happen at once. It is only important to know about them so that when they do come up, you as the leader won't be thrown for a loss by something completely unexpected. And, fortunately, you have ample opportunity to practice being a group leader every day in your relationships with individuals.

A group, as mentioned earlier, is merely an extension of the individual personalities involved. Therefore, many of the things you must do in leading a group—encouraging them, keeping them on the track, discouraging blind arguments, and so forth—you can practice in your day-to-day relationships with individuals. (This, in any event, makes good practice for you in the art of getting along with others.)

Most of the "strain" of leading creative groups in the business world comes from the knowledge that you, as the leader, have the responsibility, which you cannot duck, of making the group "pay off" for the company. This pay-off may be in the sense that you produce money-making or cost-saving ideas; or it may be that you just make productive use of the time of the individuals that you have drafted for your group. But nearly everyone has opportunities to practice group leadership, even if informally, where this strain of showing a dollars-and-cents pay-off is not present.

For example, a church group to which you belong may very well have projects or aims that could profitably use new ideas or new approaches. The same with a civic or social group. And even a friendly party of neighbors takes a certain amount of "ice breaking" to get conversations going. Any such opportunity is a chance for you to experiment, analyze, and learn without real danger of expensive waste.

Furthermore, you may find, with a little asking around, that you are not alone in having a desire to gain inexpensive experience with group leadership techniques. There is a great deal of interest in creative groups these days, and many of your contemporaries may have the same desire to experiment and share experiences. If so, you could easily form a one-night-a-week study group to work on each other's problems. (Several such groups have found that they are now able to get problems from people outside their group and are paid for solving them!)

But don't let the academic considerations of what may happen in a dynamic group discourage you from trying to gain experience. You can experiment and learn in small, nonvital ways and acquire a knowledge of what it is actually like to meet any of these difficulties before you are forced to meet them in an important way. Furthermore, you will learn what it is possible to accomplish in the way of producing ideas and obtaining concrete results. And you can learn, in a small way, what will take place when you lead your first "formal" creative group. Once you know, even on a small or unimportant scale, what may, can, and does happen, then you will have the experience and confidence to go ahead and stick your neck out when the chips are down and it *is* important.

12

The Importance of Follow-Up

In 1940, Walter Behlen, of Columbus, Nebraska, earned a gross profit of $194. In 1957, he earned over $3-million. His method? A firm belief that "Ideas are a dime a dozen—it's doing something with them that counts." In this simple principle, Behlen covers nearly all the reasons why good ideas fail to solve problems or bring their inventors justly deserved fame or fortune: having ideas is not enough; "it's doing something with them that counts."

As a matter of fact, even a "fair" idea, if it is put to use intelligently and aggressively may do more good than the most brilliant suggestion that is never followed up. So it is important when you think you have a good idea, no matter how you got it, to do *something* with it.

If it concerns a personal problem that is entirely within your control, then put it to work—try it. (And if it fails, try another one.)

If it is an idea for the company, tell your boss, or put it into the suggestion system.

If your idea is one that will involve a patent, check with your company's legal department to find out the approved company method of screening patentable ideas.

If your idea is one you think will help someone else solve a problem they have, by all means *tell* them about it. But do *something* with every worthwhile idea.

It is probably true, as some experts claim, that there are more ideas wasted in business every day than are ever used in a year because of that simple failure to do something to give the idea substance. Remember that a "raw" idea is absolutely worthless. It doesn't even merit the description of creative if it isn't allowed to produce a benefit of some kind. Many such wasted ideas are products of people who never intended to do anything with them in the first place. But many are wasted simply because the inventors didn't know how to "sell" their ideas. In fact, they may not have realized that ideas do need selling.

But there are many reasons why people in authority are apt to turn down ideas. Not the least of these is ignorance of what the idea really means. Remember that if a new idea is really good, it will also be strange. It is open to question. In many cases, the person you are submitting your idea to will not even realize that there was a need for such an idea. You may have to begin at the beginning and trace through the whole reasoning process that you yourself followed in arriving at this new idea of yours. You may even have to teach the other person the meaning of some new words that will be necessary in order to understand your idea. And, because resistance to change is perfectly natural and normal in every human being, you may have to overcome that tendency in your boss, or whoever it is you are giving the idea to.

For an executive, the necessity of "selling" ideas to overcome another person's ignorance and reluctance to change is a two-way street. The chances are you will also have people coming to you with their ideas. Remember what they are up against, and help them all you can. Many persons, when they are faced with the prospect of convincing someone else that the idea they have is good, literally get scared out. This may be the biggest cause of idea waste. But it is one that is relatively easy for you to overcome in yourself, and one you can help others overcome. It is not that people lack ability to sell their ideas. It is, rather, that they lack forethought, initiative, and resourcefulness in the way they go about it.

Let's look at some of the reasons why an idea which appears perfectly good—perhaps even "sensational"—to its creator may meet resistance and even refusal "higher up" in the company:

The most common true reason for rejecting an idea is that there is something wrong with it. If the fault is not in the idea itself, it may be in what would happen if the idea were put into use. Most of the time, if the idea's creator had taken pains to think his proposition through, he could have found such flaws himself. And, having found them, he could have corrected them or marshaled his facts to counter them.

Another reason for turning down an idea is that, although the idea itself seems sound, the evidence to support it may be untrue or illogical. This frequently happens to young men right out of university or college business schools who are ready to "set the world on fire." As soon as they are established on a job, they immediately begin proposing ideas based on what their college textbooks or their professors or other sources of academic information told them was the way something should be done. Unfortunately, academic theories don't always work out in practical business, or a particular company may have a very sound reason for violating some principle of "good practice" which the young man hasn't had time to learn. Consequently, his idea is rejected for reasons that may not be directly related to its real merit. When this happens often enough to the same young man, he either "smartens up" and learns to get more information, or he becomes embittered and discouraged and stops suggesting ideas.

Another pitfall you have to watch for in presenting any new idea is *over*selling. It is easy to get too enthusiastic about an idea, especially if it is your own. And when you begin to overestimate rewards and overstate your opinion of them, it may create doubts among people who would otherwise want to give your idea serious consideration. Actually, the idea itself may be perfectly good in a more modest sort of way, but obvious overselling can frighten people out of wanting to take a chance on it.

Another reason why an idea can be rejected by a particular individual, or in a company with a certain type of atmosphere, is commonly called the "NIH"—for "Not Invented Here"— factor. This phrase was supposedly coined by an embittered scientist who felt that his ideas were being turned down by people in authority simply because they had not thought of them. In most cases, it is probably not true that an NIH factor can, by itself, kill a good idea. But there is no question that it can make a good idea more difficult to sell. And it may be that a failure to "sell," in the literal sense of the word, is the real cause of the NIH attitude. If you present an idea on the basis that it will solve all the evils of the past, you are on dangerous ground. Your superior, or whoever it is that you are presenting the idea to, is then forced into the position of having to defend that past of which he was so active a participant!

One way to overcome this particular type of resistance is to make sure you always stress the benefits to be derived from your ideas in terms of the *future*. Talk about the "good times" ahead, rather than the bad times past.

Closely allied to defending past mistakes as a cause of resistance to new ideas is pride of authorship in past methods. Many new ideas are turned down simply because the person in authority cannot bear to give up one of his own "brain children" even though that child may no longer be adequate to the job. One salesman of business forms was bemoaning this in regard to one of his customers: by cutting an eighth-of-an-inch off the bottom of a 42-inch accounting form, he could have saved his customer $18,000 a year. But the firm's treasurer had designed this form and didn't want it changed even after twenty-seven years!

Another reason why an idea can meet rejection, even though the idea may be good and sound and would be profitable, is that it would infringe on someone's real or imagined "status" in the company. This type of resistance is frequently met in proposals for the reorganization of departments or functions within a company. Once status or position or a "preferred relationship" is obtained, the person obtaining it is extremely reluctant to give it up and will fight anything that threatens his position, regardless of the true merits of the idea. Probably the best route to circumvent this kind of resistance is through some applied psychology: bring the potential objector into the act of selling the idea; make him a part of the proposal. This, naturally, means that he will have to be sold on it first.

And this brings us to the real fundamental of getting acceptance for your new idea, no matter how good it might be: *it may take more imagination, more resourcefulness, and more outright creativeness to "sell" your idea than it did to get it in the first place.*

There are not, of course, any 100 per cent sure methods of selling anybody anything. But any experienced salesman can tell you that the first principle of selling is to know the interests of the person to whom you are selling. And this is just as true in attempting to sell an idea as it is in attempting to sell a more tangible item.

To cite just two extremes: if you have an idea for a new product for your company and present it to your management, you can be almost certain they will look at it from the standpoint of how much it will cost to go into manufacture on it, and they will then compare and evaluate that cost against the cost of other projects they may be considering. If the product is produced, and it is time to sell it to the public, you can be very certain that any prospective purchaser will look at your idea in a different light. He will want to know "What will I get out of it?" before he buys.

Of course the key person in your company that you will

probably have to sell your idea to is your own immediate boss or the person who heads up the department or function that your idea pertains to. Once you can get a responsible executive to back you, then the job of selling the idea further up the line becomes much easier. And this holds true even for the president of a company. He may find he has to get at least one of the directors "on his side" in order to sell the board as a whole on a new idea or policy.

So let's look at the man on the "next level up" to whom you will be presenting your idea. Even if he is a person who has actively demonstrated a progressive attitude, the only safe way to start out is by assuming that he will *not* like your idea when it is first presented to him—unless you know that that is not true. Remember that you are proposing a change, and it is human nature to resist change. Furthermore, if he has not demonstrated a receptiveness to new ideas, it is possible that this man may be lacking the positive attitude that such receptiveness requires. He may even be what is loosely termed "unimaginative." Or he may be a "weak" executive in the sense that he has never been made to realize that it is a part of his job to encourage you, and others like you, to produce new ideas and new thinking for the company. He may have all these faults in varying degrees, but he is the man to whom you have to present your fragile brainchild, so you will have to accept his faults.

The important thing for you is that you don't waste your time, energy, and mental resources fretting about the trouble you are apt to have with this man, because such anguish won't help. The approach you should take is that of actively helping that other person understand your idea and the benefits it can bring to the company. Be particularly careful to put your own thinking in order before you go in to see that man. Be prepared to teach him everything he needs to know about the problem your idea was devised to solve, if necessary; and be ready to give him all the answers, alternative solutions, data, facts, and reasoning processes you yourself went through in arriving at the particular problem solution you are now presenting. And, in preparing all this material to educate your boss with, try to put yourself in *his* shoes all the way through: try to imagine how you would react to this idea if your positions were reversed, and you had to think of all the things your boss will have to think of; and consider all the changes that will have to be made if he accepts your idea. If you give consideration to his problems, then you will do a better job of interpreting your idea in terms he will be willing to listen to.

There are also certain "basics of buying" that you should keep in mind in planning your selling program. Here are some of the reasons people will buy a product—or accept an idea:

The idea may let them do something they have wanted to do: cut operating costs, or make more profits, or compete against other lines or brands.

The idea may improve the individual's status in a desirable group. For example, the head of the purchasing department may feel that he will gain status among all the department heads in the company if he is the "sponsor" of a successful new idea.

There are some people who will buy an idea, unfortunately, because it will make someone else look bad. It gives the person accepting the idea a sense of satisfaction to know that he is "in on" something that someone else has missed. (This is not a recommendation that you encourage this type of feeling; only a statement of fact!)

An idea can be accepted because it helps to simplify some larger problem. Or because it enables some additional move to be made against a much larger problem.

And, of course, an idea will be accepted because it gets someone "off the hook" with his boss, or with the operating committee, or with anyone else who might have authority over him. This type of idea is usually the easy one to sell.

There are, naturally, many reasons why people will *not* buy an idea. And many more reasons why they think they should not buy an idea. Probably the most common of these is the old "Well, the way we are doing it now seems to work out okay." In other words, complacency. A suggested way of overcoming this is to take the "old way" and work out as good a selling story for that as you possibly can. Then, when you present your new way, you also show the old way. If you have been honest and objective in evaluating the advantages of the old, and if your new idea is really better, it should be obvious to anyone concerned that you do have the advantage in your new idea.

There is another real and potent reason why you may fail in attempting to sell your idea: you haven't really thought through the *business* aspects of the idea itself. Too often, we get so enthused over our ideas and make out strong and detailed cases supporting them, only to find that some simple consideration of business can kill the idea completely. An example is a new product suggestion that would make it necessary for a company to hire and train a completely new sales force to call on an entirely different type of retail outlet than it now uses. This might cost more than could possibly be made from the idea in five years. So learn your business—not only your own job, department, and division, but everything you can about the business as a whole. Attend any meetings, conferences, lectures, or other training programs you can get yourself into—even if they don't pertain directly to your job. Soak up the facts about your company, its customers, its economic and financing needs, the people who work for it. Know your company inside and out so that, when you do face that job of selling an idea, you will know *exactly* where your idea fits into the total scheme of company operations.

So what are the steps in actually presenting an idea? What, specifically, should you think about in planning the presentation of this idea in which you have invested so much time and effort? Here are a few suggestions that you may be able to adapt imaginatively to suit your particular idea:

First (and though it may seem obvious, it is frequently neglected) sell yourself on the idea as the best possible solution to the problem *at this time*.

Study your idea through carefully so you are well acquainted with all the problems that will be involved in carrying it out. Refer back to the "new product checklist" in Chapter 7 for the kinds of questions to ask about a new product idea. Make up some similar kind of checklist for other types of ideas you may be proposing. And be sure that you ask the same questions about any possible alternative problem solutions to make sure that yours is unquestionably the best.

In presenting your idea, be sure to point out the real need for it; don't assume the other person is aware of the need. He may not be. Be sure to point out the benefits of your idea; don't make the mistake of thinking they are so obvious the other person can't help appreciating them. Tell him.

If it is possible to *show* your idea with sketches, drawings, models, or floor plans, by all means take the time to prepare the illustrations. Better a day later in presenting the idea than to have it rejected because the other person couldn't appreciate it from your verbal description.

If you possibly can, make your own idea presentation in person to anyone who may have the power to accept or reject it. It may be necessary to have your boss or a co-worker along, but be prepared to fight your own fight if it becomes necessary. As one successful creative man said, "The most important ingredient in selling an idea is mother love like a tiger's!"

Have a comprehensive written report to leave behind after you've presented your idea. If there are several people to sell the idea to, have copies of your report for each of them.

Avoid trying to sell weak ideas. All you will do is lose your own prestige and undermine whatever confidence other people have in you.

In presenting your idea, and also in preparing the covering report, follow a definite, logical sequence. Here is an example:

State the idea clearly. Assume you are explaining it to a ten-year-old child. You aren't, of course, but this will quickly show up any fuzziness in your own thinking.

State the value of the idea to the company. Tell *exactly* why the owners of the business should be prepared to risk *x* number of dollars on your idea. Make sure that your arguments will satisfy the toughest person you can imagine who will have to pass on the idea.

List the advantages of your idea on one side of a sheet of paper. *List the disadvantages* on the other. Then justify your reasoning that the advantages outweigh the disadvantages. Be sure to look for "hidden" advantages like public-relations benefits, filling up of slack production periods, effects on company or industry prestige. These can all be "sold" if they are present in your basic concept.

Tell where you fit in. This is a form of recommending the next step on the idea. Are you through with it now? Should you be the person to carry out further exploratory or development or implementation work? It is always a temptation to ask for the opportunity to carry an idea all the way through and thus reap whatever rewards may result from it. But it is a mistake to trap yourself into a position of having to do something that you may not have the training, experience, or temperament to do.

Restate the benefits; recommend the next step. Always make a recommendation of the next thing to be done when you present an idea. This may be to investigate further along specific lines; to check out costs; to conduct a study to determine the effect of the idea or consumer reactions to the idea; or to appoint someone to activate the idea. But always make a specific recommendation as to what should come next. The aim is to make it easier for the person with authority to keep the idea moving than to put up with the uncomfortable feeling that an idea is hanging in suspension while he decides what should be done with it. Tell him what to do.

And suppose your idea *is* accepted and put into practice—

either into actual use or into a development stage. What do you do then?

This is where many idea men fail on the following through, and where many ideas fail to hold their own against all the destructive forces that can cut down their effectiveness and even kill them. If it is *your* idea, don't stop once it is sold—continue to follow through even if you can only do so from the sidelines.

Keep open-minded about improvements. It is one thing to resist changes in your idea that may undermine and weaken it. It is quite another to think that you are the only person who understands the idea sufficiently well to improve or "polish" it. Look for any opportunity to improve an idea yourself, and at least listen with an open mind to suggestions from others.

Know when to fight—and when not to. If your idea is really important and really creative, there is probably a "heart" to it that should not be changed. But surrounding that heart will be dozens of details that can be changed in hundreds of ways without hurting the main idea. You can always concede on these details so long as it won't hurt the big idea. It takes judgment and a sense of timing to know when to fight and when not to. But too much fighting at the wrong time or about the wrong thing has resulted in the loss of many worthwhile ideas.

Keep people sold. This is important as your idea passes from the stage of theory into that of application. Remember that your management probably felt they were taking a chance, even if they felt the odds were in favor of success, when they approved your idea. So keep them sold: report any and all successes; stay enthusiastic yourself; try to communicate that enthusiasm to your boss, to his boss, all the way up the line. Keep everyone firmly behind your idea until it takes over itself by demonstrating success.

Get other departments in on your idea. This will, to a large extent, depend on the particular idea. But don't hesitate to let someone else in on it or ask for someone else's help in making your idea succeed. You may get some valuable cross-fertilization of thinking that can "beef up" your original idea immensely.

Keep adding to your idea. If, for example, it is a packaging idea for one product, show how the same basic concepts can be adapted to other packages in your line, or to the shipping container, or to the point-of-sale display piece. If it is for a new type of product, look for possible related products or for other possible uses in addition to the original one. If it is an idea for a departmental reorganization, try to carry the basic principles down into individual operating sections, or on up into division operations to improve efficiency as a whole. Use your original idea as a seed for spreading the benefits in as many different directions as you can.

Expect to be sniped at. Remember that it is always easier to see the 10 per cent bad in an idea than the 90 per cent good. So you can expect any idea—particularly a really bold or new one—to be sniped at. In this respect, you should develop into your own best sniper. You should, of course, be the sharpest sniper of all because you will know more about your idea and its weaknesses than anyone else. So keep looking for flaws yourself. And listen to other people's suggestions on flaws. And when they suggest, don't damn in defending. Remember, they may be right and you may have to make a change. Leave yourself the opening to make it gracefully.

Know when to quit. It often happens that a promising idea just will not prove out when put into practice. No matter what the creator does in the way of refining, improving, combining, or otherwise strengthening the idea, it just won't work. The thing for the creator to do then is to drop it. Quit it completely, no matter how much it hurts. And then go on to another idea. And the creator should be the first to know that his idea is no good. He should be the person to "blow the whistle on it." It will be far better for you in the long run to get the reputation of being a person with the courage to admit you were wrong, than to be branded a "stubborn damn fool who doesn't know a good idea from a bad one!"

13

Creating the Creative Climate

Thompson Products, Inc., of Cleveland, had a problem: expensive polishing belts used in one of their operations kept fraying and breaking. Engineers couldn't find an answer, but one production employee did: Emma Gabor put nail polish on the belt edges, "Just like stopping a runner in my hose." The company paid her over $6,000 for the idea; the idea saved the company about $43,000 a year.

One of the greatest photographic laboratories in the world spent hundreds of thousands of dollars trying to develop a film that would take pictures in color. But when color film was successfully developed, it was by two traveling dance-band musicians who had been using their hotel bathtubs as "laboratories."

During World War II, regular production employees of the B. F. Goodrich Company turned in over three thousand ideas a year—a third of which were good enough to merit cash awards. And General Motors says that today they receive about thirty thousand usable ideas a year from their employees.

A new method of assembling electronic components saved the Army (and U.S. taxpayers!) $4,200,000 the first year it was in use. The inventors were two Signal Corps civilian employees, Stanislaus Danko and Moe Abramson, who received $10,000 for the idea. The award was made within the framework of the government's Incentives Awards System which, in one year, received over 294,000 suggestions from government and military workers; adopted 79,000 ideas for use; paid out $2,365,000 in awards.

Today, developing and building airplanes is a multimillion-dollar business. Huge research and engineering staffs constantly strive to improve planes, to make them better, safer, and more efficient. And who started all this? The Wright brothers—two bicycle mechanics.

One final example: in Minneapolis, an "ordinary" machinist, who had never been to college, received a check for over $50,000 from a company that manufactures giant "electronic brains" because he was able to give them something that even one of their million-dollar "thinking machines" couldn't—an idea on how to make a troublesome mechanism operate better.

These are just a few examples to demonstrate that imagination isn't confined to a select few people who happen to have positions in an organization chart indicating that they are responsible for thinking. A leading industrial personnel man recently said that if Thomas A. Edison or Alexander Graham Bell were to try to get a job in the research department of nearly any large corporation today, they probably wouldn't be hired because they didn't have the technical knowledge to be inventors! It is a fact that when Mr. Bell first got his idea for the telephone, he didn't know anything about electricity—he had to learn everything he needed to know about the science, right from scratch, before he could develop his invention!

It seems to be true that most businesses underestimate the ability of their "ordinary" workers to produce ideas. In fact, it often appears that some of the "professional" idea men underestimate the abilities of other idea men to produce ideas! But it is also true that there is only one place to get the ideas that any business needs for survival today—from people.

Regular production, clerical, office, and salaried employees in any organization probably represent the greatest untapped potential for new ideas that any company has. But you have to make them *want* to give you the ideas they have. You can't order people to be creative. You can't really "buy" ideas from them. You can't threaten or otherwise intimidate them into thinking creatively about your company problems. They have to want to do it first. This means you need what is generally termed a *creative climate*.

The general objectives of a creative climate are to encourage more creative thinking about company problems; to make sure that new or original ideas are never blocked or sidetracked without serious consideration by the company; and to provide whatever training, indoctrination, and encouragement is necessary to help workers think constructively and creatively about everything the company does or may need to do. Building this climate, or atmosphere, or attitude is a top-management and executive responsibility. It has to start with the "brass" demonstrating that they are receptive to new or radical solutions to problems. The example that there are no "sacrosanct" ways of doing things must come from the top.

A creative atmosphere in a company is much like water in a hose. There must be a reservoir to provide necessary pressure— and the pressure source must be *above* any outlets. Just as a faucet or valve can completely shut off the flow of water, a division or department head can close off the flow of encouragement for ideas. A kink in a hose can stop the flow of water; a poor foreman or supervisor can cut off the flow of ideas. If you puncture a hose, you cut down the pressure and the flow of water. If workers are subjected to negative attitudes and reactions from co-workers and immediate supervisors, it will cut down the flow of their ideas and dissipate the effects of the pressure from above to be creative. And once water reaches the nozzle outlet, you can spray it—in which case it is at the mercy of the wind to carry it about—or you can direct it in a steady, forceful stream against some particular object. And, by giving your "creative climate" some direction, you can do a better job of directing it against specific problems and objectives that are most important.

One of the most successful attempts to build a creative climate within a company is that of the AC Spark Plug Division of General Motors. This company began several years ago to see what they could do in the way of encouraging more ideas from their people. The man most responsible for this program was Mr. Joseph A. Anderson, Vice President of General Motors and the General Manager of AC. His interest in developing a creative program stemmed from the fact that he was impressed with the high cost of ideas in a company which are *not* thought of, or that come too late, or are never developed to their fullest potential. Too often, he says, we examine a new idea and say to ourselves, "We should have had this ten years ago—if only someone had thought of it."

Mr. Anderson believes strongly that top management must lead in creative development and that the urge for new ideas must be infused into all management in order to clear the way for ideas from below. "Management can bring out creative effort, and management can also stifle creative effort," he says. "Most management does some of each. That is because good management is made up with a high degree of good judgment; whereas, high creativity involves risks and taking chances."

His conclusion: A good manager, exercising good judgment only, could easily become a barrier to creativity.

With this consideration in mind, probably the first step an executive should take to begin building a creative climate in his company is to make a soul-searching analysis of his own attitude toward creativity. The first requirement for a creative manager is that he himself really wants new ideas—that he himself will have the capacity to change with the changes that new ideas require. He must be receptive to new, and even radical, propositions; he must be *sincerely* interested in them.

The man who really does want more ideas can begin to demonstrate it by following some advice that is so old, it is almost trite:

Maintain an open-door policy. Most executives have heard this, and many practice it. But the reason it doesn't always work for those who do practice it is that the door is often the only thing that is really open—the mind beyond the door is not.

Many executives who consider themselves to be completely approachable actually discourage any employees from approaching simply because the boss does not really mean it. A "boss" must be easy to talk to. He must, himself, assume the burden of making the interview successful when an employee comes in to submit an idea. After all, many employees don't really know (because they haven't been taught) how to present an idea. Furthermore, the average employee may lack confidence in his own idea. This comes, in part, from lack of experience. The organized effort to promote more creatively is a relatively new force in our culture. If yours is an average company, you may as well assume that, up to now, no one has ever tried to encourage your workers to use their imaginations; no one has ever made them conscious of ideas, or what ideas are, or how to go about having them. You have the job of developing the confidence if you want the creativity. Therefore, it is up to you to pave the way. You must be a good listener when an employee comes to you with an idea; you must resist any temptation to reject the idea before you have given it enough thought to make sure that you fully understand it yourself.

If you, as an executive, have not formed the habit of trying to encourage your people to submit ideas, you will also have to watch out for another personal pitfall: that of prematurely rejecting an idea through false pride. This, unfortunately, happens quite frequently. It may stem from the executive's chagrin that he didn't think of the idea himself—or from his fear of admitting to superiors that one of his subordinates was ahead of him on a problem. This makes it difficult for the executive to be objective in evaluating the idea, and, if it is your problem, will mean an added burden for you of always checking to be sure that you are being scrupulously fair to both the idea and the employee before rejecting or accepting any new suggestion.

It has been said of Igor Sikorsky, one of the great aeronautical designers of all times and a creative man in tune with creative minds, that whenever a subordinate came to him with a suggestion, he would say, "Excellent! Now let's work it out this way" —and, busily sketching, he would often make radical changes. When the part got into production, it was often Sikorsky's design, but so well had he handled it that the employee believed it was his!

The executive must also form the personal habit of both acknowledging and praising usable ideas if he wants to continue to receive them. In the first place, it is not very intelligent for anyone to assume the credit for the work of others. As an executive it is your job to get results on company problems, so you will automatically receive the credit no matter where an idea came from. It is also a universally understood rule of administration that an executive is responsible for developing the people under him. An executive who fails to report personal progress of subordinates, in the production of ideas or otherwise, may be suspected of "credit grabbing" or of not living up to his responsibilities as a leader.

The reverse of giving praise is also true: never reject an idea without giving as full an explanation as possible, and, if you want the employee to try again, be sure to say so. This situation is probably one of the touchiest of all to handle and, if it is bobbled, may turn a potentially good idea-producer into a completely negative worker. Criticism is difficult to give when you want to preserve a positive attitude. And the best rule for giving it is, "Be slow to."

It is easy to find fault with any idea, and frequently it is easier to criticize an employee than to praise him. But in many instances it is not necessary to criticize an idea to reject it. Furthermore, the idea-hunting executive will never abuse an employee for a bad idea, never ridicule any idea, and particularly never ridicule an idea in front of others or to others.

The "freedom to fail" must be an integral part of any creative climate. Charles Kettering once made the statement that "I can take any group of young people and teach them to be inventors if I can get them to throw off the hazard of becoming afraid to fail. A study made some years ago said that the more education a man has, the less likely he is to be an inventor. Now the reason for that is quite simple. It is because, throughout his life, he has been taught the danger of failure. From the time he enters the first grade until he graduates from the university, he is examined three or four times each year; if he fails, he is out and, in many cases, disgraced. In research and invention work, you fail hundreds, and even thousands of times; and, if you succeed once, you are in."

But probably the single most important trait an executive can acquire is that of personal enthusiasm for ideas. Be positive in your approach to problems, and to the problems of solving them. An enthusiastic, confident-appearing leader can do more to set a creative example or attitude in a company or department than all the special procedures or techniques put together.

This does not, of course, mean you should blind yourself to anyone's shortcomings, or forget anything you have learned about evaluating and judging ideas. An executive who could not sensibly evaluate an idea could be a positive danger to his company and this, of course, is just the opposite of what you should be trying to accomplish. But it is just as dangerous to operate on the antiquated theories that workers can't understand your problems and therefore can't possibly contribute ideas, or that everything must be judged by how it will appear on the quarterly balance sheet.

Another tool for building a creative climate in a company is that of training for creativity. This training includes the steps and methods an executive can use to educate his workers where he can exercise some control over the materials of education.

In practice, training for creativity or idea production may use many of the same methods used for any other type of worker training: conferences, discussions, literature study, outside guests and speakers. The basic difference is in aims and objectives.

Standard training programs are aimed at teaching set procedures for accomplishing a given task or assignment. Creative training usually goes in the other direction: it is aimed at teaching the worker to use his own mind to figure out better ways of handling standard tasks or assignments. Rapidly coming into general usage, however, are the training methods that combine both: they utilize the standard procedure of teaching a worker a specific job with specific methods, but integrate into such training the thought that nothing about these methods is final, that if the worker can think up a better way of doing something, his ideas will certainly be welcomed.

The worker is further encouraged along these lines by being exposed to information that will increase his ability to think in creative ways. As examples: a conference on methods will include background on the development of the method—including the "why"—so the worker can project that "why" in terms of any ideas he may later get to improve the method. Specialized reading material, such as rack booklets on idea-production methods, are made available. Outside speakers or instructors are brought in to conduct indoctrination sessions on principles, practices, and methods of solving problems creatively; or regular company training personnel may be sent to special seminars or institutes to familiarize them with creative training methods. Still another alternative is to assign selected workers to prepare reports on idea-stimulating helps and problem-solving techniques.

A fairly common practice in larger corporations when they want to "season" a promising executive is to rotate him through a variety of job assignments. This is the cross-fertilization principle and it can, in modified forms, be extended to help develop promising line workers, foremen, and other supervisory personnel. It can also be used to acquaint representative workers with problems and solutions from other departments or plants to broaden their own frames of reference for ideas pertaining to their jobs.

Some companies, including AC Spark Plug, report good results from specialized courses in creative thinking or creative problem-solving methods. These are usually aimed at developing potentials among middle-management executives, or men who are considered good prospects for the middle-management corps. The objectives of such specialized training are, first, to increase the individual's own creative output, and secondly, to make the executive more receptive to ideas from others. Generally, a man who has invested eighteen to twenty hours in a classroom studying and experiencing the creative processes will be more conscious of the need for a creative climate than one who has never had such specialized instruction and practice.

Along with any more or less formal training program should go some form of development program. This differs from training to the extent that development is usually something you can guide a worker into, but probably not control to the extent you can a training program. It is usually aimed at helping the employee gain self-confidence and to develop as a person. In far too many companies, workers are made to "live by the book"—required to do only what they are told to do. In time, they become as helpless as an unfeathered baby bird in exercising initiative. On the other hand, in companies where authority is delegated and workers are tested with responsibilities by being put "on their own," they do make mistakes, but simultaneously, they also develop initiative, exercise their imaginations, and grow as people. If you can guide employee or executive development in the direction of a more creative approach to living and to problems, the company will, needless to say, also benefit.

Since this guidance does not always allow dictation of direction, your efforts will probably be limited to making imaginative suggestions of things the particular employee should take an interest in. Encourage him to study company problems—which means, of course, letting him know what the problems are and cooperating in his efforts to get information for the study. Encourage questioning—and, if it is you that is being questioned, be sure your answers really do answer. Try to explain a problem or situation in full, but without prejudicing or restricting subsequent thinking by the worker. Another method, fairly obvious, is to encourage workers who have ideas to try them out.

A few other development devices worth considering: memberships in job or industry-related organizations; company social activities outside the plant; participation in outside study courses, with time off to do so. All of these have the advantage of exposing workers to other people with other problems, methods, ideas, and thinking patterns to help build an "idea background" the worker can utilize in solving the problems you give him.

A frequently overlooked tool, even in companies that have made some attempts to get more ideas from the general working force, is an organized and complete plan for *two-way* communications: a simple, orderly procedure for getting ideas from the workers to the people who need those ideas and, just as importantly, a continuous, all-inclusive system for keeping workers informed of problems that need solving and the rewards for solving those problems. An executive or company that follows that archaic policy of "Tell 'em nothing!" can only expect payment in kind so far as worker interest is concerned.

Actually, channels of communication from the "bottom" to the "top" are probably already set in your company, and if you want to use them for carrying ideas, it is only necessary to make sure they are not clogged or booby-trapped by unsympathetic supervisors, foremen, or junior executives. The channels for communicating problems downward are probably in existence also: house organs, pay envelope enclosures, bulletin boards, meetings, supervisors, and training programs. These can be utilized for implementing a creative program, providing the "technicians" manning the communication network understand what is being sought. Probably the only general guide necessary on this is that creativity thrives best on informality. The atmosphere for communicating ideas and for publicizing the need for them should be friendly in *both* directions.

The type of information to be communicated downward is

something else again. It is not enough to present a cold, bald problem and expect such a presentation to stimulate ideas (although it occasionally has for some companies—probably proof that *any* communication is better than none!). With the problem statement should go enough background to enable the average worker to understand it; the limitations, if any, on solutions; some suggestions to get thinking started, i.e., the kinds of ideas that are already under consideration and where they seem to fall short. A pitfall to watch for is that your initial suggestions do not restrict or hamper fresh thinking.

If the problem is being presented on an individual contact basis, some elementary psychology will often prove fruitful. The executive who ends up his problem indoctrination with "What would you do if you were in my shoes, Bill?" can usually expect a better reception than if he stopped with "That's the problem—take care of it!"

For any kind of sustained program, one good system corresponds to the way you handle promotional or sales campaigns: For one week, or month, the whole communications effort aims at getting ideas on a particular production problem; the following week or other period, the objective becomes waste reduction. The next period may be on product improvement, or increasing selling effectiveness; another could be on plant safety. This way workers have specific targets to shoot at in their thinking, rather than the broad, amorphous "Give us ideas."

Every plant should, of course, make use of suggestion boxes. However, it would be a mistake to limit channels of idea-suggesting to the boxes, and it is also a mistake to assume that just because the boxes are there and painted an attractive color, the workers will use them without further efforts on your part. Your communications program should include frequent reminders of the need for ideas, and should stress and restress the point that ideas are wanted and, if possible, will be rewarded.

One of the most difficult tasks in setting up any formal idea-seeking program is certainly that of arriving at suitable rewards and incentives for ideas submitted. On the one hand, there is the very real need for something to motivate workers to "give" more than just the minimum effort needed to hold their jobs; and on the other, there are all the complications of union agreements, the moral issues such as fairness and equitability of the reward, and, certainly, the company's ability to pay.

It may be, however, that motivating for creativity is being needlessly overcomplicated. We read and hear so much about impressive monetary rewards for new suggestions, methods, patents, etc. that we often forget there are other ways to appeal to people. When you are dealing with an individual who may be under your supervision, for example, you may find, with a little gentle probing and a great deal of understanding, that money really isn't too important. Individual motivations differ. This means that you can use different incentives to spur people to think.

If, for example, your company morale is high and your *esprit de corps* is strong, it may be enough just to let workers know that you would appreciate their ideas on such and such a problem. The only reward needed then will be recognition and perhaps praise for the idea-giver who succeeds, and sincere thanks for those who did not quite make it. On the other hand, if your plant morale is low, it may be that demonstrating some real creative leadership can help raise morale to the point where it will become the factor that motivates for you.

Other nonmonetary rewards to consider include such things as adaptations of "service awards" like lapel pins for workers who submit acceptable ideas: a bronze pin for five ideas; silver for ten; gold for twenty-five; etc. Another way would be to bring the family into the rewarding: instead of cash for ideas, give points tied in with one of the established incentive-reward merchandise catalogues so familiar in sales promotion.

AC Spark Plug uses a program of giving supervisory employees point credits for ideas submitted. Points range from 10 to 200 per idea. Each supervisor has a personal goal of 100 points a year. These point scores are used in considering promotions and salary increases. Nonsupervisory personnel receive cash awards for their suggestions and may earn as much as $5,000 for an idea.

At Lincoln Electric Company, the creative contribution each worker makes is one of the basic factors in determining the amount of annual incentive bonus he earns. Lincoln evaluates each person's contribution in new ideas, new methods, and new thinking. This plan, although rewards are monetary in nature, is tied in with profit-sharing, a less costly way of paying, and pays off directly to the worker who has ideas that can help the company reduce costs, increase output, improve quality, or help the company in its relations with its customers and the public.

For a continuing program, you might consider a weekly or monthly award for the most original idea submitted, regardless of whether or not it can actually be used. This offers a double opportunity: it maintains worker interest in submitting ideas, and it forces management to set up a system for regular review of all submitted ideas.

Of course, any rewards made for ideas should be well publicized throughout the company. The best encouragement you can give any individual to break out of the rut of conformity and to explore new possibilities for the company is the knowledge that others who have done so have met with both management support and some form of reward and recognition.

It could be very possible for a company to have all the theoretical requisites for a creative atmosphere and fail to get any ideas from it. This is frequently the case in smaller companies where, by virtue of favorable social and environmental factors, morale and *esprit de corps* are already high. But idea production is low. Creating the atmosphere is usually not enough. Workers must also be stimulated to take advantage of that atmosphere. In fact, it may be necessary to do something as basic as calling attention to the fact that the atmosphere exists. In the comfortable acceptance of established and recurring work habits, workers may forget that new ideas are really wanted. So it is necessary to repeat the attention-calling periodically until acceptance of the new creative policy itself becomes a habit.

Suggestions for stimulating idea production are many and varied. Some are simply communications techniques borrowed from advertising and editorial fields. Some companies have, however, experimented with actions that can be taken, and here are a few of their ideas:

Idea Breaks. These can range all the way from daily or weekly half-hour sessions, where employees are encouraged to do nothing but sit and think, down to informal meetings wherein an idea-trained foreman calls his group together during the coffee break and presents a problem for them to "kick around." Such sessions may or may not employ some of the formal group creative techniques described in Chapter 10. A more ambitious type of idea break is that used in several large research organizations where researchers are theoretically free to spend up to 20 per cent of their paid time working on projects of their own choosing.

Experimental Facilities. Many companies have successfully encouraged profitable developments through the expedient of offering the use of such standing company facilities as laboratories, model shops, and machine shops for experimental work on new ideas related to company problems. This is usually tied in with the program of giving a percentage of company time for such work. In other cases, only the facilities are made available, and the worker, if he wants to use them, does so on his own time. Many workers are willing to do this, particularly if they know that the company will be generous in rewarding them for a successful development.

Discussion. Regular or periodic discussions of problems are, of course, a standard in-company communications technique. But the practice of setting them up on a scheduled basis, with the sole object of stimulating workers to produce ideas on company problems, is well worth considering if a company needs or wants ideas. Closely related to this is the use many organizations make of the

Brainstorming technique. They frankly admit that the ideas actually produced in the Brainstorm session may be of secondary value. What they are after is the stimulation that Brainstorming a problem gives the participants to continue thinking about it on their own.

Competition. Considering that Americans are basically a competitive people, it is surprising that more has not been done to encourage friendly competition among workers for ideas. It is fairly common to pit departments or sections or plants against one another in campaigns to reduce absenteeism or production rejects or accidents. It should also be possible to develop similar competition to stimulate idea or improvement suggestions.

Display. Every plant has lobbies, entrances, bulletin boards, or other "dead" space that could be used for idea-stimulating displays. For instance, a display of models of basic machinery and machinery modifications in your industry could easily tie in with the rewards for inventing such machinery. Another display might serve to encourage some of the more timid souls by tracing out a few of the ridiculous or impractical inventions of the past and demonstrating how applied creativity developed them into useful machines or products. Still another type of display could use photos or models from some of the "world of the future" magazine articles and features that are so popular today. This, if well planned, could serve to orient workers' minds toward the future and stimulate speculation on how your company's products or services can be made to fit in.

Follow-up. No program of creative stimulation can be considered complete unless it includes a planned system for follow-up and action on the ideas produced. This is so essential that it might even be wise to plan what you are going to do with ideas before you worry about how you are going to get them.

The follow-up cycle must provide for such factors as screening and evaluating ideas, determining suitable awards or rewards, and an air-tight, iron-clad, welded-to-the-floor procedure to make sure that some action—whether investigative or activating—is taken on *every* promising idea. Your company can generate a thousand million-dollar ideas, but until some action is taken, they will not be worth the paper they are listed on. And last, but certainly not least, your follow-up system must provide for individually communicating with every worker on the ideas he submits, whether they are accepted or rejected.

This worker communication, ideally, is best done in person. But where that is impractical, it should certainly be a highly personalized, individually written letter from some individual whom the worker will consider important in the company.

If the letter is to *reject* an idea, it should summarize the details of the proposed suggestion; tell and explain what action was taken; and tell why the idea cannot be adopted. Give the worker enough information about your investigation of his idea to show that it was considered fairly. Then be sure to thank the suggester and ask him to try again. The whole letter should be positive in nature and show appreciation of the worker's effort, cooperation in company objectives, and his eagerness to do a better job.

If the letter is one informing a worker that his idea has been *accepted*, you follow somewhat the same general content: describe his suggestion briefly; explain the investigation and testing, if any; show him the benefits you expect from it; explain how his reward or award was computed; encourage him to submit more ideas. And, of course, express your appreciation. Remember that the successful "inventor" will "spread the word around" that they do, indeed, like good ideas "upstairs." Give him some proof in the form of intelligent information of just how his idea was handled from beginning to end.

All of this makes it apparent that building a more creative climate is not the easiest task an executive can undertake. However, the stakes are high and the rewards are tremendous. Mr. A. L. Simberg, Supervisor of Personnel, Research and Development of the AC Spark Plug Division, made a report on the four-year results of their program. He said: "While many tangible results and dollar savings have occurred either directly or indirectly because of the Creativity Program, it is impossible to list them all. In addition to specific results, many employees have made general statements along the following lines:

1. The creativity program has tended to make everyone much more aware of problems and problem areas and has increased their sensitivity to them.

2. People are much more responsive to suggestions. They are willing to try many more things than previously. The basic philosophy of the entire organization has been permeated with "green light" thinking. The first reaction to novel ideas is seldom negative.

3. The number of ideas has shown a marked up-turn. Evidentially, the theorem that quantity helps in producing quality seems to have taken effect. The first obstacle encountered seldom stops anyone any more.

4. Much value to the organization has accrued from the principle of having more than one solution to a problem. It is the rule, rather than the exception, for people to turn in three or four alternatives for solving problems.

5. The creativity program has helped our employees not only on the job, but in their home life and outside activities as well. One engineer, who also serves as a minister on Sundays, attests to its help in preparing his sermons; another talks about its uses in working through the local Youth Bureau and finding unusual and interesting tasks for the boys with whom he works.

At the Duquesne, Pennsylvania, Works of the U.S. Steel Corporation, a unique company-wide creativity program aimed at increasing safety is under way with the title "Operation Attitude." Mr. W. W. Keenan, Supervisor of Safety, reported that in the first two years of the program, the workers of the Duquesne plant had completed the study of 4,300 job procedures. Unnumbered changes in operating practice, and hundreds of pieces of equipment, large and small, were installed at the suggestion of the production workers themselves.

"Operation Attitude has the effect of giving us 6,000 safety men," says Mr. Keenan. "And having that many persons concentrating on this job is a lot more effective than relying on a few hundred management personnel or a handful of safety engineers, believe me."

He also reported that out of the study of the 4,300 standard procedures have come literally hundreds of recommendations for new or different equipment, or changes or additions to machinery already in use, in order to provide maximum safety on the job. Some of these recommendations, he said, are so simple and understandable that safety men shudder to think that they overlooked them. Others are more complex and reflect sound thinking and long years of experience on the job.

But profitable and productive as a creative climate can be, there is one caution for the executive who undertakes to build it in his company: it cannot be accomplished overnight no matter how willing or how sold you yourself are. But one thing we do know:

Creativity in any company must come from the top!

14

How to Spot
Creative Potential in Others

One of the most important responsibilities any executive must handle is seeing that his company gets "the most" from its workers. This is particularly so when it comes to creativeness—the production of the ideas upon which the company is dependent to make money, or to operate efficiently and at a profit.

Most of us, in our everyday lives, make the mistake of oversimplifying our classifications of others. We say someone is "likable" or "not likable." We call him a "pessimist" or an "optimist." We decide a certain worker is "responsible" or "irresponsible." A man is either "loyal" to the company or he is "disloyal." Our definitions are all black or white—we have no "gray scales" for inbetweens. However, most people, upon careful analysis, fall into the gray area between black and white. And this complicates the job of the executive who is trying to make certain that his company is making the most of the creative potential at its disposal.

The problem of spotting creative potential is also complicated by the fact that people do not always *think* up to their capacities. It is relatively easy to spot the highly creative person who is using his ability actively and conclusively to its fullest extent. Not so easy to spot are at least five other types of workers who have the ability to make creative contributions, but who are not contributing to their full potentials. These types are:

The highly creative person who is doing inferior work because he is asked to work at tasks that do not challenge his abilities sufficiently.

The highly creative person who is being limited by emotional problems which interfere with his proper perspective on either his work or his job or himself.

The person with a high creative *potential* who lacks sufficient knowledge of, or the instinct for, problem-solving methods to put that potential to work.

The potentially creative person who is limited by too narrow a range of interests or by attitudes opposed to creative (or any other!) endeavor.

The potentially creative person who lacks sufficient knowledge of his field or the business he is in.

It has been said that "Creativity is best revealed by what it creates." There is certainly a great deal of truth in this. But the practice of looking only at achievement for determining creative potential can cause an executive to overlook many potentially good creative workers who have never had either the inclination or the opportunity to reveal themselves as being creative.

The creativity program installed in the AC Spark Plug Division of General Motors was described briefly in the last chapter. This program has, to a certain extent, become the model for dozens of similar programs by other companies. An especially valuable part of the AC program, so far as this company is concerned, is the testing they do to uncover the various hidden classifications of creativity. These tests were developed because AC management wanted to find out if they had their most creative people working in areas where their creativity would find the best outlets. And they hoped to be able to "spread the talent around" to bolster up the idea potential of every department, based upon the need of each department.

The tests developed by AC's Personnel Research Section were validated by approved psychological measurements and were found to have a high degree of correlation with ratings of special test groups set up within the company. Test scores were also correlated against actual records of ideas, suggestions, and proposals submitted by members of the test groups.

The AC Test of Creative Ability, which was developed by Mr. Simberg and Dr. Richard Harris, is now used extensively within AC and has also been made available to other interested companies, with the following restrictions:

(1) The person or firm desiring to use it must send someone to Flint to learn all aspects of administering the test, and scoring and interpreting it. (2) If the test is used, a validation study must be conducted, using criterion groups. (3) AC Spark Plug Division must be advised of the results of such a study. It is apparent that these restrictions are more for the protection of the company that "borrows" the test than for the benefit of AC.

The AC Test of Creativity is designed to give an indication of the number and uniqueness of ideas a person is likely to have. As such, AC says, "It may or may not be a test of creative ability, depending on which one of a number of definitions of creativity is accepted. It will probably be more accurate to think of the test as an indicator of a person's ability to produce a quantity of unique ideas in a given situation."

The full test is in five parts, and requires one hour and twenty minutes to administer:

PART I: A twenty-minute test containing five common situations. A person lists as many possible consequences of each situation as he can. The part yields both a quantity and a uniqueness score.

Typical example: In a thick fog in a major American harbor, a passenger liner is moving cautiously toward its berth. While it has the latest radar equipment, it is inoperative and the radar operator is unaware of this fact. Another boat is approaching the liner amidships, and it is obvious that neither ship is aware of the other's presence. List *all* the things you can think of that *might* happen as a consequence.

PART II: A ten-minute test of general reasoning containing five unusual and not necessarily true statements. A person lists as many reasons as possible to explain the truth of the statements. This part also yields a quantity and a uniqueness score.

Example problem: Residents of Chicago consume, on the average, more Brazil nuts than residents of Omaha.

PART III: A fifteen-minute test of sensitivity to problems containing a list of five common appliances. A person lists any improvements that he feels could be made in each one. This part yields a uniqueness score.

Example: List all the things you think are wrong with, or could be improved upon in, a wrist watch.

PART IV: A twenty-minute test of practical judgment containing five problem situations. A person gives the solutions which he considers to be the least expensive and least time-consuming. This part yields a single quality score.

Example: An Air Force pilot was told to take samples of air at five different altitudes up to 10,000 feet. For this purpose he was given a small plane with a nonpressurized cabin and five bottles with small openings which could be sealed with a cork. When he was ready to take off, it occurred to him that the bottles already contained air at ground level. This air had to be removed so that air at the varying altitudes could be collected. Rather than go to the trouble of locating a pump or other special device to create a vacuum in each bottle, how could he accomplish the assigned task?

PART V: A fifteen-minute test of originality containing five common objects. A person gives as many possible uses as he can think of for each object. This part yields both a quantity and a uniqueness score.

Example: How many uses can you think of for a common paper clip?

Although AC and other companies who have used the AC test report satisfactory results from it, no company should ever feel that such testing is the panacea for unlocking, or even uncovering, creative potential with 100 per cent accuracy. All such tests measure what people *can* do under test conditions. They do not give you a completely accurate picture of what people *will* do. When carefully standardized, validated, and administered, therefore, such formal testing procedures can give you indications of a person's capabilities, but no clear-cut prediction of his performance. This is one of the reasons for the AC requirement that any company using their test come to Flint for prior indoctrination.

In practical business management, however, there are many "rule-of-thumb" tests and observations that the executive can apply to the persons under him to get a nonscientific, but possibly functionally usable, measurement of creative potential. It goes without saying that the final value of any such applications as these depends largely upon the judgment, understanding, and interpretive abilities of the person who is making the observations. Before going into the descriptions of these symptoms, therefore, it is desirable to establish some "ground rules":

First, all men are *not* created equal when it comes to imaginative abilities. Even if they were, not all would have had backgrounds and home environments that would give them both the encouragement and the opportunities to practice their creative abilities. For many persons, the chief deterrents to creativity will have been built up during their years as children under unsympathetic or noncreative parents.

Second, even psychologists and sociologists who have specialized in the study of creative people do not always agree *exactly* on the personality factors that make a person creative. These people are handicapped in pinpointing the creative characteristics by the relatively late start that has been made in this field of study—we simply have not built up the background of tests and verified case histories to be able to make accurate predictions even of "potentials."

Third, it is desirable to spot creative potential as early as possible after a person goes to work for you. (At AC, for example, the Test for Creativity is given to all new hires at the time of employment.) This is important, because creative potential will not develop unless it is given favorable conditions and encouragement to do so. A highly creative person, put in a job that does not make demands on his imagination, can quickly lose interest in applying imagination, or, worse, can become frustrated and embittered toward the company.

Fourth, the process of identifying, or encouraging, creative potential should be continuing. Remember, many people may be completely unaware that they have the ability to produce ideas. They may completely lack any understanding of problems or any knowledge of methods for solving problems. Only through patience and friendly "coaching" can you help them develop the confidence to "venture out" into the world of imagination. So although you may employ a formal or informal screening for creative potential initially, it is important that you also watch for any signs of developing potential as the worker progresses.

Finally, people with creative potential can be spotted by the executive who has an understanding of the basic characteristics, at least as we now know them, and who will apply his understanding toward interpreting the "signs" that any person gives to indicate his personality.

Mr. C. M. Sinnett, of RCA-Victor's Television Engineering Department, describes the process of interviewing to determine creative potential this way:

> If we are going to identify creativity, then we must separate and define some of the main characteristics possessed to a greater extent by the creative individual or engineer than by his less creative or even non-creative brother. In the final analysis, these characteristics may be mixed up in the genes, chromosomes, or hormones, but as far as I know, this has not been determined. We shall have to deal with factors which are visible to us, or can be found without the help of the electron microscope, radioactive materials, or the encephalograph.

In other words, we must apply common sense, experience, intuition, and a lot of plain "seat of the pants" judgment. I agree that this sounds very prosaic, but the method is quite effective after all.

Having thus removed all the glamour and most of the science from the subject, just what do we have to go on? I believe we can break it down into two basic categories: surface characteristics and mental processes. Some of the surface characteristics which can establish a basis for a first impression or judgment of an individual are (1) general appearance, (2) speech, (3) hobbies, and (4) experience. Please note that I said "first impression" because we are barely starting on our dissective road.

Let us now consider a couple of illustrative examples. These may be extreme cases, but I have seen both types many times on college campuses while recruiting. In fact, they can be found in almost any Engineering Department if one cares to take the time to look for them. On occasions we may rely too heavily on these first impressions, and then have a rude awakening as the interview proceeds. This happens so seldom, however, that I believe it is no more than the exception that proves the rule.

We shall assume that you are sitting behind a desk and have the job of interviewing several candidates for a position in your Engineering Department. Approaching you is a young man in his twenties. As he walks toward you it is obvious that he is no Beau Brummell as far as attire is concerned. There is really nothing radically wrong about it, but you have the overall impression that his mind was on many other things than his appearance when he got dressed. I don't imply that the creative person is never well-dressed, but if you will look around you and observe the highly creative people you know, you will probably find that the majority of them dress with an air of careless abandon. As your prospect comes closer, you note that he is looking straight at you; that any movement of his eyes is quick; and there is no outward sign of nervousness. In other words, he is as anxious to meet you as you are to meet him. He appears utterly self-confident and possesses an intensity of purpose that is unmistakable.

With these preliminaries out of the way, we have the next check point—his manner of speech. You note in talking to him that he will carry his share of the conversation irrespective of the subject being discussed. His grammar may not be perfect and on occasion he may not say exactly what he means, but his speech tends to be snappy and to the point. No difficulty is found in getting him to talk about anything.

As you delve into his hobbies and experience, you find that he has done many things outside school hours. He has built radio receivers or amplifiers and perhaps serviced them for his neighbors. While he was in high school, he built model airplanes, even reaching the radio-controlled gas model stage. He dabbled a bit in photography, including developing, printing, and enlarging his own prints, and can discuss intelligently such things as lenses, light meters, exposure time, film speeds, etc.

By now you are convinced this is the man you want and the only problem is how to land him. I don't know the answer to this part of the story. At any rate, there is no need to spend further time questioning him, so an offer is made and you look for the next applicant.

As this fellow approaches you, his appearance, particularly his clothes and bearing, are sort of ordinary. There is nothing unusual about him that you can detect. As he comes toward you, he may look straight at you but there is no fire in his eyes—they are not exactly listless, but his attitude seems to be one of "Well, here I am; try and find out something about me!" His handshake is perfunctory, there is no particular life to it, and you wish there was some way to strike a spark in him. So far you have a negative impression regarding his creative ability, but perhaps you are wrong. It may be that he is reticent, scared, an introvert, or able to hide his true feelings.

You start the interview by asking him questions regarding his school work, his laboratory experiments, his outside experience, etc. To all questions you get answers, but they have no particular interest factor connected with them. Delving into his hobbies indicates that he has never tinkered with electronic devices or the construction of any kind of a model. He does like to golf and fish and has always been fond of athletics. When asked why he took up engineering, he isn't too sure, but basically he feels that it is a good line to get into, particularly since there is a shortage of engineers. He feels there is not much the matter with anything you can think of; no improvements which need to be made. By this time you are convinced that he is not creative and unless some miracle occurs, he never will be creative.

It should be remembered that Mr. Sinnett's interviewing is done with the view of locating creative potential for television engineering. Hence his emphasis on previous demonstrations of interest in electronics by the candidates. An executive interviewing prospective workers in other fields should be similarly prepared to question previous experiences and interests that would indicate a real inclination toward the field the candidate is being considered for. As one example, a young man applying for an office or administrative-type job may show signs of imaginative ability through previous accomplishments as an "administrator" in one of the "Junior Achievement" groups so popular among high school students.

In beginning your rule-of-thumb testing and observations, there are a few pitfalls to avoid. Any person, understandably, tends to favor persons he considers like himself. For example, a college-educated executive might have an inclination to "look down on" a worker who may not have finished high school. But when it comes to creative ability, the actual educational level attained by a person may not be too important. A basically creative mind will have enough drive to acquire the equivalent knowledge of a college education in other ways. At the same time, a college degree, even from the same school as the screening executive's, is no guarantee of high creative potential.

Executives, being human, also tend to like the person most who is most cooperative in following company procedures, and who gets along with other people. This kind of person, in many cases, makes the executive's or supervisor's job much easier. A creatively gifted person, on the other hand, tends to be independent in thought and in his actions. He may occasionally ask embarrassing questions of an executive. He may prefer his own ways of doing things and his own methods of solving problems. In short, he may be a true nonconformist. If this nonconformity has ever been at the expense of the screening executive, he may, inadvertently, not do the best job of judging the creative worth of the person.

Although most creative persons usually know or sense where

they are going, there are many who perform erratically. The executive who happens to observe such a person when he is in a "low" may make the mistake of underestimating that person's potential. This is another argument for constant observation of a worker for signs of creative potential.

Most suggestions for informal observing and testing to spot creative potential are based on the outward signs of the basic creative characteristics and the thinking patterns of creative people. This puts quite a responsibility upon anyone trying to screen people for creative potential, because so much is dependent upon the observation and correct interpretation of the basic "signs." However, here are some general personality traits to look for:

The Observant Person. Generally, a person who is highly alert to what is around him, who sees details and relationships that others miss, has a great advantage in developing creative potential.

Knowledge. New ideas are usually combinations of old ideas, or old ideas in new forms. The greater a person's knowledge about his field, the greater his potential creativeness. Remember that field knowledge may be acquired through related experience or on-the-job instruction—it does not necessarily have to be from schooling. It is relatively easy to determine a person's knowledge of his job, field, company, or industry.

A Good Memory. This is a part of the acquisition of knowledge, but becomes more important in the less formal types of knowledge. The man who can remember an odd-shaped piece of metal he saw in the storage room at just the time such a piece is needed, may be indicating the kind of "odds-and-ends" memory that frequently typifies a creative mind.

Drive. This is a relatively easy factor to observe. It shows itself by a man's dogged determination to see a job through—or his insistence on finishing a task before letting something else interfere. Such persistence, however, may easily be confused with stubbornness or obstinacy. The determining factor will usually be the reason or motivation for persisting.

Ability to Concentrate. This is more difficult to determine.

Some persons, when they concentrate, are literally in a world of their own. Nothing can bother or distract them. Others, however, can just as easily develop a high degree of concentration in the midst of relative calamity, and may even be contributing to the calamity. But the ability to concentrate on a problem, or the solution to it, to the exclusion of other irrelevant and distracting factors, is usually a mark of a creative personality.

Reasoning Power. The ability to discipline thinking into logical reasoning patterns is another prime creative characteristic. Remember the creative mind's ability to be thoroughly organized and methodical in seeking solutions to problems, regardless of its ability to be the same with ordinary conventions such as dress, work schedules, etc. It is important, of course, to determine the *quality* of a person's reasoning, along with his methods of reasoning. It is perfectly possible for a man to follow a sound, logical, well-thought-out approach to a problem and arrive at a completely erroneous conclusion.

Communicative Ability. This is not a basic creative characteristic, but it is a highly valuable one for a creative person to have. It is mentioned here as a possible cause of misjudging a person in attempting to determine whether or not he is creative. Some creative persons can communicate their ideas and thoughts with ease. Others, of a more introverted type, may have trouble putting their ideas and thoughts into words, either written or spoken. Furthermore, it is easy to overlook the importance or significance hidden in a short memo or a quick answer by a person who has thought a proposition through in all its ramifications, and then "netted" it down to a short explanation. Communication, then, may or may not be a tip-off to creative potential; the important caution is that you do not let its lack "throw you" in your evaluation.

The Curious Person. This is an easy-to-spot trait and a key one to be alert for in another person. Chances are anyone without curiosity will not have a very high degree of creative potential. It is important, however, to distinguish between true creative curiosity and the idle type of questioning that only serves as conversation. ("How's the weather outside?" or "Where did you have lunch today?")

The Skeptic. In evaluating this quality, it is important to evaluate the quality or motivation of the skepticism. The creative skeptic doubts many things—particularly the obvious things that everyone else accepts perhaps too readily. The noncreative skeptic has destruction or belittlement as his motivation. The two can usually be distinguished by an adroit question or two. The noncreative skeptic will usually assume that things are going from bad to worse and nothing can be done about it, so why try? The creative skeptic normally feels that no matter how bad or how wrong something is, it can always be made better. He may even have some ready suggestions for betterment.

Ready Suggestions. There is a type of person who, no matter what kind of problem is presented to him, usually has several suggestions for solving it. Regardless of the value of the ideas, such a person is giving a strong indication of idea fluency. If his ideas are all hopelessly off-target, or inconceivable in the light of the limitations of the problem, it may indicate a need for some indoctrination in problems *per se.* But generally speaking, idea fluency is one of the most valuable traits in a creative person.

Pace Changes. Nobody can be creative who loses the ability to change his mental pace occasionally. This is manifested in a really creative person by his knowledge of, and interest in, many things. The ability to be "wrapped up" in a problem one minute, and then relax the mind completely with something else the next minute, is a key characteristic of the person who has developed the ability to discipline his thinking and change his mental pace. This type of person, however, should not be confused with the "activity boys"—the types who belong to every club they can join; participate in every social activity they can fit in; and manage always to keep themselves surrounded by people every minute of the waking day. Far from being a manifestation of creative ability, this frenzied activity may be just the opposite: a revelation of deep-seated feelings of inadequacy and inferiority which the individual attempts to compensate for by an enforced schedule of activities with other people. He is, in short, trying to prove to himself that other people do accept him. The really creative person may not care whether other people accept him or not.

Specification Fighting. The person who is held down to a single routine job has his horizons compressed to the point where his creative ability may not be able to exercise itself. If the creative urge is strong enough, it may show up as a constant battle to "get in on" other jobs or other functions, or at least to broaden the horizons into a knowledge of other people's work. It may also, of course, be a mere objection to authority of any kind when a person refuses to follow instructions or stick to the specifications of his job. But a persistent resistance to a narrow job specification may indicate an imagination that is not being given the freedom to imagine.

Routine Bucking. The routine bucker is closely related to the specification fighter. But in the case of the person who hates routine, it may be more an indication of a strong sense of curiosity at work—the kind of curiosity that burns at the person to explore and to venture. Routine, of course, means repetition. But the really creative mind, when it has been over a problem course once, rapidly loses interest in repeating that trip. It much prefers to go on to something new.

It can be seen from just this cursory study of the ways creative potential can show itself that creative ability can announce itself in ways which a company or an executive might not like. It is necessary to have job specifications; some people have to put up with routine; a strict "lone wolf" may be a detriment to certain operations or functions. Yet each of these may have potential as an idea man for your company. Many of the organizational and operational problems raised by the presence of such people can be solved to a large degree by the placement of them in the company. This is one of the basic aims of properly locating your creative potential in the first place. Just as it would be sheer waste of talent to put a physicist into a storeroom as a clerk, so it is also highly wasteful to put a person with problem-solving abilities in a routine job where he never has any problem greater than should he take sugar in his coffee today.

It should also be remembered that few of these "types" of personalities will ever be found in a "pure" state. They have been set out as individuals here to make it easier to distinguish among them. But many people will be mixtures and composites of any or all of these to varying degrees. The mere presence of one such trait, then, is probably not enough to immediately classify a person as "potentially creative." The detection of several or many such traits, however, should at least give the executive cause to go out of his way to really get acquainted with the worker. The result of further acquaintance may be the happy discovery of still another mind capable of coping with the company's problems in an imaginative way.

15

The Creative Executive
in Action

In the world of business, the word "leader" is one not used very often. Or, if it is applied to a man, as often as not it is in a fatuous sense.

Businessmen, perhaps through modesty or pretended modesty, seem to prefer terms like "executive," "administrator," "supervisor," "manager," or even "chief." Yet the problems inherent in all those preferred titles are problems involving leadership: making decisions; implementing policy and action; influencing the thinking and actions of others in such a way that they will want to be "followers."

Leadership, of course, comes in all sizes and shapes. The grade school youngster who organizes a game of sand-lot baseball is exercising it. So is the production worker who feels that the only solution to his problem lies in organizing a grievance committee to complain to management. So is the company president who "sells" his board on expending $5-million on a new plant.

Of chief interest to the business leader, however, are forms of leadership best described as "dynamic"—meaning leadership characterized by energetic action that is both progressive and effective. And dynamic leadership must be creative leadership. It must be imaginative and forwardly oriented to be of benefit to the company or organization in which it is applied. A man who displays energy in tackling the problems of his job, and who also produces results that are both effective and progressive for the company, is a dynamic, creative leader—no matter what his official title or what he prefers to call himself.

It is true, of course, that every business executive or leader, no matter how creative or dynamic the results he obtains, is first of all a human being. If we were to list all the virtues that an executive should have, according to all the writers and "authorities" on management, the composite results would probably be more angelic than human. Therefore, the best we can hope for in describing the traits of creative leadership are some "ideals" that are worth working toward, and even these must be generalized to a high degree.

It has been said that the qualities for success as an executive are "drive; a sense of responsibility; the ability to communicate; the ability to think; the ability to get along with people; health; good character." To these should probably be added that of having a focus or goal in life: the creative leader should know what it is he is trying to accomplish—he should know where he is going and be able to explain it to others. It is often surprising and even amazing how many men you can find who are in their middle productive years of thirty-eight to forty-two who have never asked themselves the questions, "What do I want out of life?" and "Just where do I think I am going?" But a would-be creative leader must know the answers to these because, upon them, will revolve his entire attitude toward his relationships with others.

The executive's activities in applying his own creativity to help others release their imaginations are many: he, as an individual, must be a planner, coordinator, judge, and coach. And he must do each of these jobs in such a way that it does not interfere with any of the others or weaken his position as the final authority. This, in many cases, requires the highest degrees of applied imagination!

The creative executive will, needless to say, set a creative example himself. He will always be ready to suggest courses of action on problems that will at least get action started, without, in any way, taking away from the delegated freedom to experiment or develop. This means that the executive's own idea sources must be developed. He will attend conventions; he will travel; he will visit other plants or departments and question their proceedings with a view toward finding new ideas. He will be familiar with the views of business writers and authorities in trade magazines— even in fields not directly connected to his own. He will associate with creative people and people who can spark—and even shock —his own thinking.

In attempting to obtain results through other people, the creative leader will, in a way, be a human chemist. He will think impersonally about people—as if they were human chemicals that will behave themselves in certain ways if skillfully handled. This means he will "learn" his people. He will study their natures as the chemist studies his chemical elements. The results, far from being *inhuman* or cold, will be that he can then employ the specific talents and reactions people have for creative, positive accomplishment, instead of making the mistakes that are attendant upon personal, and often prejudiced, conception and misconception.

In the role of coordinator, probably the most difficult and complex job the executive faces is that of delegation. But a manager of anyone other than himself must learn to delegate or cease to grow. His own success and ability will be measured largely by his ability to get things done through other people. The manager who will not delegate is always in danger of having the people under him work at far below their capacities. One symptom of inadequate delegation is that the executive finds himself saddled with details and so busy helping his people do their jobs that he has no time left to concentrate on and think about his own job. And, of course, by insisting on such a close supervision of subordinates' work, the executive is preventing them from growing in their own right.

It is a well-quoted maxim of management that delegation of responsibility must be accompanied by delegation of authority. Not so well known is the maxim that there must be delegation of the freedom to use imagination. This means that the subordinate must have freedom to develop his own, even completely new, ways of doing things, to develop or invent his own methods, and to keep track of his own results. Many an executive knows his job or his field so well that he can solve a problem almost instinctively. And when he sees a subordinate struggling with a puzzle that he could solve in a minute, there is an almost irresistible temptation to step in and do the job. It requires real self-control to resist that temptation. But it is the only way to ensure that, in the long run, you will end up with subordinates who are capable of doing their own thinking.

One of the best ways to accomplish this creative delegation is to do so in terms of a completed job. It is necessary to tell people what is required of them, of course. But, unless standardization is absolutely necessary, they should not be told *how* to accomplish what is wanted. The executive who is trying to encourage more creativity in his company will avoid giving detailed job instructions along with the job assignment. He will, instead, present the job assignment and require the subordinate to carry it out to the finished job when he has a "complete package" to present as his own effort.

The role of creative judge for the executive will usually overlap or interlock with that of creative coach. Beginning with the realization that unless he, or the company, has provided it, the average subordinate will not have had any training in creative problem-solving methods, the executive must then take on the job of guiding a worker through the necessary steps to solving a problem. Initially, the executive will probably be the one who is sensitive to the problem and who will recognize, define, and orient it. If, however, he has an interest in developing a worker of promising creative potential, he may ask that person (or persons) to sit in on a "problem-clinic" session and attempt to formulate a workable problem statement, with all its attendant requirements.

Next will come the job of gathering the information and data needed to work with, screening and evaluating this, and correlating the "knowns" and "unknowns" of the problem details with the data. Again, this can be assigned to a subordinate with an explanation of why the information is wanted; or it can be made a joint effort with a subordinate.

Once the principal "unknown" parts of the problem are clearly delineated, the executive is then ready to delegate these off in the form of specific problem assignments. He may, at this time, suggest certain idea-development techniques, specialist resources, or individual or group idea-gathering methods. But note "may suggest." If he *orders*, or implies that he favors a certain method over another, he will restrict the subordinate's freedom to think for himself. If he *suggests* several alternative methods, he encourages the subordinate to do some thinking on his own.

The executive should probably not get back into this picture until the subordinate has come up with recommendations he has developed on his own. It is a good technique of creative encouragement to make the idea-developing assignment one of providing "three or four" alternatives for consideration. He may or may not require the subordinate to make a specific recommendation on one of the alternatives, and he should always require that all ideas considered be available in case the subordinate's judgment is open to question.

The executive cannot, of course, duck his own responsibility for the successful completion of any courses of action that are taken under his direction. He may, therefore, have to be arbitrary in his final decision as to which of the recommended alternatives he will accept. But he should also be completely "open" in his reasons, and be sure that he is being objective and imaginative. In other words, that he is *not* just taking the "safe" way out.

And finally, if the subordinate's idea, suggestion, or recommendation proves successful, the executive *must* acknowledge and praise it. The worker must be made to feel a sense of accomplishment for having a part in the problem-solving effort, no matter how much of a "follower's" role it was. Only in this way can the novice problem-solver be given the encouragement and confidence needed to build the inner resourcefulness that will turn him into a creative problem-solver.

These few recommendations for executive coaching are based on the fact that it is up to each "boss" to give his men maximum opportunities to develop. This means the delegation of responsibility. More, it means exposing promising men to the company's problems. It means letting them "sit in" while the seniors or bosses wrestle and wrangle over problems. And it means giving them specific assignments to carry out on their own as contributions to solving the problems.

In the case of a younger subordinate, it is every bit as important to build his courage and confidence as it is to increase his knowledge of the business. He must feel free of any fear of criticism. He must feel free to make mistakes, realizing that management will consider mistakes as experience, and that they are willing to pay for that experience as an investment in his future value to the company. This does not mean, however, that he should never expect criticism. Constructive criticism is how he will learn from his mistakes. It can build his confidence, pride, ambition, loyalty, and most importantly, his determination to do better. But it does place on the executive the burden of making sure the criticism *is* constructive, positive, *and private*.

One secret of making criticism constructive, other than thinking it through well in advance, is that of trying to get on the other person's wave length. Try to see his point of view; imagine what you would want if you were the person receiving the criticism in this particular case. Mr. Fred Manchee, formerly executive vice president and treasurer of BBDO advertising agency, relates the story a friend once told him of an experience that changed the course of his business life:

"I was feeling pretty good," said the friend. "I liked my job, had a healthy family, good home. And there was a man I'd known for years, thought I knew pretty well. One day I found out what I had never known—that this man and his wife had a child who was a mindless lump. Every night of his life this man went home and helped bathe and feed the child. Never afterward did I forget that the man across the desk might be carrying a totally unbearable load. And that whatever I planned to say to him might be the last straw that would send him out the window!"

And it was Charles Schwab who said, "There is nothing that so kills the ambitions of a man as criticisms from his superiors. I never criticize anyone. I believe in giving a man incentive to work. So I am anxious to praise, but loath to find fault."

Much has been said in this book about the necessity of a questioning or challenging attitude as a requisite for creativity. Therefore, the creative leader will keep firmly in mind that he must not only set the example in this, but must encourage others to follow his example. It is all too easy for an executive to fall into the habit or the trap of feeling that he or his contemporaries on the same level are the only persons capable of creative or progressive thinking. But the executive who rebuffs questions himself, or who discourages questions on the part of subordinates, runs a grave risk of shutting himself off from either a new idea or what would ultimately be a profitable line of investigation. Therefore, the executive leader himself must be open to questions and should, in fact, respect and encourage them if he is interested in developing and releasing creativity in his subordinates.

Perhaps, in our generalizing, we can sum up the personal attributes necessary to be a creative leader with these observations:

He must be receptive to other people's ideas; he must, in fact, actively seek other people's ideas and help to supplement his own imaginative resources.

He must, at the same time, be able to plant his own ideas in the minds of others, and to compliment them on their ingenuity and resourcefulness.

He must be sufficiently placid to see a subordinate make a mistake, and to charge it off as an investment in the development of his most valuable resource: a creative, progressive worker.

He must forever forego the luxury of that most satisfying of experiences, "blowing his top" over the mistakes or shortcomings of his assistants. He must never, under any circumstances, berate or criticize a subordinate or worker in front of others.

He must be able to restrain himself from telling the sales manager how to sell or the comptroller how to keep accounts, no matter how much knowledge or experience he, the boss, has had in these fields. He will, rather, content himself with exercising broad direct and indirect control over obtaining results.

As was stated in Chapter 13, creativity in a company must come from the top—top and middle management must pave the way. This is so because only at the management level do the conditions exist for the encouragement, development, and recognition of both creative potential and the results of creative action.

Furthermore, it must be an executive responsibility because the most difficult talent to develop in business is that of executive replacement. Not only is such replacement in short supply, but also the quality of it needs a great deal of upgrading. In this respect, it is worth paying particular attention to the current shortage of so-called "generalist" executives: those with the breadth of knowledge and far-sighted vision to be able to cut through the limiting thought patterns of the specialists and think in terms of the over-all good of the company.

In this respect, creative encouragement and even "formal" creative training may prove to be the most efficient and effective method yet found for developing generalists. What is needed to make a generalist is a broad understanding of many different types of problems, and the capacity to think in terms of many different approaches to solving all the problems encompassed in any particular company's activities and interests. With the increasing complexity of business today, even in such "formularized" functions as accounting and traffic management, it is extremely doubtful that any company can set up an executive training program which will teach its future managers everything they might possibly need to know about every problem they might conceivably be called upon to solve. Far more efficient would be a program aimed at teaching them to be "at home" with problems of any kind, and to use their imaginations and resourcefulness to produce creative solutions to those problems.

With regard to the business leader's own attitude, he should realize that if, indeed, it is habit that takes us back to where we were yesterday, then it is only an improper attitude that keeps us there. A leader, to be a creative leader, must believe there is a better way before he will be able to find it. He must believe that, in most cases, there is more than one way. He must recognize that he will never have the ultimate in human accomplishment, but that through utilizing his own imagination and the creative potentials available to him, he can, with persistence, accomplish results that will at least be superior to what he has now. He must make sure that his own scope does not become too narrow and that, if he is going to fail, he will at least fail forward. He may not accomplish all that he sets out to do, but he will at least carry his company forward beyond today.

And the creative executive will look to his own and his workers' strengths as well as their weaknesses. He will learn to work with, and make the most of, the values his company *has*, while he tries to develop those that don't exist. He will utilize his own courage as an example—rather than give in to his fears of the unknown. And he will not retreat from those things he believes in, even when he finds that he is alone among his peers in his beliefs.

For a business executive to grow in stature and quality in the

Appendix

Review Questions and Exercises

The following questions and exercises may be used to gain a greater familiarity with and understanding of the principles and procedures covered throughout the book; or as topics for group discussions based on the book contents; or as class exercises for problem-solving courses utilizing this book as text.

Chapter 1 · Why Be Creative?

1. Consider some social institution or concept with which you are familiar—church, marriage, public schools, democracy, or the like.

   a. What changes will take place in it in the next twenty years?

   b. What new ideas have been introduced into it in the last hundred years?

   c. What forces exist to slow up or accelerate the changes in the next twenty years?

2. It has been stated that technological knowledge—that pertaining to the sciences—is increasing at a rate of 22 per cent a year. What changes in thought patterns, ways of working, and job responsibilities will this require for a salesman? purchasing man? office manager? production engineer? retailer?

coming years, he will need to be able to compete creatively-not with other candidates for promotion, but with other bus nesses, with technologies of competitors, and even with nationa and international developments. This means that management' preference for the "sound" executives who are able to conform and administer according to set standards and procedures will, of necessity, be forced to give way to a search for executives who will challenge all such standardized thinking and who will be able to apply creative thinking to upgrading the company in every phase of operations.

Ideas are probably the most valuable products any company or organization ever produces. Therefore, under the common law of investment and return, you cannot reasonably expect the job of securing them to be an easy one. It takes persistence, determination, and dedication to make yourself more creative. It takes persistence, determination, dedication, planning, and, above all, *imagination* on the part of the executive to get more imagination and develop a creative spirit in his company or organization.

As mentioned, this creative spirit is not something you can accomplish throughout a complete organization overnight—no matter how willing or sold you yourself are. But it could easily be that your personal road to fame, fortune, and success in your company, field, or industry will be that you will use your own imagination to analyze, develop, and solve the problem of infusing your organization with both the necessity and the means of getting all-out, imaginative, creative thinking from everyone.

3. Do you agree with Mr. Brower's statement, "This in America is the high tide of mediocrity, the great era of the goof-off, the age of the half-done job?" If yes, why?—if no, why not? Think of at least three examples to support your reasoning.

4. *a.* How can the increasing amount of leisure time, due to the shorter work week, cause a social problem in this country?

b. Other than get a second job, what should you personally be doing now to make sure you won't waste this coming leisure in "escapist recreation"?

5. Think in terms of your own company or organization: what problems that you have today could be aggravated by the growing shortage of executives and administrators? What do you think your company should be doing about this shortage now?

Chapter 2 · What Is Creative?

1. In your own words, distinguish between the terms "original," "talented," "imaginative," and "creative." Name at least one person among your own acquaintances who exhibits primary symptoms of each.

2. Give examples of progressive innovations in some commercial product, other than the automobile, since it was first developed.

3. Suggest at least ten ways the introduction of frozen food into supermarkets was a destructive force so far as "established" methods were concerned.

4. The text traces out the history of what happened as a result of John Dunlop's pneumatic tire being applied to the bicycle. Construct a similar history beginning with the Wright brothers' first successful airplane.

5. What would be the benefits to your company if you could cut 50 per cent of the cost out of your most important product? Suggest at least five.

Chapter 3 · Characteristics of Creative People

1. *a.* Write down the name of the "most creative" person you know.

b. Write a short statement of the reasons why you think this person is creative.

c. Relate each of your reasons to the creative characteristics given in the text that come closest to describing the characteristics exhibited by this person.

2. Suggest at least five things in your own business that are not being done as well now as they could be. For each of these, give at least two suggestions of how it might be improved.

3. Dr. John Arnold has said, "If the creative individual wants to be an inventor, he cannot be a specialist." Assume this is true. What are the implications? How do they pertain to you in your job?

4. What are the advantages of idea fluency? How can it also improve both flexibility and originality?

5. Suggest at least five ways that the creative characteristic of "drive" can help overcome deficiencies in some of the other characteristics?

Chapter 4 · Blocks to Creativeness

1. Think of the last major business problem you had to solve.

    a. Make a list of the mental steps you went through in solving it.

    b. Take some current personal problem and try to work out a solution following the same general steps.

2. What is your concept of the kind of *security* a creative person should strive for? How can he keep a desire for security from becoming a block to his development as a creative individual?

3. List five examples of how people you know (you may include yourself) conform to "accepted" patterns *not* involving questions of morality.

    a. Why do you think each of these patterns is "accepted"?

    b. Are any of the original conditions of acceptance outmoded today?

    c. What are the dangers of conforming to such outmoded patterns?

4. List at least five "unwritten laws" governing personal behavior where you work. Do any of these tend to inhibit the freedom to create for the company? What would be the results if you were to challenge any of them?

5. List at least ten habits that govern your daily living.

    a. Which of these tend to simplify the details of living to leave your mind more free for thinking?

    b. Which tend to restrict your thinking so as to inhibit you from finding new and better ways of doing things?

    c. For each of the restricting habits you list in *b* above, suggest at least three things you could do to help yourself replace the bad habit with a good one.

Chapter 5 · The Nature of Creative Thought

1. What specific meaning might the word "idea" have for each of the following?
    a. An artist
    b. A chemist
    c. A salesman
    d. A poet
    e. Your company president
    f. A composer
    g. The U.S. Secretary of State
    h. Your office mailboy
Give a specific example of each type of idea.

2. Einstein's mind has been described as "slow and contemplative"; John Von Neumann's as "lightning quick—stunningly fast." Both men made outstandingly creative contributions in the field of mathematics. What implications do you draw from this?

3. List at least three advances (product, operation, methods, organization) in your own business that came about as a result of a combination or relation of two or more previously unrelated ideas.

4. If you were given the assignment of developing a new way to clean carpeting without the use of liquids, suggest at least three things you could use as the "commonplace" to start your thinking. Do the same for developing a more efficient organization of your present job.

5. Consider either of the two problems in 4 above. Make a ten-step outline showing how you might alternate "involvement" and "withdrawal" thinking in hunting for the solution to the problem.

Chapter 6 · The Nature of Problems

1. List at least ten problems of any kind that are currently occupying your thinking in one degree or another. Which of these are caused by forces outside your own control (such as the fact that the problem was assigned to you by someone else)? Which are problems that you have made for yourself?

2. a. Think back over the last month. How many of the "problems" you had to meet passed the "ten-year test" of importance?

   b. Think back to ten years ago. What problem solutions did you produce then that are still affecting your life today?

3. Here are several analytical problem statements. Restate each to open them up to possibilities for more creative solutions:

    a. Design a better automobile.

    b. Reduce company personnel costs 20 per cent.

    c. Design a new box for a tube of toothpaste.

    d. Devise a new way to teach American History.

4. For each of the following, list at least five experiences you have had that might be of value to you if you were suddenly confronted with the problem (include vicarious experiences such as reading a book about it):

    a. Developing an executive training program for your company

    b. Organizing a bird-watchers club

    c. Planning an annual convention for some industry

    d. Designing a new vacuum cleaner

    e. Provisioning a two-man rocket for a sixty-day trip to the moon

5. *a.* Every company would like to increase profits by making more money. Suggest at least three *direct* ways you could uncover opportunities for your company to increase their income.

    b. Every company can also increase profits by saving money. Suggest three direct ways your company could begin saving money immediately without harming either product quality or customer service.

Chapter 7 · Steps in Deliberate Problem Solving

Case study: You have a promising junior production engineer, Bill Brown, transferred into your department. He is intelligent, enthusiastic, and has a high scholastic rating. He has an unusual flair for shaving costs on production problems. However, he also has the ability to exasperate all his associates to such an extent that they actually resist valuable suggestions simply because they come from him. You have talked to him twice about the need for tact and diplomacy in working with others, but he doesn't seem to care. In any event, he has failed to reform.

You now have in blueprint form a new item on which the saving of every fraction of a cent will be highly important. You have been counting on Brown's help to make the savings. You also have a request in with your company's finance committee for funds to buy new production equipment. The comptroller has tipped you off that the committee's decision may be influenced to some degree by the size of your profit margin on this new item.

At the same time, the morale of your production unit is at the lowest

ebb ever because of Brown's unpleasant personality. In a particular
slump is a veteran of twelve years' experience who knows the practical
side of manufacturing like the back of his hand. He is in a completely
negative frame of mind and refuses to consider any of Brown's suggestions whatever. But you need him almost as much as you need
Brown.

1. On the basis of the facts given, how would you orient this problem? Be sure to break out all subproblems.

2. *a.* What facts are given in the study that will have to be reconciled
with any solution you propose?

b. What facts do you feel are still needed?

c. How would you go about getting the additional facts—either
directly or indirectly?

d. How could you prove the validity of any facts you turn up?

3. Working with what you have developed so far, list at least twenty
possible ideas—good, bad, or indifferent—you might try as a means of
solving your problem. Try to do this on an "ideas only" basis, without
evaluating their merits as you produce them.

4. Read over your original orientation of the problem. Does this
suggest any additional ideas to you? Read over the list of facts you felt
were important to the problem. Can you add any additional ideas now?
Reread all the ideas you have listed so far. Can you add another five?
Ten?

5. *a.* Establish at least five criteria points that any solution to this
problem must meet. (Remember to consider the original facts that you
said must be reconciled into a solution.)

b. Evaluate each of your ideas against the criteria you have developed. Which idea seems to offer the best possibilities for immediate
solution of the problem?

6. Assume that none of the ideas you produced and tried had any
effect on resolving the conflicts caused by Brown's personality and attitude. List at least ten alternative courses of action you might be able to
take. Do any of these satisfy the criteria for solution?

7. Assume you decide to fire or transfer Brown. Orient the problem
you would then have of making up for the loss of his specialized abilities.

Chapter 8 · Help Yourself to More Ideas

1. When was the last time you made a written note of something you
wanted to remember? What did you do with the note? What could
you have done with it that would have made it more useful?

2. Devise or plan a note-making and note-using system for your particular needs that will be efficient, convenient, and simple.

3. Make a list of all the things you could change or eliminate in your daily schedule to "clear" at least one hour a day for uninterrupted thinking about problems and/or opportunities. Try processing this as a problem, following the five-step method suggested in Chapter 7.

4. Use a clock or kitchen timer for this one: In ten minutes, try to meet a quota of twenty ideas on how you could raise a son so he would grow up to be a creative person.

5. Assume you have decided to submit one new idea a day to your company's suggestion system. Devise a checklist with at least twenty points on it that you could skim through every day to stimulate your mind to produce the needed idea-a-day.

6. Make up a list of ten questions about your company that, if you had the answers, might help you produce profitable ideas. Work out a simple plan to get the answers to those ten questions.

7. *a.* List at least three basic attributes of each of the following: A lead pencil; a flashlight; the chronic tardy worker; the daily coffee break; transparent window glass.

b. For each of the attributes you have listed, suggest at least three possible changes.

Chapter 9 · When to Use Creative Groups

1. What are the implications in the statement, "Most great advances in technology occur when two sciences get together?" How is this apt to "transfer" to other branches of business: administration, finance, personnel?

2. *a.* What are the dangers of overemphasizing competition with others to the neglect of cooperation?

b. From your own experience, can you think of a cooperative effort that would have been better handled by an individual?

3. For each of the following, make up a list of six other people in your company who might be able to help you in finding a solution to the problem:

a. Improving union-management relationships

b. Designing a new product to augment your present line

c. Improving interdepartmental communications

d. Obtaining a 10 per cent increase in production without increasing labor costs

4. The "power jockey" can thoroughly disrupt any cooperative group effort. How could you, as a meeting chairman, enlist his support to help you make the group effort a success?

5. Your company has just learned that they are in danger of losing one of their oldest and most profitable accounts because of several recent instances of failure to keep promised delivery dates. You have been given the dual job of getting to the cause of the trouble and correcting it and of pacifying the customer. You may call on anyone else in the company that you feel can help you solve the problem. What kind of group would you put together? What specific contributions would you expect of each member?

Chapter 10 · Creative Group Techniques

1. Analyze in detail the last conference you attended—a sales meeting, church or civic club, family conference, or one you called yourself. List in particular the anticreative things that were done.

2. Consider the general problem of new inventions (products, methods, materials, etc.) needed in your business. Find an open-minded teammate and process the problem, following the steps given in the Creative Team outline. Analyze your results.

3. Consider the general problem of encouraging workers to take a greater interest in improving product quality:

   a. Suggest where or when you could profitably use a Buzz group on this problem.

   b. Suggest where or when you could profitably use Brainstorming.

   c. Write out the specific problem statement you would give the Brainstorm panel.

4. Consider the general problem, "What new products, not now available, are needed in the home?"

   a. Make up a list of ten people you think could effectively contribute to a Brainstorming session on this problem. Give a brief statement of why you selected each person.

   b. Make a list of ten categorical questions you could use in leading the session on this problem.

   c. List at least five "wild" or "blue-sky" ideas of your own you could use in the course of the session to keep it relaxed.

5. Assume you have conducted a Brainstorming session on the problem of improving the frame design for an electric motor used in a window air-conditioning unit. A panel of engineers and designers produced

eighty-nine unduplicated ideas. Exactly how would you go about determining which five of these ideas you would recommend for laboratory testing.

6. Write a five-minute talk you could use to explain Brainstorming to a group of people who had never heard of it before.

7. The text gives several general suggestions for problems in which you could use Brainstorming:

    a. Exploring the possibilities in a product or situation

    b. Creating a list of new needs

    c. Discovering potential uses for new products or new materials

    d. As a "crash program" knowledge-pooling device

    e. As a group test

For each of these, give a *specific* problem your company has on which you could consider the use of Brainstorming.

8. This problem is listed as "Vital to the National Defense" by the National Inventors' Council:

Needed: A personal built-in heating unit. The armed services want a device that can be built into a man's suit to distribute heat over his body in subzero weather. The device...

Must operate without a restricting power source

Must operate eight hours (minimum) without refueling

Must permit rapid discard

Must not hamper agility

Must be reasonably lightweight

Must be fully reliable

Assume you are going to conduct an Operational Creativity session to find an idea for this problem.

    a. Determine your "subject" word or phrase.

    b. Make up a list of at least ten leading questions that you, as the leader, could use to keep discussion going without revealing the exact problem.

Chapter 11 · How to Lead Creative Groups

1. Do you agree with the statement, "Any female member of a conference or meeting can go only so far in challenging a male opinion or thought before she is in danger"? Why or why not?

2. You have assembled a creative group of ten people from sales, design, and production to tackle the problem of designing a new thermos bottle. List at least five things you could do or say in the first

three minutes of the meeting to "break the ice" and motivate each of those people to contribute to solving the problem.

3. You are conducting a fast-moving Brainstorming session aimed at producing ideas on a major problem for your company. Suddenly one of your most important members stands up and says, "This is ridiculous. I've never seen such a waste of time before. I'm going back to my desk where I can spend my time profitably!"

a. How would you calm this member down and win back his support?

b. How would you get your meeting going again without loss of the creative momentum?

4. As the leader of a creative group, you notice that one of your members is not participating at all. You know this person is a rather shy-type personality, but quite brilliant and capable of original thinking. Suggest three things you could say or ask that would bring him into the discussion without "pressuring" or otherwise embarrassing him.

5. In the interests of giving yourself "inexpensive experience," suggest at least three problems on which you could lead creative groups for

a. Your church

b. Your PTA

c. A Boy Scout troup

d. Your favorite charity

e. A political action group

f. Your family

Chapter 12 · The Importance of Follow-up

1. For a twenty-four-hour period, write down every idea or suggestion you hear someone else make and about which you are pretty certain nothing will ever be done. For each of these ideas, try to suggest at least three things you could do to put the idea into action, assuming it's a good one.

2. Assume you have a new idea for improving coordination of the sales, production, and shipping departments of your company. If you had only *one* hour to check the validity of your facts before presenting this idea to top management, how would you go about it?

3. Your office is about to be redecorated. It is the standard practice for the office manager, a man two years short of retirement age, to

pick out colors and furnishings. You would prefer a professional decorator who would be compensated by his commissions on the paint and furnishings. Suggest a plan that would get the office manager "on your side" even though it would take away one of his status prerogatives.

4. Your management has accepted your idea for a new package for the company's most profitable product. The package will give the product better protection in shipment, and cost 23 per cent less than the previous method. The whole suggestion has now been taken away from you and turned over to an outside supplier to produce. Suggest at least five ways to build on your initial success with this idea.

5. Consider the last idea you submitted to anyone that was rejected. Plan a detailed "selling" presentation for this idea that will overcome the previous objections.

Chapter 13 · Creating the Creative Climate

1. Suggest at least five things your company could do to make sure that employee-suggested ideas are not discouraged or blocked by noncreative supervisors.

2. Suggest at least ten things your company should do to make general employees more conscious of the company's need for new ideas.

3. Employee Tom Anderson has submitted a completely useless idea on a production problem. You have sent him a polite note explaining in detail why his idea was turned down. But today, as you are walking through the plant area where Anderson works, he stops you and loudly and rudely begins to berate you, your judgment, and your appreciation of ideas. Approximately a dozen other workers are looking on and taking it all in. How would you handle the situation?

4. Outline a five-hour program that would give junior executives and supervisory personnel in your company an indoctrination into and an appreciation of the principles of creative problem-solving.

5. Select one of your company's standard training programs with which you are familiar. Suggest at least ten changes that could be made in it to give the participants a greater appreciation of the need to think imaginatively, without in any way cutting down on the quality of the training.

6. In addition to those given in the text, suggest at least ten forms of nonmonetary rewards to give to workers for worthwhile ideas.

Chapter 14 · How to Spot Creative Potential in Others

1. Suggest at least three things a manager could do in attempting to correct each of the following situations:

 a. A highly creative worker in a job that does not make full use of his capabilities

 b. A worker with creative potential who does not exercise it because he is "at war" with his supervisor

 c. The worker who occasionally produces good ideas, but is not interested in taking on "extra" problems in spite of the possibilities of receiving generous rewards

2. Suggest a specific indication, such as a way of speaking, a pattern of action, or an approach to an unfamiliar situation, that might serve to indicate the presence of each of the following characteristics in a particular individual:

 a. Problem sensitivity

 b. Idea fluency

 c. Flexibility

 d. Originality

 e. Drive

 f. Creative expectancy

3. Develop a list of ten basic conversational questions you could ask of any prospective new employee to get answers which might indicate either creative potential or the lack of it.

4. Make up a specific question you could ask a prospective employee to determine if he

 a. Is observant

 b. Knows his field

 c. Has a good memory

 d. Can concentrate for any length of time

 e. Can reason effectively and accurately

 f. Can communicate his thoughts and ideas

 g. Is curious

 h. Can change his mental pace

 i. Can work within problem limits when necessary

 j. Can ignore apparent problem limits when they are not truly restrictive

Chapter 15 · The Creative Executive in Action

1. List at least ten things you can do, on your own, to improve your relationships with other people.

2. List at least ten ways in which you could make better use of your own imagination in

    a. Your job

    b. Your marriage

    c. Raising your children

3. *a.* Write down the name of the most dynamic leader you have ever worked under.

    b. Analyze, in detail, the qualities that you believe made him that way. (Note: "Quality" cannot be expressed in one word!)

    c. What shortcomings did he have?

4. List at least ten things you can do in the way of developing your own imaginative resources to enable you to be a better creative "coach" for others.

5. Your company is about to introduce a new electric dishwasher. You believe it is superior to any other on the market, but you will have to build a dealer organization from scratch. You, as General Sales Manager, have decided that Fred Smith is the most promising man to head up the job of planning and executing the marketing strategy. He has never had appliance marketing experience before, but he will have the assistance of your advertising agency. Write the memo telling Smith of his new assignment; delegate his specific responsibilities; and instruct him to write a similar memo to the agency detailing how he would like them to work with him.

6. Suggest at least twenty things you personally can do to promote more imaginative thinking throughout your company.

Bibliography

The following list of books, reference works, and selected articles relative to creative thinking was compiled by the Creative Education Office of the University of Buffalo (N.Y.), under the guidance of Dr. Sidney J. Parnes, Director. Reprinted by permission.

Arnold, John, et al. *Summer Session Notes* (1955, 1956). Creative Engineering Laboratory, Mechanical Engineering Department, Massachusetts Institute of Technology, Cambridge.

Clark, Charles H. *Brainstorming*. Doubleday & Company, Inc., Garden City, New York, 1958.

Crawford, Robert P. *How to Get Ideas*. University Associates, Lincoln, Nebraska, 1950.

————. *The Techniques of Creative Thinking*. Hawthorn Books, Inc., New York, 1954.

Cros, Gamble, Mraz, Whiting, et al. *Imagination. Undeveloped Resource* (A Critical Study of Techniques and Programs for Stimulating Creative Thinking in Business, prepared by a student research group in the Manufacturing Course, Class of 1955, Harvard Graduate School of Business Administration, Cambridge, Massachusetts). Creative Training Associates, P.O. Box 913, Grand Central Station, New York, 1955.

> NOTE: A second study, *Individual Creativity and the Corporation,* is now in preparation by a group of students in the same class in 1958.

267

Guilford, J. P., Christensen, Paul R., and Wilson, Robert C. "A Bibliography of Thinking, Including Creative Thinking, Reasoning, Evaluation, and Planning." Department of Psychology, University of Southern California, Los Angeles, California, July, 1953.

Kogan, Zuce. *Essentials in Problem Solving*. Arco Publishing Company, New York, 1956.

Osborn, Alex F. *Applied Imagination*. Charles Scribner's Sons, New York, 1957.

——. *Teacher's Guide*. For Use in Conjunction with the Revised Edition of the Textbook "Applied Imagination." Creative Education Foundation, 1614 Rand Building, Buffalo 3, New York.

——. *Wake Up Your Mind*. Charles Scribner's Sons, New York, 1952.

——. *Your Creative Power*. Charles Scribner's Sons, New York, 1948.

Parnes, Sidney J. *Creative Retailing*. Department of Public Instruction, Harrisburg, Pennsylvania. (An instructor's manual for a course in creative retailing.)

Smith, Paul (Editor). *Creativity*. Hastings House, New York, 1959.

Von Fange, Eugene K. *Professional Creativity*. Prentice-Hall, Inc., Englewood Cliffs, New Jersey, 1959.

Wertheimer, M. *Productive Thinking*. Harper & Brothers, New York, 1945.

Whiting, Charles S. *Creative Thinking*. Reinhold Publishing Corporation, New York, 1958.

Creative Education Foundation. *Compendium of Research on Creative Imagination*. Buffalo, New York, 1958. Reports of 30 research studies concerned with identification and development of creative ability, and additional studies under way. (A separate "List of Available Materials" regarding creative thinking is also published by the Creative Education Foundation.)

Creative Problem Solving Institute, University of Buffalo. Proceedings of first through fourth annual institutes, 1955–1958. Detailed proceedings of the institutes involving the creative problem solving process, emphasizing the methods of Alex F. Osborn (*Applied Imagination*).

Foundation for Research on Human Behavior. *Creativity and Conformity*. Ann Arbor, Michigan, 1958. A report of research on creativity and conformity in organizations.

Industrial Relations News. *Company Climate and Creativity*. New York, 1958. A study of the impact of the business and industrial environment on creative people, with special reference to engineers and scientists, and how to establish a favorable creative climate.

———. *Creativity* (a bibliography). New York, 1958.

Industrial Research Institute. *Bibliography on Creativity* (1919 references). Prepared by Creativity Sub-committee of Research Personnel Committee, 1955.

———. *The Nature of Creative Thinking* (a monograph). New York University Press, New York, 1952, 73 pp. This monograph contains a series of articles dealing with creativity and creative thinking, as presented at a symposium on creative thinking sponsored by the Industrial Research Institute.

Institute of Contemporary Art, Boston, Massachusetts. Reports of conferences on the creative process, 1956–1957. Three detailed reports of proceedings of conferences, emphasizing the William J. J. Gordon Operational Approach to Creativity.

University of Utah, Salt Lake City. Reports of the 1955 and 1957 *Research Conference on the Identification of Creative Scientific Talent*. Papers presented by a variety of researchers working in the area of scientific creativity and its identification.

*Papers and Articles Relevant to Research in
Creative Thinking*

In preparing this bibliography, *Psychological Abstracts* were reviewed from January, 1950, through April, 1958. Articles were obtained chiefly from this source and from the files of the Creative Education Foundation and the University of Buffalo Creative Education Office.

Bergler, Edmund. "Unconscious Mechanisms in Writer's Block." *Psychoanalytical Review*, 1955, vol. 42, pp. 160–167. The author discusses what he believes to be the four main hurdles which hinder creative thinking.

Bristol, Lee H., Jr. "The Application of Group Thinking Techniques to the Problems of Pharmaceutical Education." *American Journal of Pharmaceutical Education*, 1958, vol. 22, no. 2, pp. 143–146. This article offers the reader a résumé of the Brainstorming principles and procedures. Suggestions on how to set up a session are also included.

Bromiley, Dennis B. "Some Experimental Tests of the Effect of Age on Creative Intellectual Output." *Journal of Gerontology*, 1956, vol. 11, pp. 74–82. This article deals with a study of the Shaw Test of creative intellectual output. The results yield information concerning the relationship of quantity and quality of output to age.

Burack, Benjamin, and Mass, Donald. "Effect of Knowing the Principle Basic to Solution of a Problem." *Journal of Educational Research*, 1956, vol. 50, pp. 203–208. The results of an experiment show that "knowledge of the principle underlying the solution of a problem does not necessarily lead to solution of the problem."

Burchard, Edward M. L. "The Use of Projective Techniques in the Analysis of Creativity." *Journal of Projective Techniques*, 1952, vol. 16, pp. 412–427. The author reviews some contemporary psychoanalytic theories of creativity, as well as certain studies of creativity which have utilized the projective technique.

Bush, George P., and Hattery, Lowell H. "Teamwork and Creativity in Research." *Administrative Science Quarterly*, 1956, vol. 1, pp. 361–372. In view of the fact that traditional methods of administration cannot always be applied to scientific endeavors, the author suggests three areas which should receive more emphasis.

Chorness, Maury H. "Increasing Creativity in Problem-Solving Groups." *Journal of Communication*, 1958, vol. 8, pp. 16–23. This article discusses some possible methods for increasing creativity in problem-solving groups, as well as the results of a number of studies on creativity conducted under government contracts.

Coon, Arthur M. "Brainstorming—A Creative Problem-Solving Technique." *Journal of Communication*, 1957, pp. 111–118. This article offers the reader a concise history and description of the Brainstorming technique. Dr. Coon elaborates on the theories behind the four Brainstorming rules and discusses Brainstorming's place in the fields of business and education.

Gordon, William J. J. "Operational Approach to Creativity." *Harvard Business Review*, 1956, vol. 34, pp. 41–51. This article deals with the approach called "Operational Creativity," which is a theory of how creative groups function. Gordon lists and discusses what he has observed to be the six themes or elements of the creative process. He also goes on to illustrate how these themes are exercised in group creativity.

Gough, Harrison G. "Researcher's Summary Data for the Differential Reaction Schedule." Institute of Personality Assessment and Research, University of California, Los Angeles, 1957 (mimeographed). The paper includes a discussion of Gough's Differential Reaction Schedule containing five scales which yield six scores.

Guilford, J. P. "Creativity." *American Psychologist*, 1950, vol. 5, pp.

444–454. Creativity is discussed as patterns of primary abilities containing certain factors, such as sensitivity to problems, ideational fluency, flexibility of set, synthesizing ability, and analyzing ability.

———. "Some Recent Findings on Thinking Abilities and Their Implications." *Informational Bulletin*, Training Analysis and Development, TA&D Directorate, Deputy Chief of Staff Operations, Hq. ATRC, Scott AFB, Illinois, Fall, 1952, vol. 3, pp. 48–61. This article deals with the hypothesis that creative individuals possess certain characteristics; and the author presents research results which support the hypothesis. Various approaches to the measurement of originality investigated at the University of California are also discussed.

———. "Creative Abilities in the Arts." *Psychological Review*, 1957, vol. 64, pp. 110–118. From this investigation Guilford sets forth a set of hypotheses concerning factors and abilities involved in artistic creative talent.

Hart, Henry H., M.D. "The Integrative Function in Creativity." *Psychiatric Quarterly*, 1950, vol. 24, pp. 1–16. This article introduces some psychoanalytical viewpoints concerning creativity. The author deals primarily with the integrative function in its relation to creative effort.

Joelson, Edith A. "Creative Thinking." *Journal of the American Society of Training Directors*, September, 1957, pp. 7–13. Cultural factors which act as impediments to creativity are discussed.

Lehman, Harvey C. "The Creative Years of Long-lived versus Short-lived Individuals." *American Psychologist*, 1950, vol. 5, p. 365. This paper reports the results of a study designed to investigate the effects of increasing life span upon quantitative creative production.

Lincoln, John W. "Developing a Creativeness in People." *Proceedings*, Fourteenth Annual Conference, American Society of Training Directors, 1958. A discussion of the theory of Synectics or Operational Creativity is the main theme of this article.

Mooney, Ross L. "Groundwork for Creative Research." *American Psychologist*, 1954, vol. 9, pp. 544–548. In this article the author discusses the nature and importance of creativity in scientists and its relationship to the training functions in the university.

———. "Perception and Creation." *Proceedings*, Fourteenth Annual Conference, American Society of Training Directors, 1958. The author discusses the intrinsic potentiality of man as a creative being. Experiments in perception and in group influence on judgments are also reviewed.

Morgan, Douglas N. "Creativity Today." *Journal of Aesthetics and Art Criticism*, 1953, vol. 12, pp. 1–24. This paper presents an analytical review of certain philosophical and psychological studies of creativity. It also suggests an analytical definition of the creative process and discusses certain contemporary psychological inquiries into the subjects.

Munn, Norman L. "Theoretical Creativity in Psychology." *Main Currents in Modern Thought*, 1954, vol. 11, pp. 35–39. This article deals with creativity within the field of psychology from the early schools to present.

Murphy, Gardner. "Creativeness." *Menninger Quarterly*, June, 1957, pp. 1–6. Creative acts are discussed as involving four developmental phases. The various effects that culture has upon these phases are illustrated throughout the article.

Rhodes, James Melvin. "The Dynamics of Creativity; an Interpretation of the Literature on Creativity with a Proposed Procedure for Objective Research." *Dissertation Abstracts*, 1957, vol. 17, p. 96. The author not only reviews various literature on creativity but also offers a comprehensive theory of creativity as well as a new procedure for investigating the dynamics of creativity.

Rogers, Carl R. "Toward a Theory of Creativity." *ETC: A Review of General Semantics*, 1954, vol. 11, pp. 249–260. Rogers sets forth a theory of creativity, focusing on such aspects as: (1) the nature of the creative act, (2) the necessary inner conditions for its occurrence, and (3) the desirable external conditions which foster it.

Scientific American, September, 1958, vol. 199, no. 3. The entire issue of the magazine is devoted to articles regarding the creative process, the physiology and psychology of imagination, and innovation in the sciences.

Stein, Morris I. "Creativity and Culture." *Journal of Psychology*, 1953, vol. 36, pp. 311–322. Beginning with a definition of creative work, this article dwells upon the various stages involved in the creative process, with particular emphasis on the stage of hypothesis formation.

Taylor, Donald W., and McNemar, Olga W. "Problem Solving and Thinking." *Annual Review of Psychology*, 1955, vol. 6, pp. 455–482. This article contains a review of experimentation centered around the areas of problem solving, concept formation, decision making, and creative thinking. An extensive bibliography is also included.

Thurstone, L. L. "Creative Talent." *Report from the Psychometric Lab.*, The University of Chicago, December, 1950, no. 61. This paper focuses upon hypotheses concerning the nature of creative talent and the means by which they may be investigated. Proposed types of experimental studies are discussed in some detail.

———. "The Scientific Study of Inventive Talent." *Report from the Psychometric Lab.*, The University of Chicago, July, 1952, no. 81. In this paper Thurstone further elaborates upon hypotheses concerning the nature of creative and inventive talent.

Tumin, Melvin. "Obstacles to Creativity." *ETC: A Review of General Semantics*, 1954, vol. 11, pp. 261–271. The author views creativity as an aesthetic experience which is "self-consummatory in nature." He also explains how modern social conditions have created four "social pathologies."

Veatch, Jeannette. "The Structure of Creativity." *Journal of Educational Sociology*, 1953, vol. 27, pp. 102–107. This article contains a discussion of the effects of the creative and democratic climate in the classroom as well as in society. Results are reported of an experiment investigating the effects upon children of participation in creative activities.

Wilson, R. C. "An Operational Definition of Originality." *American Psychologist*, 1951, vol. 6, p. 297. Wilson's presentation deals with the development of an objective method for the measurement of originality, which he defines as "The ability to produce ideas which are statistically infrequent for the population of which the individual is a member."

Index

275